D0875727

# T S Eliot:
## poems in the making

For Eleanor

Gertrude Patterson

# T S Eliot: poems in the making

Manchester University Press
Barnes & Noble Inc., New York

Published by the University of Manchester
at the University Press
316–324 Oxford Road, Manchester M13 9NR

ISBN 0 7190 0416 0


*USA*
Barnes & Noble, Inc.
105 Fifth Avenue
New York, N.Y. 10003

ISBN 0 389 04086 X

Printed in Great Britain by
W & J Mackay & Co. Ltd, Chatham, Kent

# Contents

Acknowledgements                                        *page* vii

I     'That poetry is made with words'                      1

II    The Imagist experiment: the fragment poem            19

III   The Symbolist method: fragments as structures        38

IV    Ezra Pound: fragments into action                    57

V     Fragments into poems                                 87

VI    'The Waste Land'                                    134

VII   The final pattern                                   169


Bibliography                                             186

Index                                                   193

# Acknowledgements

The research for this book was carried out under the supervision of Professor Philip Edwards, formerly Professor of English at Trinity College, Dublin, now Chairman of the School of Comparative Literature at the University of Essex. To him I owe a special debt of gratitude for his sympathetic and informed advice at every stage of the writing. The book has been read several times by Professor Frank Kermode of University College, London. His examination of my work has been painstaking and I am most grateful for his valuable comments and suggested revision.

I should also like to thank Mrs Valerie Eliot who gave me permission to examine 'The Waste Land' manuscripts which are now part of the Berg Collection in the New York Public Library. Mrs Eliot has since read the passages concerning the manuscripts and I am very grateful to her for her permission to include them in my text. I appreciate the help given me by my publishers in making my visit to New York possible. To Dr L. Szladits, Curator of the Berg Collection, I owe a further debt. Without her co-operation and help during my research in New York it would have been impossible to bring this book completely up to date.

I should finally like to thank my parents and many friends for their encouragement and help during the preparation of this book, especially Mrs Barbara Young, who not only typed the manuscript, but also helped with the correction.

This is the common ground of the arts, this combat of arrangement or 'harmony'. The musician, the writer, the sculptor, the higher mathematician have here their common sanctuary.

It does *not* mean that the poet is to describe post-impressionist pictures, or that the sculptor is to carve allegorical figures of the dramatist's protagonists.

In different media, which are at once the simplest and the most complex, each artist works out the same and yet a totally different set of problems. And he uses the medium for which the combination of his talents most fits him.

His 'agreement with fellow artists' is in many senses a matter of no importance. I mean if he has the sense of *this* common ground.

My brother artist may, and probably does, disagree with me violently on all questions of morals, philosophy, religion, politics, economics; we are indissolubly united against all non-artists and half-artists by our sense of this fundamental community, this unending adventure towards 'arrangement', this search for the equations of eternity.

Ezra Pound
*Gaudier-Brzeska,* 1916

# I    'That poetry is made with words'

After the scholarly studies of critics like George Williamson[1] and Grover Smith,[2] which set out to explain the meanings of Eliot's poems to us, it seems clear that nothing further can be added in this direction. Having acknowledged that these critics in particular have added greatly to our understanding and appreciation of the early poems, it may seem somewhat ungrateful to suggest that by laying such stress on the need to find out what the poems are 'about' and—as in the case of George Williamson —to produce a kind of 'plain man's guide' to them, they have had to direct their attention away from the far more important aspect of the poetry, its method of composition. In fact, in order to 'make sense' of many of the poems—'The Waste Land' in particular—they have deliberately had to ignore a structure which overtly defies 'meaning' in the traditionally accepted sense of 'paraphrasable content'. While the critic concerned with finding out what the poet is seeking to communicate must start off with an elucidation of the parts which go to make up the complete poem—and for this Grover Smith's study is invaluable —he should not assume that by putting these meanings together, one after the other, he will be able to piece together the 'statement' that the poem illustrates. A need has arisen to look again at the earlier poems on their own terms and by re-examining and re-affirming the principles behind Eliot's fragmentary method of composition come to a more accurate understanding of them. While critics like Williamson and Smith have proved that the poems can be made to make sense in the conventional way and have probably gained for Eliot a wider audience than he might otherwise have enjoyed, by supplying a statement of meaning for them, a careful look at Eliot's theory of poetic composition will show that they have denied his stated intentions by doing so. The whole method and structure of the

[1] George Williamson, *A Reader's Guide to T. S. Eliot* (first published Gt Britain 1955).
[2] Grover Smith, *T. S. Eliot's Poetry and Plays: A Study in Sources and Meanings* (first published 1956).

poems deliberately set out to avoid the singleness of meaning which is the particular reading of any one critic. Although comment like this is not new, it seems necessary to make it again.

Graham Hough, in *Image and Experience*, has expressed the view that 'the real roots and novelty in modern literary practice have been very little examined'.[1] C. K. Stead and a number of other critics, including Graham Hough, rightly see these roots in the Imagist experiment, and Stead's comments on the nondiscursive Imagist poem are useful in approaching Eliot's method. Nevertheless, there has been strangely little attempt to relate the Imagist movement to the experimentation in the arts in general at the turn of this century. Both the nature and scope of Stead's study *The New Poetic*[2] preclude the sort of comprehensive examination which Mr Hough thinks is necessary. While I could not hope to supply a study of the range and depth indicated in Hough's comment, it is, nevertheless, the purpose of this book to offer a re-definition of the principles underlying Eliot's early method and to examine them in relation to the background roots of the modernist movement in general, rather than concentrate on a few, individual, well-known influences.

At the outset we must underline our earlier statement that when Eliot speaks of the 'meaning' of poetry, he understands by it something more comprehensive than the paraphrase that the critic can make of any single poem. As he himself put it in 1942:

> If, as we are aware, only a part of the meaning can be conveyed by paraphrase, that is because the poet is occupied with frontiers of consciousness beyond which words fail though meanings still exist.[3]

In other words, it is the business of the poet to find the means of exploring a new world of meaning beyond the limitations of normal understanding, meaning for which ordinary expression is useless. The rôle of the poet needs some clarification, however, for Eliot is not here suggesting that he is some sort of inspired seer reporting to his audience the discoveries he makes in some pure realm of infinity. The need seems to have arisen once again to separate Eliot from the Romantic tradition which produced 'radiant truth out of space and time'[4]—Frank Kermode's

---

[1] Graham Hough, *Image and Experience* (1960), p. 51.
[2] C. K. Stead, *The New Poetic: Yeats to Eliot* (1964).
[3] 'The Music of Poetry', *On Poetry and Poets* (1957), p. 30.
[4] Frank Kermode, *Romantic Image* (1957), p. 2.

definition of the Romantic Image. Eliot's whole theory of the impersonality of art, and moreover, his refusal to recognise the personality of the poet as the sole qualification for artistic practice, are difficult to reconcile with the super-confidence of the Romantic poet in the self-sufficiency of his own sensibility. While Professor Kermode illustrates the autonomy of the Romantic Image well, he clearly indicates that it proceeds from an imagination glorying in its visionary sense. He defines it as

> The free, self-delighting intellect which knows that pain is the cost of its joy; the licence to look inward and paint, as Blake and Palmer painted, a symbolic world; to make a magical explanation of a divine order—all this represents the victory of Coleridge, of Blake and the French; it is the heritage, delightful and tragic, to which Yeats was born.[1]

In Professor Kermode's terms, the Romantic looks inwards for the Image, and overcome with the joy of finding it there, is left with the agonizing task of communicating it. Eliot's poetic exploration beyond the 'frontiers of consciousness' is, on the other hand, in the terms of this study, not a voyage of self-discovery, for as I hope to demonstrate, it is an attempt to transcend the perceptual limitations of any single personality.

The statement quoted above from 'The Music of Poetry' was made considerably outside the historical scope of this study but is, nevertheless, appropriate here, in that it places Eliot quite firmly in the modern movement of the arts in general which started early in the 1900s. Artists, in whatever medium they work, have all sought from the beginning of this century to break down the barriers of conventional expression and to reveal to us new meanings, new perceptions of reality beyond the 'frontiers of consciousness'. They assume that at any precise instant one can see only one view of an object, one can feel only one emotion. The eye can, nevertheless, move very quickly to take in the object from several different aspects, just as emotions can vary from moment to moment to make up a complex reaction to the particular object or event in our consciousness. The field of human vision is fixed, however, and the range of our emotions before a given object limited, according to our individual personalities. The ideal way to see an object in its totality would be,

[1] ibid., p. 26.

presumably, if human perception could experience all aspects of it at once. Although the human eye is physically incapable of moving all the way round an object in a single moment of consciousness, the painter of the early twentieth century believed that by arranging various views of the same object simultaneously together on a canvas, the spectator could experience something of its 'total existence',[1] which would be a new and exciting discovery for him. For poetry this meant that the poet no longer wished to confine himself to a single point of view, or to concentrate on one aspect of an emotion, but to attempt to catch within the duration of the single poem the mind as it oscillates between one view and another and to include other people's experience of the same emotion as well. In both these art forms 'time' has a special significance. Each artist wishes to show us all aspects at the same time, since this is the most accurate way of expressing the 'reality' of his object or emotional experience. Just as the camera has advanced from the daguerreotype 'still' picture to present an object in its composite perspective by moving itself or catching the object as it moves, so the painter and poet aim at expanding their medium to bring to the 'still' form of their art something of this cinematic technique. The aim common to both painter and poet can be summed up in the Impressionist desire to:

. . . seize, in passing, the variations in aspect which the same scene assumes at different moments and to fix them on the canvas with precision.[3]

The attempts of twentieth-century artists to deal with reality in new ways have as their background a whole field of scientific and philosophical thought, the work of philosophers like Henri Bergson, Alfred North Whitehead and the one who is most interesting for the early Eliot, F. H. Bradley. In 1893, Bradley produced *Appearance and Reality* and it was *Essays on Truth and Reality* which was the subject of Eliot's doctorate thesis *Knowledge and Experience in the Philosophy of F. H. Bradley*.[3] The ideas which Eliot examines in this thesis are not easy to

[1] André Salmon, *La Jeune Peinture Française* (Paris, 1912), quoted by Wylie Sypher, *Rococo to Cubism in Art and Literature* (1960), p. 260.
[2] Duret, *Manet and the French Impressionists*, quoted by Wylie Sypher, ibid., p. 183.
[3] Written in 1916, published 1964.

follow and a detailed analysis of Bradley's thought is outside the scope of this study. In so far as one can summarize basic ideas to illustrate the trend of modern thought, however, Bradley stated that reality has no absolute contours but varies according to the way one looks at it. A single view of any object therefore presents a very limited view of its reality and, in Bradley's terms, is only an 'appearance'. Although appearances are partial realities, they are, nevertheless, the only means we have of approaching the total reality of an object:

. . . appearance without reality would be impossible and reality without appearance would be nothing.[1]

While the *identity* of any object depends on our actual experience of it, its *reality* is made up of the multiplicity of its various 'appearances'. Thus the reality of any object—and Eliot takes for illustration of Bradley's theories a red flower—is the sum of its total appearances:

The real flower, we can say, will be the sum of its effects—its actual effects upon other entities—and this sum must form a system, must somehow hang together.[2]

Ideas like these obviously lay behind the Cubists' theory of composition, for they define the objects of their pictures in practically identical terms:

An object hasn't any absolute form. It has many: as many as there are planes in the domain of meaning . . . autant d'yeux à contempler un objet, autant d'images essentielles.[3]

For the Cubist painter 'reality' could therefore only be expressed by assembling multiple images of it. The more views the artist could incorporate into his picture, the more accurately would he express the reality of his object.

And so we can now turn to the ways Eliot has applied his view of reality to the task of the writer. As his criticism indicates, Eliot finds the greatest poetry written by those poets who have

---

[1] F. H. Bradley, *Appearance and Reality* (1893), quoted by Wylie Sypher, op. cit., p. 272.
[2] T. S. Eliot, *Knowledge and Experience in the Philosophy of F. H. Bradley* (1964), p. 30.
[3] Gleizes and Metzinger, quoted by Wylie Sypher, op. cit., p. 268.

achieved poetic 'comprehensiveness'[1] by sacrificing the elaboration of a single view in their poems. I. A. Richards, one of the
chief spokesmen for this poetry of 'inclusion', as he chooses to
call it, writes in *Principles of Literary Criticism*:

A very great deal of poetry and art is content with the full ordered
development of comparatively special and limited experiences, with a
definite emotion, for example Sorrow, Joy, Pride, or a definite
attitude, Love, Indignation, Admiration, Hope, or with a specific
mood, Melancholy, Optimism, or Longing. And such art has its own
value and place in human affairs. No one will quarrel with 'Break,
break, break', or with 'Coronach', or with 'Rose Aylmer', or with
'Love's Philosophy', although clearly they are limited and exclusive.
But they are not the greatest kind of poetry.[2]

Eliot has consistently defined 'great' poetry or classical poetry
in terms similar to these. While he praises eighteenth-century
writers for the way in which they display classical virtues in the
act of composition, they do so by excluding the finer shades of
feeling and thought from their subjects:

In the eighteenth century, we are oppressed by the limited range of
sensibility, and especially in the scale of religious feeling.[3]

Writing much earlier of Marvell's satires, Eliot praises him for
his 'equipoise'—'a balance and proportion of tones'—which make
him a classic in ways which Gray and Collins are not; they
cannot be accredited with the title because they 'are comparatively poor in shades of feeling to contrast and unite'.[4] Tourneur,
for all Eliot's praise of him, is an immature artist and *The
Revenger's Tragedy* might be the work of 'a highly sensitive
adolescent with a gift for words'.[5] Eliot quotes Churton
Collins's comment in support of his views:

'Tourneur's great defect as a dramatic poet . . . is undoubtedly the
narrowness of his range of vision': and this narrowness of range might
be that of a young man.[6]

The highest form of poetry, according to Eliot's definition of it,

[1] 'What is a Classic?', *On Poetry and Poets*, p. 67.
[2] I. A. Richards, *Principles of Literary Criticism* (1926 edition), pp. 249, 250.
[3] 'What is a Classic?', *On Poetry and Poets*, p. 60.
[4] 'Andrew Marvell', *Selected Essays* (1951 edition), p. 302.
[5] 'Cyril Tourneur', ibid., p. 189.
[6] ibid.

should, on the other hand, 'express the maximum possible of the whole range of feeling'.[1] In order to achieve this ideal the artist, as all these comments indicate, should first of all aim at the greatest possible maturity in his personal outlook. This necessitates his becoming more and more objective and less concerned with expressing the singleness of vision to which a purely individualist view would commit him. Aristotle, Eliot believes, had this maturity of outlook which made for his perfect critical method. The 'ordinary' intelligence, he writes, like that of the brilliant man of science, for example, will like one particular poet because he expresses ideas with which he can agree and emotions which he can admire. The 'universal intelligence' of Aristotle enabled him, on the other hand, to look:

. . . solely and steadfastly at the object; in his short and broken treatise he provides an eternal example—not of laws, or even of method, for there is no method except to be very intelligent . . .[2]

It is this same 'universal intelligence' which the poet should bring to bear upon the 'objects', the emotions with which he wishes to deal in his poem.

The 'depersonalization' of the artist as a preliminary step towards the comprehensive or inclusive poem is a major preoccupation of the early Eliot: the cult of an 'impersonal' or 'universal' apprehension which can see in every experience 'other kinds of experience which are possible'.[3] This 'impersonality' needs careful definition, however. C. K. Stead, for example, sees it as the poet's escape from self into a deeper self of soul:

It is the voice of the poet's 'soul'—that part of his being which is unknowable, even to himself. It expresses itself, not in 'thought', but by a recreation of diverse experience into 'feeling', which in turn becomes . . . the essential texture of the poem.[4]

In a way, therefore, according to Stead, the more impersonal Eliot appears, the more deeply, if unconsciously, personal he actually is. Stead thus sees 'Prufrock' and 'Gerontion' as expressions of 'the dark stain of some intense suffering'[5] in

---

[1] *On Poetry and Poets*, p. 67.
[2] 'The Perfect Critic', *The Sacred Wood* (1950 edition), p. 11.
[3] 'Andrew Marvell', *Selected Essays*, p. 303.
[4] Stead, op. cit., p. 144.          [5] ibid., p. 157.

Eliot, but of which even he is unaware; and it is this same suffering which is carried over into 'The Waste Land'. The implication that the emotions articulated in the poetry can all be found
in the poet's inner soul is a reading of Eliot's impersonality
which seems to deny Eliot's whole theory of composition. Eliot's
implied poetic method of apprehending the 'objects' of reality can
only be described, in the poet's own terms, as the means whereby
the poet attempts to transcend the bounds of his empirical self
and look on his poetry as a medium whereby a comprehensive
vision of reality can be presented. Hence Eliot writes in 'Tradition and the Individual Talent':

. . . the poet has not a 'personality' to express but a particular
medium, which is only a medium and not a personality, in which impressions and experiences combine in peculiar and unexpected ways.
Impressions and experiences which are important for the man may take
no place in the poetry, and those which become important in the poetry
may play quite a negligible part in the man, the personality.[1]

In the same essay he says:

It is not in his personal emotions, the emotions provoked by particular
events in his life that the poet is in any way remarkable or interesting.
His particular emotions may be simple, or crude, or flat. The emotion
in his poetry will be a very complex thing, but not with the complexity
of the emotions of people who have very complex or unusual emotions
in life.[2]

Eliot therefore writes of the depersonalizing process whereby the
man becomes a poet as 'a continual self-sacrifice, a continual
extinction of personality'.[3] The mind of the poet should be
solely

. . . a receptacle for seizing and storing up numberless feelings,
phrases, images, which remain there until all the particles which can
unite to form a new compound are present together.[4]

Although personal emotions may and do form the *initial* urge to
write, as we shall see, the poem should present them only as part
of a far more comprehensive structure of related emotions. The
significance of the personal element will therefore be superseded
in the poem by the greater importance of the total integration.

---

[1] *Selected Essays*, pp. 19, 20.       [2] ibid., pp. 20, 21.
[3] ibid., p. 17.                         [4] ibid., p. 19.

Eliot implies the artistic process by which the simple emotion becomes complex, the personal view of the artist, the impersonal and comprehensive view of the poem, in his definition of the impressionistic method of Symons's criticism. While he may not hold that this is the perfect method of criticism, he seems to indicate that it is the best method for poetry:

For in an artist these suggestions made by a work of art, which are purely personal, become fused with a multitude of other suggestions from multitudinous experience, and result in the production of a new object which is no longer purely personal, because it is a work of art itself.[1]

One obvious way to achieve universality and comprehensiveness would simply be to express the general look of the object, and by excluding the personality of the poet, iron out his individual response to it. Eliot's 'generality' is reached in a more complex way, however. In the perhaps little-known article 'That Poetry is made with Words',[2] he speaks of the uselessness of the general statements of science for the artist and in particular of the uselessness of the knowledge of psychology for the creation of dramatic characters. The findings of modern psychology, he says, simply illustrate the sameness of one man to another, making his responses wholly predictable, 'always unconvincing and usually false'. The passage is worth examining, for it appears to provide a contradiction of what we have just said about the impersonality of art:

The great characters of drama and prose fiction may themselves provide material for study to psychologists; but out of the psychologists' abstractions no character can be put together. The dramatist must study, not psychology, but human beings; and to what he observes, dissects and combines he must add something from himself of which he may not be wholly conscious.

In another essay, on Blake, he writes of the danger of 'general' education for the artist:

It is important that the artist should be highly educated in his own art; but his education is one that is hindered rather than helped by the ordinary processes of society which constitute education for the ordinary man. For these processes consist largely in the acquisition of

1 *The Sacred Wood*, p. 7.
2 *New English Weekly*, XV No. 2, 27 April, 1939.

impersonal ideas which obscure what we really are and feel, what we
really want, and what really excites our interest. It is of course not the
actual information acquired, but the conformity which the accumula-
tion of knowledge is apt to impose, that is harmful.[1]

What Eliot is here suggesting is that the personal interests of
the poet and the particular observations which he makes of
human character *should* be the starting point of poetry. He goes
on, in 'That Poetry is made with Words', to say that, if poetry:

. . . is not to be a lifeless repetition of forms, [it] must be constantly
exploring the 'frontiers of the spirit'.

How then can a poet achieve comprehensiveness and
impersonality, if at the same time he is concerned with himself
and his own particular observations? Eliot explains that the
'frontiers of the spirit' are not necessarily always the personal
emotions:

[They] are not like the surveys of geographical explorers, conquered
once and for all and settled. The frontiers of the spirit are more like the
jungle which, unless continuously kept under control, is always ready to
encroach and eventually obliterate the cultivated area. Our effort is as
much to regain, under very different conditions, what was known to men
writing at remote times and in alien languages.

It is therefore 'the endless battle to regain civilization in the
midst of outer and inner change' as much as 'the struggle to
conquer the absolutely new' which is the aim for the mature poet:

Just as history has constantly to be re-written, because everything is
gradually altered by the lengthening perspective, so also the poet needs
an alert consciousness of the past, in order to realize in its particular
concreteness the moment at which he lives.

The poet must therefore bring to his particular and individual
awareness of the moment at which he lives the acquired awareness of the past. To do this, he must not simply substitute
'modern furniture for the furniture of a previous period' in his
*mise en scène*. A dramatic scene in modern terms always differs
in 'emotional quality' from a similar scene at another time; the
individuality of the modern scene must be preserved at the same
time as the poet discovers the old. In other words, the historical

---

[1] 'Blake', *The Sacred Wood*, p. 154.

sense must inform the particular moment at which the poet lives; it should not cancel it out. The poet thus starts from the particularity of his own time, the individuality of his own personal view and then, by surrounding it, in the context of the poem, with other views, works up a comprehensiveness, a universality which will transcend this particularity. The universality of the final poem is therefore a quality which is assembled from the particularity of the individual parts of which it is made up. Just as Bradley defined reality of an object as the sum of its individual appearances, so Eliot's generality, his comprehensiveness, is made up by assembling particular observations, personal views. The 'subject' of a poem will be what the poem finally is, not the initial personal emotion from which it started. In 'The Music of Poetry' he speaks of the autonomous nature of this kind of poetry:

. . . when I learn that a difficult sonnet was inspired by seeing a painting on the ceiling reflected on the polished top of a table, or by seeing the light reflected from the foam on a glass of beer, I can only say that this may be a correct embryology, but it is not the meaning.[1]

The 'meaning' will be something which has no referent in the single experience either of the poet or of the audience because it will be 'beyond the frontiers of consciousness' of both.

We can now return to our initial comments on the theory of modern art in general and show how Eliot's practice subscribes to its main tendencies. He clearly wishes to achieve the same 'total vision' as that of the Cubists by bringing as many aspects of his 'object' as are possible into the poem:

Autant d'yeux à contempler un objet, autant d'images essentielles.[2]

This linking of Eliot's method with that of the painters of the same period is not one which he himself might have approved. As Herbert Read points out in a 'Memoir' published in a recent collection of essays, Eliot had very little interest in the visual arts of his time:

If pressed he would no doubt have admitted that the tradition that led from Poe and Baudelaire to Laforgue and Rimbaud and his own poetry

[1] *On Poetry and Poets*, p. 30.
[2] Wylie Sypher, op. cit., p. 268. See p. 5.

could not be entirely divorced from the tradition that led from Delacroix and Cézanne to Matisse and Picasso, but he would not himself
have made much of the comparison.[1]

While this is so, the fact remains that the two methods *are*
analagous and provide interesting ground for comparison. We
can sum up Eliot's method of composition in terms similar to
those we used to describe a Cubist painting. The poet starts off
with his 'subject', an emotion as he feels it in the present, the
'object' which he wishes to examine. His immediate reaction to
it forms one 'appearance'. By surrounding it with other related
'appearances' either for the similarity or contrast they provide,
he achieves inclusiveness or comprehensiveness. When these
'appearances' include what other poets in other languages, in
times past, have felt about the same 'objects', then his poem will
have gained 'universality' and timelessness, Eliot's special view
of traditionalism. It is 'reality' showing itself in the multiple
appearances which go to make it up, the eternal manifesting
itself in the transitory which Eliot seeks to present in his poetry
and to which he brings his 'mature' intelligence.

When the poet has these aims constantly before him and has
achieved maturity of intelligence and the historical sense, the
will to sacrifice his own personal and limited view in favour of an
impersonal and comprehensive one, he is then in a position to
concentrate on his craft—the problems of the poet as opposed to
the problems of the man. In his most recently published article
on Dante, he expresses what these problems are:

The task of the poet, in making people comprehend the incomprehen-
sible, demands immense resources of language; and in developing the
language, enriching the meaning of words and showing how much
words can do, he is making possible a much greater range of emotion
and perception for other men, because he gives them the speech in
which more can be expressed.[2]

It is only through his artistic medium, language, that the poet
can present this comprehensive vision of reality. By concentrat-
ing on his own language the poet makes possible new emotions;
by rediscovering the language of the past he rediscovers lost
emotions. In the article to which we have already referred, 'That

---

[1] *T. S. Eliot: The Man and his Work* (1967) (ed. Allen Tate), p. 33.
[2] T. S. Eliot, *To Criticize the Critic* (1965), p. 134.

Poetry is made with Words', he indicates clearly the close relationship that exists between the language of poetry and the comprehensive vision. He discusses Maritain's distinction between two types of poet, the one who is solely interested in 'la découverte de soi-même' and the other in 'l'action poétique elle-même'. Neither preoccupation should exclude the other, he writes, and he suggests instead that the poet's task should be 'the problem of what he can do with his language':

A ceaseless care, a passionate and untiring devotion to language is the first concern of the poet; it demands study of how his language has been written in both prose and verse, in the past, and sensitiveness to the merits and shortcomings of the way in which it is spoken and written in his own time.

That is not to say, however, that the poet should concern himself solely with words and craft. In his essay on Swinburne he has made this clear; after speaking of the 'morbidity' of poetry which dwells exclusively among words, he writes:

. . . the language which is more important to us is that which is struggling to digest and express new objects, new groups of objects, new feelings, new aspects . . .[1]

On the other hand these 'new objects', 'new feelings' are not exclusively the poet's interior discovery of himself. As we have seen from the earlier part of this chapter, the 'frontiers of the spirit' are emotions as they were felt and expressed in the past. It is the occupation of the poet, therefore, in acquiring knowledge of the past, in exploring beyond the frontiers of the spirit, to discover and rediscover language:

. . . what would make me most apprehensive about the future of the language—and that implies the future of sensibility, for what we cease to try to find words for, we cease to be able to feel—would be to observe a decreasing level of literacy amongst poets.[2]

The ultimate task for the poet, then, is to render his language comprehensible, and this makes enormous demands on the poet's medium—words. Translated into terms of poetic craft, what Eliot along with contemporary poets in France and Pound in England were attempting to do, was to transcend the limitations

[1] 'Swinburne as Poet', *Selected Essays*, p. 327.
[2] 'That Poetry is made with Words', op. cit.

of words themselves in poetry; to break down the singleness of meaning of words in order to explore a richer multiplicity of meaning through them. Eliot's point of departure in this objective is the language as it is at present:

Even if the language is deteriorated, the poet must begin from where he is, and not from a point at which be believes the language to have been superior.[1]

The initial task of the poet is therefore to render the language of his own time more exact for the immediate observations which he makes of 'new objects'. Just as the completely comprehensive poem must rise from the particular to the general, from the immediate to the timeless, so language must start from the particular. 'General' words, such as those used by Swinburne, are of no use, for it is 'but the vague associations of idea that the words give him.[2] Swinburne has not his eye on a particular place, a particular object, in his poetry:

When you take to pieces any verse of Swinburne, you find always that the object was not there—only the words.[3]

'Language in a healthy state', he goes on, 'presents the object, is so close to the object, that the two are identified.' If it is the particular aspect in the concrete language of his own time from which the poet must start, how then can his language become comprehensive? In the same way that the particular observation was assembled into a complex structure to make the comprehensive poem, so particular language is raised by connotation within the context of the poem to include a wide multiplicity of meaning. It is the purpose of the chapters which follow to examine how this is achieved, to examine the formative process by which Eliot discovers a new concrete language capable of expressing the 'appearances' of his world and the ways whereby these 'appearances' are arranged in a pattern-structure to achieve a comprehensive meaning. By the pattern which the poet makes with words and images, he aims to reach a universal 'still point', the point where time, representing the meanings of the here and now, intersects the timeless, the associations which the same words have had for all poets in all time. The development of the

[1] ibid.
[2] *Selected Essays*, p. 326.        [3] ibid.

early poetry from 'Preludes' to 'The Waste Land' represents the various stages by which he achieves this aim. He himself expresses the 'stillness' of this timeless vision of art in 'Burnt Norton':

> Only by the form, the pattern,
> Can words or music reach
> The stillness, as a Chinese jar still
> Moves perpetually in its stillness.[1]

If the comprehensive poem involved the breakdown of the singleness of meaning of words, it also meant the breakdown of conventional structure; a break-up of classical transition which dictated that one part of an artistic structure should follow logically after the other. In classical drama, for example, the audience was taken from event to event from the beginning to the end in the same way that traditional linear perspective in painting related every object to all other objects. Just as in painting, this perspective involved a single point from which to view the object, so classical structure involved a single line of thought progression. The arts of the twentieth century all oppose this type of progression. Instead, they supply a different kind of logic, the logic of juxtaposing. These artists do not want to move from point to point in a linear fashion, but in a circuitous locus, where they can bring all aspects of the object to the view of the spectator simultaneously. The object in painting is to make us see all aspects at once, in a single moment; and in poetry, to conceive of various attitudes at one and the same time, which include, in Eliot's most ambitious poems, aspects and views from the past. The technique was called, significantly enough, by Delaunay, 'simultanéisme'.[2] In technical terms, its principle was simply that the parts of the poem were to be kept deliberately at random, until the artist was ready to assemble them in his poem. The unity of the resultant assemblage depended not on the logical way in which the artist worked out his thoughts from the beginning to the end, but on the intensity of awareness which he achieved through the interpenetration of the parts which made it up. Unity was not provided by a careful guidance through the successive parts of the poem; it was not

[1] *Collected Poems*, (1963 edition), p. 194.
[2] William Seitz, *The Art of Assemblage* (1961), p. 15.

*progression,* but awareness of a still point where all the parts of the poem could be felt to exist in a continuous present. Roger Shattuck discusses these ideas in his chapter on Apollinaire in *The Banquet Years,* and describes this unity in almost Eliotic terms:

Unity becomes not progression, but intensification by standing still, a continuous present in which everything is taken together and always. Memory and attention, the two prime faculties of human consciousness, can be trained to conceive intuitively in simultaneous occurrence as well as historically in chronological unfolding.[1]

If the poem 'moves', it moves circuitously. In Eliot's words:

> Not the stillness of the violin, while the note lasts,
> Not that only, but the co-existence,
> Or say that the end precedes the beginning,
> And the end and the beginning were always there
> Before the beginning and after the end.
> And all is always now.[2]

Like the poems of Gertrude Stein, Eliot's poems have neither beginning nor end; they are all middle:

All things in that universal middle exist in the rudimentary order (apparent disorder) of conflict, an order we conceive only when we perceive its parts as simultaneous.[3]

Of Stein, Shattuck says:

Her poems and narratives do not progress from one point to another, but establish themselves deeper and deeper in a perpetual mode of existence.[4]

It is the same kind of structure which Eliot assembles out of the parts of his poem. It is what Shattuck calls 'the juxtaposition of parts around a moment of profound awareness'. This moment cannot be reached in the poem itself, since it is 'beyond the frontiers of consciousness',[5] only in the areas of association outside it to which its parts act as directives.

All art is a formative experience and the final art form the

[1] Roger Shattuck, *The Banquet Years* (1959), p. 268.
[2] 'Burnt Norton', *Collected Poems*, p. 194.
[3] Roger Shattuck, op. cit., p. 268.
[4] ibid.
[5] *On Poetry and Poets* (1951), p. 30. See also p. 2.

record which the artist leaves of it. The variations which the
history of art reveals within this general intention simply
illustrate the various stages at which the artist declares his work
to be done. The conventional or traditional stage is where he
analyses and rationalizes his experience and hands it over to the
audience as his conclusive thoughts on the subject. The artists of
the twentieth century leave off at an earlier stage—where they
are still in the act of discovery for themselves. Their art is the
art of recording the very act of thinking, feeling and discovering.
The artist working in a conventional medium tells us what to feel
and think in his art form; the artists of this century invite us to
share their discoveries simultaneously with them. There are no
conclusions, for conclusions are ultimately a personal and therefore limited assessment or appraisal of an experience. If they
have left through their medium the right words in the right
order, that discovery should be made easier for us. Instead of the
interpretation of reality being the interesting part of the artist's
work, it is now the psychological exactitude of the way he
perceives it. Herbert Read, examining the new art of this
century, writes:

Art is for the first time clearly conceived, not as a mere reproduction of
a ready-made, given reality, but as the discovery of reality, which
discovery is communicated in symbolic form.[1]

Artistic activity is not a retrospective, distilled analysis of
experience, but a symbolic means of perceiving—as useful as the
scientist's or the philosopher's methods of classifying the modern
world. The art of this century therefore seeks its own reality, its
own right, to independent status. Its discoveries are as autonomous as the discoveries of science, for the artist as rationalist and
thinker has disappeared and with him the singleness of the
individualist's view. What we are left with is the poem, the
means of discovering reality in something approaching its 'total
existence'. The poet of this century, by perfecting his medium as
far as he can, relies on it alone to induce the reader to co-
operate in this discovery. In the method of mature criticism,
Eliot writes:

. . . the critic must not coerce, and he must not make judgements of

1 Herbert Read, *Art Now* (1960), p. 41.

worse and better. He must simply elucidate; the reader will form the correct judgement for himself.[1]

It is the same method which is the method of mature poetry.

This study sets out to examine Eliot's 'means of elucidation', the method whereby he induces us to co-operate in his discovery of a world of meaning beyond 'the frontiers of consciousness'. As his first concern was with the language of his own day, we shall begin by examining the means whereby he renders it more exact for the articulation of the individual 'appearances' of modern reality; the method whereby these 'appearances' are assembled to form a comprehensive or universal 'vortex of perception',[2] to borrow the terms by which Hugh Kenner describes the similar 'meaning' of Pound. We shall finally consider the art-object itself, the poem, and its right to independent status as an instance of art.

[1] *The Sacred Wood*, p. 11.
[2] Hugh Kenner, *The Poetry of Ezra Pound* (1951), p. 189.

# II  The Imagist experiment: the fragment poem

Eliot was not alone and not the first to see the necessity for a new poetic language to express 'the new objects, new groups of objects, new feelings'[1] which were the poet's particular reaction to the modern world. Sometime during the year 1908, T. E. Hulme, then a comparatively unknown student of aesthetics, proposed the formation of a Poets' Club,[2] and from the moment of its first meeting, there began the earliest attempts in England to emancipate poetry from the devitalized forms and idioms of a failing Romantic tradition which characterized contemporary poetic effort. Nineteenth-century Romanticism had long since passed the climax of its achievement and as Hulme was later to express it in *Speculations*:

We shall not get any new efflorescence of verse until we get a new technique, a new convention, to turn ourselves loose in.[3]

The way in which Hulme argued that the end of Romanticism had come and a new age of Classicism was about to dawn is elaborated in the large part of *Speculations* devoted to a discussion of humanism, which need not concern us here. It is primarily interesting, however, for the emphasis which it places on poetic language and craft and the necessity for the poet to concentrate on his medium. Central to Hulme's argument for a neo-Classical revival was the idea that poets had gone far enough in seeing themselves—to use Stephen Spender's term—as 'writer-prophets';[4] who, by setting themselves above the situation in which they lived, allowed themselves the privilege of judging and making philosophical pronouncements on it in the form of poetry. Such fond illusions about their superior gifts and the worth of their 'message' encouraged them, as Hulme believed, to conceive of themselves as God. The Classical poet by comparison never forgets his finiteness, his human limitations:

1 'Swinburne as Poet', *Selected Essays* (1951 edition), p. 327. See Ch. 1, p. 13.
2 Glenn Hughes, *Imagism and the Imagists* (1960), p. 10.
3 T. E. Hulme, *Speculations* (1924), p. 122.
4 Stephen Spender, *The Struggle of the Modern* (1963), p. 71.

He remembers always that he is mixed up with earth. He may jump, but he always returns back; he never flies away into the circumambient gas.

You might say that the whole of the romantic attitude seems to crystallize in verse round metaphors of flight. Hugo is always flying, flying over abysses, flying up into the eternal gases. The word infinite is in every other line.[1]

The material with which the poet has to deal should therefore be the realm of finite things and his task that of rendering his observations of these things in the most accurate way possible. From this point the theory gains in complexity, for the 'revolution' which Hulme was initiating was not a belated form of French Parnassianism. Hulme saw the artist as a person who has the ability to see things more accurately than the normal person whose perception of things has been conditioned or hardened into certain stereotyped responses. The normal man sees things according to the use he can make of them, whereas the artist is the man

. . . who on one side of his nature is born detached from the necessities of action.[2]

He can therefore see things as they are, in a disinterested way, which is the most accurate way of perceiving them. This detachment is not complete, however, for the artist also has his human limitations. The most he can do, therefore, is

. . . to pierce through here and there, accidentally as it were, the veil placed between us and reality by the limitations of our perception engendered by action.[3]

In other words, the artist perceives things as they really are, only in moments, and it is these 'exquisite moments' or the 'vivid patches of life' which Hulme has in mind when he speaks of the 'reality' of poetry:

Literature, like memory, selects only the vivid patches of life. If literature (realistic) did really resemble life, it would be interminable, dreary, commonplace, eating and dressing, buttoning, with here and there a patch of vividness. Life is composed of exquisite moments and the rest is shadows of them.[4]

[1] T. E. Hulme, op. cit., p. 120.      [2] ibid., p. 155.      [3] ibid., p. 147.
[4] T. E. Hulme, *Notes on Language and Style*, quoted by Glenn Hughes, op. cit., p. 21.

A poem then could be clearly defined in Hulme's terms as an accurate presentation of the reality of 'exquisite moments', without 'moaning or whining about something or other'[1] or a moralizing attitude on the part of the poet. He then goes on to sum up the general aims of art in terms which we have already identified as being typical of the artists of this century:

. . . art must be always individual and springs from dissatisfaction with the generalized expressions of ordinary perception and ordinary language.[2]

Like them, he sees that the problem for the artist is ultimately a struggle with his medium. Ordinary language, as it is used conventionally, only expresses the stereotyped or 'general' perception. The important part of the artist's experience, its particularity and individuality, is left out:

The straightforward use of words always lets the individuality of things escape. Language, being a communal apparatus, only conveys over that part of the emotion which is common to all of us. If you are able to observe the actual individuality of the emotion you experience, you become dissatisfied with language. You persist in an endeavour to so state things that the meaning does not escape, but is definitely forced on the attention of the reader . . . It is because language will not carry over the exact thing you want to say, that you are compelled simply, in order to be accurate, to invent original ways of stating things.[3]

And so we come to the practicability of this theory for poetry. The new and original ways of saying things, which Hulme found necessary if poetry was to be accurate, were to be found in a new kind of imagery: fresh, unusual metaphors and analogies:

Plain speech is essentially inaccurate. It is only by new metaphors, that is by fancy, that it can be made precise.[4]

This precise analogy was otherwise known as the Image.

Such were the main tendencies of Hulme's thoughts about poetry which, although they were discussed at the various meetings of the Poets' Club, were not published by Hulme himself until *Speculations* appeared in 1924. F. S. Flint, a founder member of the Club, wrote 'The History of Imagism' which appeared in *The Egoist* for 1 May 1915[5] and anticipates many of

---

[1] *Speculations*, p. 126.      [2] ibid., p. 153.      [3] ibid., p. 162.
[4] ibid., p. 137.               [5] See Glenn Hughes, op. cit., p. 11.

the ideas which were later to be elaborated in *Speculations,* and
when Ezra Pound joined the movement, the famous Imagist
Manifesto was set down in the form of a Preface to the 1915
Imagist Anthology. I shall quote it only in part:

To allow absolute freedom in the choice of subject. It is not good art to
write badly about aeroplanes and automobiles; nor is it necessarily bad
art to write well about the past. We believe passionately in the artistic
value of modern life, but we wish to point out that there is nothing so
uninspiring nor so old-fashioned as an aeroplane of the year 1911.

To present an image (hence the name imagist). We are not a school of
painters, but we believe that poetry should render particulars exactly
and not deal in vague generalities, however magnificent and sonorous.
It is for this reason that we oppose the cosmic poet who seems to us to
shirk the real difficulties of his art.

To produce poetry that is hard and clear, never blurred nor indefinite.

Finally most of us believe that concentration is of the essence of poetry.

The importance of Pound's personal comprehension of the Image
will be dealt with in another chapter. For the moment we can sum
up the essential principles from which all Imagists proceeded,
resulting from Hulme's initial speculations about the nature of
poetry, as 'absolute freedom in the choice of subject' and 'to
present an Image'. It is the means whereby the poet finds the
words to express this Image which are of the utmost importance
for this study of Eliot's method, for it is with similar objectives
and resulting from identical procedure that Eliot presents us
with the images which form the individual 'appearances' of his
early poems, lines like:

> When the evening is spread out against the sky
> Like a patient etherised upon a table;
> > 'The Love Song of J. Alfred Prufrock'

> His soul stretched tight across the skies
> That fade behind a city block,
> Or trampled by insistent feet
> At four and five and six o'clock;
> > 'Preludes'

> Midnight shakes the memory
> As a madman shakes a dead geranium.
>
> > 'Rhapsody on a Windy Night'

> I an old man,
> A dull head among windy spaces.
>
> > 'Gerontion'

> Son of man,
> You cannot say, or guess, for you know only
> A heap of broken images, where the sun beats,
> And the dead tree gives no shelter, the cricket no relief,
> And the dry stone no sound of water.
>
> > 'The Waste Land'[1]

The Image has been defined and redefined by the Imagists themselves, but basically it is the immediate reaction on the sensibility of a poet to an event which strikes him forcibly. The effort of the poet to realize an Image is the most significant part of his work. Stephen Spender in *The Struggle of the Modern* has described this effort as 'the kind of concentration in performance which remains faithful to the moment in which an idea, visualized, first purely occurs and asserts its claim that it is capable of further definition'.[2] The whole process by which the Imagist poet proceeds is beautifully summed up by him in the same chapter:

When I ask myself the question: 'Is this image suitable for poetry?', the answer I give is revealing of my innermost convictions about the nature of the kind of poetry I believe I ought to write. I might say, for example, 'Yes, if it is beautiful or if it can be conveyed in words which are poetic, or if it fits into a stanza form which I already have in mind.' The imagists insisted that the answer should be simply: 'Yes, if I feel the force of an image.' And if I then protested: 'I do see an image, but I don't feel it suitable for a poem.' They then replied: 'There is no such thing as unsuitable.' 'Yes, but I can't see this image as music or pattern.' 'Well then, do without music or pattern, simply use the best words in the best order to realize the image.'[3]

If the poet is true to his 'Imagistic' experience, the resultant poetry will be accurate, clear and precise, because it will be direct communication between poet and audience, so direct in

[1] T. S. Eliot, *Collected Poems* (1963 edition), pp. 13, 24, 26, 39, 63.
[2] Stephen Spender, op. cit., p. 111.     [3] ibid.

fact, that he will not take time to 'translate' it into the exposi-
tory prose sentence with the normal grammatical rules of syntax. So we are led back to the primitive situation where the job
of the poet is to let us see how his mind 'thinks'. It is in this that
the Imagists were attracted to the French Symbolists and their
champion, Rémy de Gourmont. De Gourmont had stated that

On pense au moyen d'images[1]

which is otherwise stated by T. E. Hulme:

Thought is prior to language and consists in the simultaneous presentation to the mind of two different images. Language is only a more or
less feeble way of doing this.[2]

It would then follow in de Gourmont's terms, paraphrased by
Taupin, that

L'émotion étant à la base de toute connaissance, l'art se doit de chercher
les moyens d'opérer la communication directe entre l'émotion et
l'expression, entre l'artiste et le public.[3]

and for T. E. Hulme:

The direct language is poetry, it is direct because it deals in images.[4]

This leads Hulme on to his conclusion on the subject of 'inspiration':

Thought is the joining together of new analogies and so inspiration is a
matter of an accidentally seen analogy or unlooked for resemblance.
It is therefore necessary to get as large as possible change in sense
impressions . . . the more change of shapes and sights there are,
there is the more chance of inspiration.[5]

Poetic activity is thus physical or physiological and so, in order
to arrive at an image, a poet must, in René Taupin's words,
'frapper les sens' in order to bring about 'mots-images', 'mots-
sensations'.[6] It is also a matter of having great learning, of being
conscious of the European tradition of literature. The greater the

[1] Rémy de Gourmont, *Problème du Style*, p. 69, quoted by René Taupin, *L'Influence
du Symbolisme Français sur la Poésie Américaine* (1929), p. 84.
[2] T. E. Hulme, *Notes on Language and Style*, quoted by Herbert Read, *The True
Voice of Feeling* (1953), p. 109.
[3] René Taupin, op. cit., p. 84.
[4] T. E. Hulme, op. cit., quoted by Herbert Read, op. cit., p. 107.
[5] ibid., p. 109.        [6] René Taupin, op. cit., p. 126.

poet's knowledge of other poets, other literatures, the wider will be the scope of his sensibility. Herein lies the essence of Imagist and 'modern' traditionalism.

The Image is a clear, hard, accurate observation and the articulation of it is a poem, a direct communication between poet and reader, where there is no need for logical coherence. It is an autonomous creation and is, as we say, 'a world of its own', for it is no longer a stream of discourse into which the poet introduces metaphors and similes in order to make his 'statement' more clear. Stead illustrates this point well in examining the following brief poem by H.D.:

Whirl up, sea—
Whirl your pointed pines,
Splash your great pines
On our rocks,
Hurl your green over us—
Cover us with your pools of fir.

He describes it thus:

From H.D.'s single moment of experience the world of values is totally excluded; but the rare point is achieved at which discourse can disappear without communication being eliminated. An experience is suggested in which the persona behind the poem lies in a forest while wind moves the pines overhead. The correspondence between the pine forest and the sea is one of shapes, colours, and above all (implied, not stated) sounds—the sound of waves breaking and of wind in pines.[1]

In other words, the poem is not a moral evaluation of life which the poet illustrates with images of a pine forest and the sea, but an art-form in which the poet, having seen the correspondence between the two, calls into being the new autonomous world of the poem where one can actually become the other by the manipulation of the poet's language. Ezra Pound describes this autonomy well in his Gaudier-Brzeska study:

The point about Imagisme is that it does not use images as *ornaments*. The image itself is the speech. The image is the word beyond language.[2]

[1] C. K. Stead, *The New Poetic* (1964), pp. 102, 103.
[2] Ezra Pound, *Gaudier-Brzeska* (1916), p. 102.

The poem is an impersonal thing, for the emphasis is firmly placed on presentation and not personal expression. 'Craft' should, therefore, be the preoccupation of the poet, and for Hulme, craft is the task of finding 'the exact curve of what he sees, whether it be an object or an idea in the mind'.[1] Craft is style and style is, in de Gourmont's terms, the man, for it is 'de sentir, de voir, de penser et rien de plus'.[2]

The value of the Imagist experiment at the precise moment in the history of English poetry at which it occurred cannot be over-estimated. It introduced into poetry a technique whereby any experience could be of value to poetry and allowed a poet to introduce 'unpoetic' metaphors and similes into the form of his poem, making of the entirety of experience a 'musée imaginaire', as Malraux called it, from which successors could draw. Its greatest importance, however, was that it pointed the way in which English poetry could develop from the non-discursive Image. Stead again, perhaps, sums this up best when he writes:

The English poetic tradition has always occupied the middle ground between pure discourse and pure Image. At times it has striven hard towards the Image; at others it has been content to be scarcely distinguished from prose except by its metrical form. On the other hand the number of occasions on which it has become pure Image are so few that no generalizations can safely be made about them. Two points at which this purity has been significantly achieved are 'The Waste Land' and 'Ash Wednesday'.[3]

One cannot talk of direct Imagist 'influence' on T. S. Eliot. 'Influence' is an overworked word in any case and generally speaking is applied where we are comparing two poets with a view to discovering where one consciously 'imitates' the methods of the other. The sense in which I use the word 'influence' could be defined as those areas of experience which one poet indicates as possible for exploration, which subsequently appeal to another. Nowhere in Eliot's critical writings do we find an acknowledgement of a 'debt' to the Imagists, except in passing, in dealing with Pound. His most direct acknowledgement of the values of Imagism was made in a *Criterion* Commentary dated July 1937:

[1] T. E. Hulme, *Speculations*, p. 132.
[2] Quoted by René Taupin, op. cit., p. 110.          [3] Stead, op. cit., p. 177.

The period which may be said to have begun about 1910 had its own
critical requirements which were not those of a general assessment of
the literature of the past. What was needed was a critical activity to
revivify creative writing, to introduce new material and new techniques from other countries and other times. The accomplishment
of the Imagist movement in verse seems to be, in restrospect, to
have been critical rather than creative, and as criticism very important.

Eliot goes on to state that he is not simply thinking of F. S.
Flint's valuable studies of French poetry, or of the philosophical
theories of T. E. Hulme. He asserts in the same article that
Hulme's 'influence' at this time was a result of his conversations
with his fellow poets.[1] Whether Eliot knew Hulme is not quite
certain. What we do know is that in 1916 Eliot became editor of
*The Egoist*, a paper which Pound and the Imagists had taken
over from Harriet Shaw Weaver and Dora Marsden, who had
published it under its original title *The New Freewoman: An
Individualist Review*.[2]

The bulk of the content of *The Egoist* was written by the
Imagists themselves, poets like Richard Aldington, Ezra
Pound, F. S. Flint, H.D. and Amy Lowell, to name but a few,
so that even if Eliot did not know Hulme he must have been
made very aware of his ideas and the various developing
principles of the Image put forward by the poets with whom he
was then working. Certainly, while Eliot was to carry Imagist
technique far beyond the limitations which were intrinsic to such
a purist movement, there is much common ground for comparison between the theory of Imagism and the poetry and criticism
written by Eliot around the time of his association with Imagist
poets.

Eliot's chief concern in the early days, as has already been
touched on in the previous chapter, was with technique and
craft. Bearing in mind the theory of the Image, we can now go on
to examine in further detail the practical implications which this
preoccupation held for his method. In the 1928 Preface to *The
Sacred Wood*, a collection of essays written between the years
1917 and 1920, he writes:

[1] *Speculations* as we have already noted, was not published until 1924 and therefore
could not have had any direct 'influence' on poetry written before then.
[2] See Glenn Hughes, op. cit., p. 30.

. . . the problem appearing in these essays, which gives them what
coherence they have, is the problem of the integrity of poetry, with the
repeated assertion that when we are considering poetry we must consider it primarily as poetry and not another thing.[1]

In going on to call poetry a 'superior amusement', an amusement
'pour distraire les honnêtes gens', he is not making of it a game
or a facile entertainment but suggesting that it is not

. . . the inculcation of morals, or the direction of politics; and no
more is it religion or an equivalent of religion, except by some monstrous abuse of words. And certainly poetry is something over and
above, and something quite different from, a collection of psychological data about the minds of poets, or about the history of an epoch;
for we could not take it even as that unless we had already assigned to
it a value merely as poetry.[2]

In taking his stand on the nature of poetry Eliot is on common
ground with the Imagists. But it is his definition of the nature
of poetic activity and the material out of which poetry is made
which is even more significant. Like Hulme, Eliot believed that a
poet should perceive reality more vividly and accurately than
ordinary men. As he was to express it in a much later essay,
'What Dante means to me', published in *To Criticize the Critic*:

Perhaps it could be best expressed under the figure of the spectrum or
gamut. Employing this figure, I may say that the great poet should not
only perceive and distinguish more clearly than other men, the colours
or sounds within the range of ordinary vision or hearing; he should
perceive vibrations beyond the range of ordinary men, and be able to
make men see and hear more at each end than they could ever see
without his help.[3]

Eliot, like Hulme, emphasizes that the writer should only
*present* his observations to the reader, for he, like them, is a
limited finite being:

. . . the explorer beyond the frontiers of ordinary consciousness will
only be able to return and report to his fellow-citizens, if he has all the
time a firm grasp upon the realities with which they are already
acquainted.[4]

Eliot's demand is therefore for accurate presentation of reality.

[1] T. S. Eliot, *The Sacred Wood*, p. viii.          [2] ibid., p. ix.
[3] *To Criticize the Critic*, p. 134.                  [4] ibid.

Returning to *The Sacred Wood*, we find in the essay 'The Possibility of a Poetic Drama' further definition of literature as presentation:

Permanent literature is always a presentation: either a presentation of thought, or a presentation of feeling by a statement of events in human action or objects in the external world.[1]

It is, he goes on to say, 'the labour of the intellect' by which the poet will refrain from 'reflection' by 'putting enough into the statement to make reflection unnecessary'.[2] Aristotle is a great *writer* because he 'presents thought, stripped to the essential structure'.[3]

Eliot believed then that great writing should present thought 'stripped to the essential structure'. In terms reminiscent of de Gourmont and Hulme he describes what he means by this essential structure of poetic 'thought'. I quote from an article entitled 'A Sceptical Patrician' published in *The Athenaeum* for 23 May 1914:

It is probable that men ripen best through experiences which are at once sensuous and intellectual. Certainly many men will admit that their keenest ideas have come to them with the quality of sense perception and that their keenest sensuous experience has been as if the body thought.

The Imagists, as we have seen, emphasized the physical nature of poetic thought and demanded of the poet the primitive situation where thought became the experience of seeing the analogy between two objects. Eliot finds this realized in Donne and the Metaphysicals, along with the later Elizabethan dramatists. In his 1921 essay 'The Metaphysical Poets', he writes:

A thought to Donne was an experience; it modified his sensibility.[4]

Donne was to be compared with Tennyson and Browning who were unable to feel their thoughts as 'immediately as the odour of a rose'.[5] In Chapman, Eliot found 'a direct sensuous apprehension of thought, or a re-creation of thought into feeling'.[6] The mind of the metaphysical poet was to be distinguished from the

[1] *The Sacred Wood*, pp. 64, 65.      [2] ibid., p. 65.
[3] ibid.          [4] 'The Metaphysical Poets', *Selected Essays*, p. 287.
[5] ibid.          [6] ibid., p. 286.

'ordinary man's', in being more 'perfectly equipped for its work', because it was 'constantly amalgamating disparate experience':

. . . the ordinary man's experience is chaotic, irregular, fragmentary. The latter falls in love, or reads Spinoza, and these two experiences have nothing to do with each other, or with the noise of the typewriter or the smell of cooking; in the mind of the poet these experiences are always forming new wholes.[1]

Thus the perfect poet, for Eliot, as for the Imagists, is he who out of the width of his emotional range acquired by vast learning and knowledge of European literature, is always finding, by experience, new analogies and presenting them objectively to the reader.

The Imagists' effort to present the analogy resulted in the Image, but Eliot chose to describe it in other terms. He speaks of the 'clear visual images'[2] of Dante, 'verbal equivalent for states of mind and feeling' in 'The Metaphysical Poets'[3] and 'objective equivalents' of feelings in the famous 'Hamlet' essay.[4] This 'objective equivalent' is given further definition in the famous passage from 'Hamlet' which has been quoted so often as to make further mention of it seem somewhat superfluous. We must look at it again, however, for it provides us with Eliot's most comprehensive statement of how the poet should go about expressing his particular observations of reality:

The only way of expressing emotion in the form of art is by finding an 'objective correlative'; in other words a set of objects, a chain of events which shall be the formula of that *particular* emotion; such that when the external facts, which must terminate in sensory experience, are given, the emotion is immediately evoked.[5]

Compare this with Ford Madox Hueffer's definition of poetry:

Poetry consists in so rendering concrete objects that the emotions produced by the objects shall arise in the reader . . .[6]

This is in effect exactly what Hulme demanded from the Image— a form of direct communication.

[1] 'The Metaphysical Poets', *Selected Essays*, p. 287.
[2] 'Dante', *Selected Essays*, p. 242.        [3] ibid., p. 289.
[4] 'Hamlet', ibid., p. 145.        [5] ibid.
[6] Quoted by T. S. Eliot, *To Criticize the Critic*, p. 181.

It is interesting to compare the way in which both Eliot and the Imagists realize the Image or 'the objective equivalent of feeling' in an impersonal form. Pound used the behaviour of particles of metal in the presence of a magnet as an image by which to describe the process whereby material was shaped in the poet's mind to become art. The poet's mind acts as a magnet in drawing his materials together into a 'dynamic form':

The 'forma', the immortal 'concetto', the concept, the dynamic form which is like the rose-pattern driven into dead iron-filings by the magnet, not by material contact with the magnet itself, but separate from the magnet. Cut off by the layer of glass, the dust and filings rise and spring into order.[1]

Herbert Read describes the Imagistic poetic process as the way in which the poet 'seizes' the physical phenomena which is his world—which Hulme had already described as the world of finite things—and finds their verbal equivalence:

Thought begins with the simultaneous presentation to the mind of two distinct but related images. Poetry is what then *happens*. Prose is a post-mortem on the event.[2]

Eliot saw the same process and asks us to consider, in terms similar to Pound's, the action which takes place when 'a bit of finely filiated platinum is introduced into a chamber containing oxygen and sulphur dioxide':

When the two gases previously mentioned are mixed in the presence of a filament of platinum, they form sulphurous acid. This combination takes place only if the platinum is present; nevertheless the newly formed acid contains no trace of platinum and the platinum itself is apparently unaffected; has remained inert, neutral, and unchanged. The mind of the poet is the shred of platinum.[3]

The chemical reaction which takes place when oxygen and sulphur dioxide meet in the presence of a catalyst results in the formation of sulphurous acid; the analogous reaction which takes place in the mind of the poet forms the objective correlative, for the poet himself is detached from his materials and only acts like the catalyst in bringing them together.

[1] Ezra Pound, 'Culture', p. 152, quoted by Hugh Kenner, *The Poetry of Ezra Pound* (1951), p. 234.
[2] Herbert Read, *The True Voice of Feeling*, p. 115.
[3] *The Sacred Wood*, p. 54.

The qualities which Eliot finds to praise in Dante, the Meta-physicals and the later Elizabethan dramatists were qualities which the Imagists themselves strove for, but their creative achievement was far below the standards of their critical demands, as Eliot has himself pointed out.[1] It is possibly for this reason that Eliot, while echoing their theories, leaves their poetry and turns to the more vital sophisticated poetry of the past.

The limitations and the failings of the Imagists are obvious, as a quick glance at the poems they produced and the immediate reactions of contemporary critics to them show.[2] The Imagists made the mistake of regarding the single Image as an end in itself, a poem. They believed that once the Image was realized in poetic form, the work of the poet was done. Professor William Ellery Leonard of the University of Wisconsin published a series of articles in the *Chicago Evening Post* between 18 September and 9 October 1915, entitled 'The New Poetry—a Critique', in which he attacks the narrowness of their range of vision:

Imagists, doubtless, hear things more wonderful than Beethoven's symphonies in the buzz of the mosquito on the flats back of Chicago, and they whiff more than all the perfumes of Arabia in the summer steam of a Jersey dunghill.

Their physical eye is abnormal. They are often myopic: little minutiae of life, the shadow on a half leaf caused by the upcurling of the other half, the white lines between the bricks of a chimney, . . .

. . . details which a de Maupassant or a Tennyson would perhaps weave harmoniously into a larger picture or situation, become for the Imagists the whole horizon.[3]

The same point is taken up by Conrad Aiken in 'The Place of Imagism', in the *New Republic* of 22 May 1915. He describes Imagist poetry as 'a gentle preciosity of sound and colour'. The field for this kind of thing, he says, is 'the semi-precious in experience'. The Image is therefore, in the words of another critic, O. W. Firkins, in *Nation* for 14 October 1915, 'a drifting, homeless, expatriated thing':

[1] *Criterion*, July 1937, cited, pp. 26–7.
[2] I am greatly indebted to Glenn Hughes for the excellent references and biblio-graphy which he provides in *Imagism and the Imagists*. He indicates a most useful and interesting series of articles by contemporary critics of Imagism.
[3] Quoted by Glenn Hughes, op. cit., p. 56.

It is destitute alike of a place in a charted globe and a function in a civilized order. It has no history, no prospects, no causes, no sequels, no association, no cognates, no allies.[1]

What the Imagists did not see was that the Image alone, while valid for short poems, like the 'one-Image' poem, as Pound called it,[2] would not do for longer poems. When we read these poems, often only two lines long, they read like fragments, like notes for longer poems. Hulme's 'Autumn' reads like a fragment and so perhaps does his best poem, 'Conversion':

> Light-hearted I walked into the valley wood
> In the time of hyacinths,
> Till beauty like a scented cloth
> Cast over, stifled me. I was bound
> Motionless and faint of breath
> By loveliness that is her own eunuch.
> Now pass I to the final river
> Ignominiously, in a sack, without sound,
> As any peeping Turk to the Bosphorus.[3]

As illustrative of the technique of Imagism, these lines are good, but as a poem they are simply a fragment, an accurate description, without being anything more.

This view of the Image as nothing but a fragment is emphasized by the particular view of reality held by contemporary philosophers which has been examined briefly in the previous chapter. If, as Bradley or Bergson believed, our immediate awareness of an object indicates only part of its reality, it follows that the Image which expresses this awareness will only be a partial observation of it. The Imagist poets tended to be content with the elaboration of a single visual Image, with the accurate expression of one 'appearance' of their world. It was left to their successors to show how to set such Images into a complex relationship with one another in order to make a more comprehensive poem.

Lewis Worthington Smith makes an important point when he sees Imagist poets as minor poets who cannot stand the strain of the sophisticated complex world in which they find themselves, and so 'relax and take their experiences one at a time'. In the

[1] ibid., p. 61.
[2] Ezra Pound, op cit, p. 103.
[3] T. E. Hulme, *Speculations*, p. 267.

*Atlantic Monthly* for April 1916, 'The New Naïveté', he sees that

Poem after poem in this sort is full of the simple wonder of a child picking up pebbles on the beach and running to some other child with yellow hair in happy wonder at finding the pebble and the hair of like colour. The big-eyed recognition is about as far toward correlation of their material as the Imagists or the writers of free verse ever get.

Imagist poetry is too 'easy'—the poet 'content merely to look at things, like a child, open-eyed and open-mouthed, to report the retinal image to the brain, to transfer it to innocent blank paper, and lastly to impose it on a credulous world for poetry'. Nevertheless, this spontaneous and open-eyed wonder, has been seen by many artists—Rousseau in painting, Satie in music, Jarry in the theatre and poets like Rimbaud—to be a necessary preliminary step in the development of an accurate adult response, as the 'primitivism' of each of their art forms shows. The cult of innocence carried to an extreme becomes ridiculous, however, and was indeed laboured by the artists in all media in the earlier part of this century. The discoveries of these earliest modernists needed to be resolved or integrated into a more sophisticated movement.

The emphasis on the force and the speed with which the poet set down the immediately felt analogy also contributes to the fragmentariness of the Imagist poem. Words like 'immediately', 'suddenness', in 'an instant of time', are words which occur again and again in Imagist theory. Gustav Kahn writes:

Ne pouvant connaître que ce qui se passe en nous, il nous faut nous résoudre à le clicher le plus rapidement et le plus sûrement possible en son essence, sa formule et son impulsion.[1]

The Image is liberated with the speed and immediacy of shock, with the aim of evoking immediately in the mind of the reader this same emotion. René Taupin describes the pleasure derivable from such practice when he writes:

. . . le plaisir de leur poésie, ce n'est pas le bonheur de deviner peu à peu, mais celui de saisir d'un seul coup et dans son maximum de vie, l'image, fusion de la réalité dans l'expression.[2]

Such 'shock' treatment is possible in short poems where the

---

[1] Gustav Kahn, *Symbolistes et Décadents*, p. 92, quoted by Taupin, op. cit., p. 98.
[2] ibid., p. 101.

emotion is a single one, but not for longer poems where the poet is concerned with arousing a complex emotion.

The above comments may be very relevant criticism of Imagist poems, but not of their basic technique. As Glenn Hughes writes:

If a hard, clear, objective poetry were to be developed, a certain number of blackboard exercises were necessary before anything important should be done.[1]

The poems we may now regard as useful, preliminary experiments in the development of a more mature and comprehensive poetry of which Eliot alone is master.

Eliot's technique was similar to that of the Imagists and his poems form elaborate assemblages of the single-Image poems. Each part of the complex structures of the early poems is an Image, unconventional in the analogy it makes, forcing us, in typical Imagist fashion, by the speed and compression with which it is set down, to share the experience of the poet. Let us look at a line from 'The Love Song of J. Alfred Prufrock':

I have measured out my life with coffee spoons[2]

Here is a precise image, which shows us by the smallness and daintiness of the visual coffee-spoon measure, Prufrock's awareness of the smallness of bourgeois 'life' as it was meted out to him. The whole of 'Prufrock' is made up of similarly intensely felt 'surprise' images:

The yellow fog that rubs its back upon the window-panes,
The yellow smoke that rubs its muzzle on the window-panes,
Licked its tongue into the corners of the evening,[3]

And the afternoon, the evening, sleeps so peacefully!
Smoothed by long fingers,
Asleep . . . tired . . . or it malingers,
Stretched on the floor, here beside you and me.[4]

Here is 'direct sensuous apprehension of thought'. Eliot does not wish to express the abstract thoughts of Prufrock. What he wishes to do is to present an uneasy state of mind, and so he correlates Prufrock with the evening and presents the resultant

---

[1] Glenn Hughes, op. cit., p. 69.          [2] T. S. Eliot, *Collected Poems*, p. 14.
[3] ibid., p. 13.          [4] ibid., p. 15.

image in the form of a sense-image, visible and concrete. The analogy between Prufrock and the evening is so condensed, so immediate that the two are identified. This single image, however, will not communicate all that Eliot wishes us to feel about Prufrock and so he takes more images, and the group together forms a whole, and makes, as we shall see, a complete articulation of the complex view of the world which Prufrock represents.

The early poems are made up of similar immediately felt analogies or 'emotional equivalents of thought'. 'Preludes' makes an articulation by a series of visible images in the form of scenes:

> The winter evening settles down
> With smell of steaks in passageways.
> Six o'clock.
> The burnt-out ends of smoky days.
> And now a gusty shower wraps
> The grimy scraps
> Of withered leaves about your feet
> And newspapers from vacant lots;
> The showers beat
> On broken blinds and chimney-pots,
> And at the corner of the street
> A lonely cab-horse steams and stamps.[1]

This passage is in itself an Imagist poem, a fragment. It is only when we examine it in relation to the other images in the same poem that we can gather its more comprehensive 'meaning'— Eliot's modernist vision. Each image which makes up the complete poem is clear, sharp, accurate, visible and is in René Taupin's words 'une équation du premier degré immédiatement solvable'.[2] A complex view of the world cannot be expressed by a fragment in the form of a first degree equation. What Eliot maintains is that a *series* of such fragments *can*, however, and so he makes elaborate constructions of his images. The way in which he does this and the nature of the poetry which results is subject matter for another chapter.

It is true that Eliot makes further extension to Imagist method where he uses correlatives which he 'found', as well as objective equivalents which surged from within. Kristian Smidt gives as

[1] T. S. Eliot, *Collected Poems*, p. 23.      [2] René Taupin, op. cit., p. 102.

an example the way in which Eliot came by the title of 'La Figlia che Piange', recalling how Eliot tried to find an old sculpture of that name in a museum in Northern Italy. He was unable to find it and so never saw it.[1] The name stuck in his mind, however, and became the title for his poem. In 'finding' lines from other poets and being struck by them as forcibly as by the sight of an object, he is also 'finding' emotional equivalents.

What is important to stress here is the value which the Imagist experiment had in the development of Eliot's method of objective presentation. What Eliot did was to construct *on* the Image, to connect it with symbol and myth and show it in complex relationship to other Images. For the Imagist, the Image was a unit, and this unit was a poem. For Eliot, this fragment became the unit of poetry, the point from which he began the difficult task of 'constructing' the complex assemblages which are his poems.

[1] Kristian Smidt, *Poetry and Belief in the Work of T. S. Eliot* (1961), p. 41.

# III The Symbolist method: fragments as structures

In the previous chapters I have emphasized the fragmentary nature of the Imagist poem, but concluded that the Image itself became the unit of poetry from which Eliot began the difficult task of constructing the complex architecture of his poems. This is not the starting point which Eliot himself would have and has acknowledged, for we know from his assertion, that it was to France that he turned for the assistance needed so badly by English poets to take up the task of articulating their modernist vision.

The reason why such emphasis is laid by Eliot on the examples of his 'elder brothers', the French, as well as being one of personal kinship and similarity of attitude to the modern predicament, is also that the example of the French offered him the intensification and extension of Imagist theory which was necessary and found lacking in its practice. It is interesting to note that while Symbolism as a movement preceded Imagism, it provided such an intensification. Yet, as Imagism had its limitations, so had Symbolism, and it is necessary at the outset to stress that one must examine the achievements and failings of one school alongside those of the other in order to come to an understanding and appreciation of Eliot's method.

The most significant objection to Imagist practice was that it made the job of the poet too 'easy'. All one had to do to become a poet was to 'see' an unusual analogy, write it down as quickly as possible and a poem was made. The Image, perceived with the immediacy of sense perception, must be preserved in its eidetic state and required no further reference to other elements in the poet's experience. This made of it a fragment and absolved the poet from any obligation to place his Image in a poetic structure. In Herbert Read's terms, however,

Art . . . always involves an original act of creation—the invention of an objective reality which previously had no existence. The projection of a symbol or image from the unconscious is not an act of creation in that sense: it is merely the transfer of an existing object from one sphere to another—from the mental sphere, for example, to the verbal or plastic sphere. The essential function of art is revealed on a co-ordination of images (whether unconscious or perceptual does not matter) into an effective pattern. The art is in the pattern which is a personal intuition of the art and not in the imagery.[1]

The 'art . . . in the pattern' lays stress on structure and form which the Imagists left very much to chance or defended under the title of *vers libre*. Stephen Spender called such 'easy' verse structure verse which did not 'arrive':

. . . although the verbalised image may with excellent poets be the flash point from which the poem starts, it does not have that richness and strangeness which enables poetry to 'arrive'. Departures but few arrivals.[2]

Eliot has consistently denied the usefulness of any 'free' verse form of this sort. In 'Reflections on *Vers Libre*', he writes:

*Vers libre* has not even the excuse of a polemic; it is a battle cry of freedom, and there is no freedom in art. And as the so-called *vers libre* which is good is anything but 'free', it can better be defended under some other label . . . but I am not here concerned with imagism, which is a theory about the use of material; I am only concerned with the theory of verse-form in which imagism is cast. If *vers libre* is a genuine verse-form it will have a positive definition. And I can define it only in negatives: (1) absence of pattern, (2) absence of rhyme, (3) absence of metre.[3]

The last two of these negative definitions we can ignore, for the purpose of our examination is not the metrical or rhythmical structure of Eliot's early verse, but the 'pattern', which we take to be the structure of images into a meaningful, if complex, pattern.

Eliot at the outset has himself asserted the importance of form and structure in verse. His admiration for the accurate, perceptual sense which Dante possessed and which the Imagists, on their part, constantly strove for in their poetry was at the basis of one of our reasons for identifying Eliot's principles with those of the Imagists, and we have given examples to show that Eliot's early poetry was largely made up of such visual or concrete observations. We must now examine further what Eliot

---

[1] Herbert Read, *The Philosophy of Modern Art* (1952), p. 53.
[2] Stephen Spender, *The Struggle of the Modern* (1963), p. 112.
[3] T. S. Eliot, *To Criticize the Critic* (1965), p. 184.

continued to admire in Dante, for what Eliot stressed absolutely in his early essay in praise of the *Divine Comedy* was Dante's sense of form and structure:

. . . no emotion in Dante is contemplated by Dante purely in and for itself.
. . . If the artistic emotion presented by any episode of the 'Comedy' is dependent upon the whole, we may proceed to inquire what the whole scheme is. The usefulness of allegory and astronomy is obvious. A mechanical framework, in a poem of so vast an ambit, was a necessity . . . It is not essential that the allegory or the almost unintelligible astronomy should be understood—only that its presence should be justified. The emotional structure within this scaffold is what must be understood—the structure made possible by the scaffold. This structure is an ordered scale of human emotions.

And Eliot continues:

. . . Dante's is the most comprehensive, and the most *ordered* presentation of emotions that has ever been made.

The structure of emotions, for which the allegory is the necessary scaffold is complete from the most sensuous to the most intellectual and the most spiritual.
. . . it is evidence of this greatness that the significance of any single passage, of any of the passages that are selected as 'poetry', is incomplete unless we ourselves apprehend the whole.[1]

It is thus easy to see why Eliot's early preoccupation with 'pattern', wholeness of construction and a 'structure' made out of emotions, should lead him away from his contemporary experimenters in England towards the more sophisticated and comprehensive attempts at articulate coherence which had already taken place in France.

It is difficult to isolate among the heterogeneous 'bundle of tendencies'[2] which made up what we call the Symbolist movement any one particular unifying principle which might have made an appeal to Eliot, but we can assert that all Symbolists—whether they succeeded or not in their practice—emphasized the importance of structure in their verse. Poe, one of the forerunners of the movement, saw the task of the poet similar to that of 'a

[1] T. S. Eliot, *The Sacred Wood* (1950 edition), pp. 167–70.
[2] William Wimsatt and Cleanth Brooks, *Literary Criticism: A Short History* (1957 edition), p. 596.

craftsman who brings his intelligence fully, and even coldly to
bear upon the problem of organizing words into specific literary
structures'. For him a poem had an architecture, and it was 'well
or ill built'.[1] Symons described Laforgue as 'mathematically
lyrical',[2] and for Mallarmé poetry was a problem of craftsmanship:

> Mallarmé was concerned that nothing in the poem be the effect of
> mere chance, that the articulation of every part with every other part
> should be complete, each part implying every other part, and that the
> meaning of the poem should be inseparable from its formal structure.[3]

Baudelaire was greatly impressed with Poe's notion that the
shape of a poem ought to reveal 'the precision and rigid con-
sequence of a mathematical problem'.[4] Rimbaud's poetry, even
after his most extravagant attempts at becoming 'voyant' by
taking drugs, Brooks calls 'a *systematic* exploitation of symbols'.[5]

The Symbolist movement was historically a rejection of the
rigid Parnassianism which preceded it and the conventional
forms in which the poems of that school cast their realistic,
external descriptions. It counteracted Parnassian materialism by
a mysticism which led to a final and complete rejection of the
phenomenal world as fit material for poetry. The cry of the
Symbolist is that of Axel in Villiers de l'Isle-Adam's poem of
the same name:

> Oh, the external world! Let us not be made dupes by
> the old slave, chained to our feet in broad daylight,
> who promises us the keys to a palace of enchantments
> when it clutches only a handful of ashes in its clenched fist![6]

Symbolism, however, did not consistently remain a voyage of
exploration towards the realms of Ideal Beauty or the world of
essences, and various groups were formed in France to counteract this element in its theory. It is thus impossible to unite all
Symbolists under this banner. We may identify two trends,
however—those poets who formed an 'Ecole Romane' and

---

[1] ibid., pp. 588, 589.
[2] Arthur Symons, *The Symbolist Movement in Literature* (1899), p. 108.
[3] Wimsatt and Brooks, op. cit., pp. 592–3.
[4] Edgar Allan Poe, *The Philosophy of Composition*, quoted by Wimsatt and Brooks,
op. cit., p. 589.
[5] ibid., p. 594. (My italics.)
[6] Translated by Edmund Wilson, *Axel's Castle* (1931), p. 263.

favoured a return to ancient law and order, and 'the exotic experimentalists',[1] the disciples of Tristan Corbière, Jules Laforgue and Arthur Rimbaud. We must therefore define the areas of Symbolist theory which appealed to Eliot, for, although we have his own explicit acknowledgement to Arthur Symons who led him to Laforgue, Corbière and Baudelaire, we shall have to 'place' them more precisely than we have done above, in the Symbolist perspective. This will lead us to a new definition of Eliot's 'Symbolism'—the object of so many critics of Eliot's work—for Eliot is far from being a 'pure' Symbolist poet.

While the mystic element of Symbolism was not one of its unifying features, the implications which it held for French poets between 1885 and 1900 united them in their attitude towards language and the rôle of the poet. It implied for Mallarmé, the 'elocutionary disappearance of the poet':[2]

. . . For the Symbolist poet there is no question of describing an experience; the moment of illumination only occurs in its embodiment in some particular artistic form. There is no question of relating it to the experience of a lifetime, for it is unique, it exists in the poem alone.[3]

Hence the world of denotation, the world of exposition, held no value for them. The theory thus became a theory of the suggestiveness of words. If 'logical thought' was irrelevant in poetry, then poets were free 'to explore the rich possibilities of intimation, suggestion, and all the other modes of linguistic indirection'.[4] Wallace Fowlie, writing on Mallarmé, says of the Symbolist theory in this regard:

Whether a real school of symbolism ever existed, remains a problem of speculation . . . Each poet developed and represented a single aspect of an aesthetic doctrine that was perhaps too vast for one historical group to incorporate . . . But more than on any other article of belief, the symbolists united with Mallarmé in his statements about poetic language . . . It is language possessing extraordinary affinities with music and dreams.[5]

---

1 Glenn Hughes, *Imagism and the Imagists* (1960), p. 6.
2 Quoted by Arthur Symons, op. cit., p. 135.
3 Graham Hough, *Image and Experience* (1960), p. 10.
4 Wimsatt and Brooks, op. cit., p. 595.
5 Wallace Fowlie, *Mallarmé* (1953), p. 264, quoted by Wimsatt and Brooks, op. cit., p. 596.

Symbolist poets were therefore all concerned with exploiting the possibilities of connotation in poetry, and it is this aspect of the theory with which we shall be primarily concerned, along with what has been stated earlier about structures.

The Symbolist poem could now be defined as a 'structure in connotation', and the method whereby the poet achieves this structure is most relevant to our study. Genesius Jones, in a very valuable study of T. S. Eliot's poetry, has examined closely the poetic method of the Symbolist poets and it is interesting to indicate here how he views the Symbolist struggle for articulation.[1] The poet starts off with his inarticulate and extremely complex 'état d'âme', an inner, alogical experience (for which logical expression would be inadequate), and so he seeks symbols with which to formulate it. He chooses his symbolic analogies not so much for what they denote as for the emotions and connotations which they have for him and which he hopes to evoke in the reader. In order that the reader will detect the same or approximately the same areas of connotation as the poet felt, it is the task of the poet to define or delimit these areas in some way. He does so by placing next to his first symbol a second symbol which will have connotations in common with those of the first; to these he will add more and more symbols, each defining and delimiting the boundaries of the others until his articulation is complete.

And so the poem is made. This series of symbols, grouped together with no 'thought' connection, forms a new whole, and, since the poet is not speaking directly to the reader, the poem is an autonomous creation. It has obvious close affinities with the method Eliot expresses in 1918 in his essay on *Hamlet*. The poetic activity is as difficult for Eliot as for the Symbolist poet. The state of mind, the emotion, for which he seeks articulation, is equally complex for logical exposition, hence:

The only way of expressing emotion in the form of art is by finding an 'objective correlative'; in other words, a set of objects, a situation, a chain of events which shall be the formula of that *particular* emotion . . .[2]

This attempt to build a poetic structure out of the suggestive

[1] Genesius Jones, *Approach to the Purpose* (1964), pp. 37 ff.
[2] T. S. Eliot, *Selected Essays*, (1951 edition), p. 145.

aspects of language alone, Yvor Winters calls a 'Qualitative Progression',[1] where the poet abandons a rational structure altogether and moves in a dislocated, stream-of-consciousness-type progression from image to image with little or no connection between them. Winters censures such a method for its vagueness and obscurity, and believes that a poet should have his experience 'rationalized'. The method is further defined and defended by Eliot in a passage quoted by Graham Hough, who echoes all the faults which Winters finds with a structure of this type:

Any obscurity of the poem, on first readings, is due to the suppression of 'links in the chain', of explanatory and connecting matter, and not to incoherence, or to the love of cryptogram. The justification of such abbreviation of method is that the sequence of images co-incides and concentrates into one intense impression of barbaric civilization. The reader has to allow the images to fall into his memory successively without questioning the reasonableness of each at the moment; so that, at the end, a total effect is produced. Such selection of a sequence of images and ideas has nothing chaotic about it. There is a logic of imagination as well as a logic of concepts.[2]

Genesius Jones defends it in terms very reminiscent of Eliot:

Denotatively the articulation may seem chaotic and nonsensical; . . . But each [symbol] will have its own 'logic of the imagination' fixed and delimited in unique formulation after unique formulation—and waiting to be discovered by the reader. The reader, faced with the formulations, will be puzzled by their strange surrealist appearance, their seeming nonsense. Only when he retreats from denotation into that world which has been built from denotation—the world of connotation—will he have a chance to understand the poet's meaning. He will be aware first of panoramas of connotation; then of delimitation; then, from each formulation, of a clearly outlined but alogical meaning.[3]

But these are vague and inadequate justifications for such a method, and if the poet has a right to hand over the burden of disentangling his meaning to the reader, then we shall have to

[1] Yvor Winters, *In Defense of Reason* (1947), pp. 31 ff. I am indebted to Wimsatt and Brooks *Short History of Literary Criticism*, which led me to this book and also to Winters's valuable book *On Modern Poets* (1959).
[2] T. S. Eliot's Introduction to St-John Perse's *Anabase* quoted by Graham Hough, op. cit., p. 18.
[3] Jones, op. cit., p. 37.

examine the method more closely in order to convince ourselves that the poet too has made sufficient effort to be articulate and has reasonable grounds for making such demands on his reader.

The Symbolist structure is defined by Jones as a 'dynamic of sensuous forms'[1] and the success of each articulation is determined by what he calls the 'convenientia':

> . . . the symbols come together because each one is needed to build up the particular pattern of evocation required . . . The *convenientia* determines whether the final pattern is adequate to the state of affairs; and itself can be declared upon only if the symbols have a delimited symbolic connotation. *It is the task of the poet so to fix the connotation that there may be no missing the evocation.*[2]

Genesius Jones examines the Symbolist structure in terms of a mathematical equation,[3] which might seem a trifle over-ingenious, but if we consider that the Symbolists—and Eliot—have spoken of structure in the terms of 'mathematical precision', and 'formula', then perhaps it is not so unnatural and is, in fact, an obvious analogy to make. The mathematical equation which Jones works out in full and uses for his illustration need not concern us here, only its poetic applicability. The 'value' of a mathematical or algebraic equation becomes the 'meaning' or articulation of the poem. Articulation is made up of a series of 'arguments' or symbols (after the manner of the Qualitative Progression to which we have already referred). In order for the equation to be useful, each symbol has to have something in its field of connotation to link it with the other symbols in the series. This common element within the connotation we may call the 'given' values in the mathematical 'argument', or the constants. In terms of mathematics there cannot be more than one variable in any single equation. If we have three variables, X, Y, Z, then we require either three separate equations for X, Y, Z, in order to calculate the value of each, or else we have to make mathematical assumptions about the values of two of them, e.g. if X=such-and-such and Y=such-and-such, etc. Applied to a poem, however, what we must have is a series of symbols whereby some 'constant' is present in each. If two or more 'undelimited' symbols are placed side by side, the result is chaos. Symbols in Symbolist poetry were too often placed with all

---

[1] ibid., p. 39.   [2] ibid., p. 39. (My italics.)   [3] ibid., p. 31.

their connotations released at once and the result, according to Genesius Jones's rightful calculation, was explosion. Eliot, in a quite different context and much later in his poetic development, described it as follows:

> Words strain,
> Crack and sometimes break, under the burden,
> Under the tension, slip, slide, perish,
> Decay with imprecision, will not stay in place,
> Will not stay still.[1]

Such overconnotation was often the poet's misuse of personal symbols in his poetry. It is understandable that when a poet is attempting to articulate what seems the inarticulate, he has to create personal symbols, especially when the 'world' with which he is dealing is the inner world of 'le rêve'. (Hence we have the vague system of 'correspondances' of which the Symbolists were so fond.) But personal symbols, such as Corbière's toad, Baudelaire's ant-hill, Mallarmé's wing beat, etc. are useful and relevant to the expression of the 'état d'âme' only if the poet allows their connotations to be built from the denotative 'constant' value inherent in them. His structural coherence depends on it. The trouble was that many Symbolist poets, Mallarmé in particular, were so carried away by their mystical search for the 'essence of things' that they were guilty of the sin of 'angelism', as Allen Tate defined it.[2] Marcel Raymond in *De Baudelaire au Surréalisme* writes of how Mallarmé in 'Les Fenêtres' turns his back upon life 'as a great frustrating force', and, facing the casement windows, now 'gilded by the chaste morning of the infinite', exclaims: 'I look upon myself and see an angel.'[3] 'Angelism' is the sin whereby man identifies himself with the angels, to use Tate's comparison, or in Hulme's terms for the Romantic poets, with God who *alone* can have perception of the fundamental nature of life. Man can only aspire towards the essences through analogy, and if he, in his pride, refuses to look on life as he knows it for his analogies, he is 'doomed to see nothing'.[4] In another essay, 'The Forlorn Demon', Tate sees

---

[1] T. S. Eliot, 'Burnt Norton', *Collected Poems* (1963), p. 194.
[2] Allen Tate, *The Angelic Imagination*, see Wimsatt and Brooks, op. cit., p. 605.
[3] M. Raymond, *From Baudelaire to Surrealism* (1949), p. 24, quoted by Wimsatt and Brooks, ibid., p. 605.
[4] ibid., p. 606.

that 'the reach of our imaginative enlargement is perhaps no
longer than the ladder of analogy'.[1] Yeats is quoted as not
having 'scorned' the ladder of analogy and in his later poetry
'did not forget the relationship of the masterful images of
accomplished poetry to the world of things'. As Stephen
Spender wrote of him:

What distinguishes Yeats from the Symbolists and post-Symbolists
is the effort he made to give external authority to his symbols. The
Symbolists and Rilke are content for the most part to translate their
experiences into terms of their own inner life and create symbols which
the reader can only understand by entering their own closed-in intellectual spheres. Yeats is consumed by a passion to project his metaphors into an external framework which supports and affirms them,
giving them as it were a life or superlife of their own, outside his own
subjectives.[2]

Mallarmé, in trying to get along without the object in his creation of 'la notion pure' and 'néant', forgot the 'ladder of analogy',
and the result was that his structure became 'a constellation of
images astronomically distant, nearly invisible to the naked
eye'.[3]

Coupled with the 'angelic imagination' of which many
Symbolist poets were often guilty, was their attempt to make the
meaning of poetry equal to musical articulation. In order to do
this, they attempted to empty words completely of their denotative quality. Mallarmé was again foremost in this and his
attempt to create the pure musical poem Eliot refutes:

We can never emulate music, because to arrive at the condition of
music would be the annihilation of poetry.[4]

Thus we can conclude that where structure is made out of
connotation and where connotation is not delimited, we have no
'meaning', no articulation.

But not all Symbolists were guilty of such arbitrariness in
structure. René Taupin in *L'Influence du Symbolisme Français sur
la Poésie Américaine* writes that the notion of poetry as Mallarmé
understood it began to be attacked and the movement 'se

[1] ibid.
[2] Stephen Spender, *The Creative Element* (1953), p. 113.
[3] Wylie Sypher, *From Rococo to Cubism in Art and Literature* (1960), p. 141.
[4] T. S. Eliot, *On Poetry and Poets* (1957), p. 87.

tournait . . . vers une poésie moins fugitive'.[1] He goes on to quote an interesting letter of Louis St Jacques in *'La Plume'*, 1 March 1897. Poets, he writes, need to:

s'inspirer directement de la vie. Plus nous nous laisserons posséder par elle et plus l'expression que nous en donnerons sera forte, mieux encore nous en suggérerons l'idée. *Nous suggérerons d'autant plus que nous nous exprimerons plus exactement.*

Such criticism did not contradict the main principles of the movement, but, as Taupin says, 'redressèrent, consolidèrent un mouvement qui tendait à se fourvoyer dans la rêverie, loin du réel'.[2]

The need for and desire of certain Symbolists to bring their symbols within the range of 'the ladder of analogy' and to avoid 'angelism' is the meeting point of Imagism and Symbolism. For it was the attempts of the 'nouveaux symbolistes' as Taupin calls Rimbaud, Claudel, Corbière and Rémy de Gourmont, which attracted the Imagists to the Symbolist movement. Flint writes of Claudel in *Poetry*, July 1915:

In the 'Art Poétique' he has said that his art is based on 'la métaphore, le mot nouveau, l'opération qui résulte de la seule existence conjointe et simultanée de deux choses différentes' . . . and the whole of his work is constantly upheld by the intensity of his visual imagination constantly creating new metaphors that have the power of the primitive.

In our original remarks about Imagism, we defined the Image as a single, direct analogy and here among the Symbolist poets we find the symbol taking on some of the characteristics of the Image—a new word, an unusual analogy, something concrete, something visual, which will present itself to the reader. But Claudel was a Symbolist, concerned as all Symbolists were with the evocative power of his image, so while he wishes to present a symbol directly to the reader, he also wants to suggest something by it. And so the situation comes about in Symbolist poetry whereby poets 'suggèrent directement'.[3] The Symbolist-Image, as we may now call it, retains its exactness,

[1] R. Taupin, *L'Influence du Symbolisme Français sur la Poésie Américaine* (1929), p. 103.
[2] René Taupin, op. cit., p. 104.        [3] ibid., p. 104.

but by its connotative value raises (as a mathematical symbol can be raised) the Imagist equation to a higher intensity:

Elle ⌈speaking of l'Image⌉ exprime la perception puis, par un pro-longement tout un mirage derrière elle.[1]

So one movement counteracts the faults and limitations of the other. The pure Symbolist in trying to do away with the perceptual or denotative quality of the symbol, failed to 'fix' its connotations and so destroyed the structure of his poem, just as the Imagist, in trying to dispense with connotation, failed to make a complex structure of his. The 'nouveaux symbolistes' tried to strike a balance between the two. Perhaps H.D. was the only one—and certainly the only Imagist poet whom Eliot praises[2]—who was successful in striking such a balance. Taupin, in praising her, speaks of her 'mystère précis':

La minutie, la précision de ces images attirent la sensibilité du lecteur qui sent certains aspects des choses qu'il n'avait pas même soup-çonnés.[3]

This development of Imagist practice is also a logical develop-ment of 'nouveau symbolisme', 'qui de plus en plus s'est tourné vers le réel, vers le vivant, y trouvant les mêmes plaisirs artistiques que dans le rêve d'une imagination fermée aux aspects du monde'.[4] Edouard Dujardin invented the term 'réalisme symbolique'[5] to give to the poetic suggestiveness which we associate with Symbolism the quality of precision which is the prime principle of Imagism.

These qualities of suggestion along with precision are the properties of all good images in poetry. So we must remind our-selves here of the principles which distinguish the two schools from any traditional forms of poetic expression. The two move-ments are joined in their conscious effort to record the actual thought process of the poet (the method of Qualitative Progres-sion), reminding us again of de Gourmont's belief, held also by the Imagists, that 'on pense au moyen d'images'. Herbert Read has spoken of the Symbolist communication as 'the

---

[1] ibid., p. 98.
[2] 'Ezra Pound', A Collection of Critical Essays (1963) (ed. Walter Sutton), p. 20.
[3] René Taupin, op. cit., pp. 105–6.
[4] ibid., p. 106.
[5] Quoted by Taupin, ibid., p. 125.

symbolic transfer of emotion' and quotes from Whitehead's
*Symbolism: Its Meanings and Effect* to elucidate his theory:

. . . it gives the reason for the importance of a rigid suppression of
irrelevant detail. For emotions inhibit each other, or intensify each
other. Harmonious emotion means a complex of emotions mutually
intensifying; whereas the irrelevant details supply emotions which,
because of their irrelevance, inhibit the main effect. Each little emotion
directly arising out of some subordinate detail refuses to accept its
status as a detached fact in our consciousness.[1]

And in Taupin's words:

Grâce à la psychologie moderne, on savait que le symbole, s'il était
total, était l'expression la plus directe qui fût. Lorsque la sensibilité
s'exprime librement, c'est en images qu'elle s'exprime, ce qui est
très évident dans le rêve, et souvent apparent dans la veille.[2]

And so we must return to our initial remarks about structure
and form. Winters is obviously justified in condemning a poet
who believes that, by simply jotting down impressions as they
come to him and leaving it at that, he is a poet, for a poet is
above all a craftsman, whose function it is to impose some sort of
order on his experiences. The Symbolists, where they failed,
failed because, although they were conscious of their artistic
obligation to impose order on chaos, were not sufficiently strict
in their practice. The value of an 'emotional structure' or a
'connotative structure' depended on their 'fixing' the suggestiveness of their symbols in some way, or as Eliot said, in speaking
of Dante, placing them in some form of 'scaffold'. It would be
wrong to suggest, however, that a poet like Mallarmé never
made an attempt to 'fix' his connotations and that his poems
never made a structural whole. Sometimes he actually gave the
'meaning' of his mathematical equation, so that the reader could
'place' each symbol within the delimited framework which it
provided. An obvious example is the last line of Mallarmé's
'Apparition':

La lune s'attristait. Des seraphins en pleurs
Rêvants, l'archet aux doigts, dans le calme des fleurs
Vaporeuses, tiraient de mourantes violes.

[1] Whitehead, *Symbolism: its Meaning and Effect*, p. 101, quoted by Herbert Read,
op. cit., pp. 24, 25.
[2] René Taupin, op. cit., p. 125.

De blancs sanglots glissant sur l'azur des corolles.
—C'était le jour béni de ton premier baiser.[1]

Such a method as this is also used by Eliot in a poem like 'Gerontion' where the last line

Thoughts of a dry brain in a dry season[2]

fixes the emotional framework of the aforegoing passages and defines the boundaries within which we may allow our imagination to move among the connotations of

Gull against the wind, in the windy straits
Of Belle Isle, or running on the Horn.
White feathers in the snow, the Gulf claims,
And an old man driven by the Trades
To a sleepy corner.[3]

The old man's 'thoughts' occur in visually concrete images. He 'sees' himself driven by the wind, suggesting the helplessness with which he must finally accept his end. 'White feathers in the snow' suggests the light, transitory nature of life itself. These 'images', rich in connotation, are to be placed within the limitations imposed by the last line.

Eliot avoids the lack of structural coherence, inevitable when the conventional 'rational' structure is abandoned in favour of the method of Qualitative Progression, by 'fixing' his 'personal' symbols within the 'scaffold' of myth, traditional religion and against the background of all the literature known to him. His symbols of the hyacinth and the lilac in 'The Waste Land' are well known in medieval myths and if we are acquainted with such myths we cannot miss what Eliot wishes to evoke by them. But if we are not familiar with this background, he offers us a further delimitation. 'The Burial of the Dead' is at once a denotative and connotative title. The Christian service of the burial of the dead has at its base the belief that 'the dead shall be raised incorruptible' and only out of death shall there be life. Spring flowers then are set against this background, suggesting the coming of the life and fertility of spring after the deadness of winter. Here Eliot has succeeded in fixing the connotation 'so that there may be no missing the evocation'.

[1] Also quoted by Genesius Jones, op. cit., pp. 39, 40.
[2] *Collected Poems*, p. 41.  [3] ibid.

This leads us on to the structural coherence offered by the juxtaposition of images for their ironical effect—perhaps the most satisfactory way of fusing thought images into the type of comprehensive structure defined in Chapter I. Here we must specifically mention Laforgue. Laforgue's method, in Symons's words:

. . . carries as far as that theory has ever been carried, the theory which demands an instantaneous notation, (Whistler let us say), of the figure or landscape, which one has been accustomed to define with such rigorous exactitude. Verse, always elegant, is broken up into a kind of mockery of prose.[1]

We can easily identify Laforgue as one of the Imagist-Symbolists from the above description, for here we have Laforgue, the Imagist, faithful to the carefully observed details of his visual perception, placing his fragments together, carefully juxtaposing them so that what we have in his poems are complex, ironical views of modern life.

Yvor Winters defines the structural method of Jules Laforgue as 'progression by Double Mood',[2] an ironical structure whereby the poet builds up a 'grandiloquent effect' in one passage only to 'demolish it by ridicule or ridiculous anticlimax in another'.[3] In effect, this structure is a Qualitative Progression heightened by irony, for Winters distinguishes it clearly from the ironical structure of a classical poet like Pope or Dryden, whose sophisticated self-assurance enables him to 'rationalize' his poetic experience and make his poems explicitly ironical attacks on other people. The structure of Qualitative Progression has been justified earlier in our study as the most direct means of communication and therefore the most accurate. ('Statement' poetry is the logic which we afterwards impose on our experiences, reminding us of what Hulme said about 'intensive' and 'extensive' manifolds.) When the Qualitative Progression is heightened by Double Mood it takes on added qualities. It becomes 'dramatic' in that this art form shows us by a succession

[1] Symons, op. cit., p. 105.

[2] Yvor Winters, *In Defense of Reason*, pp. 65 ff. Discussed also by Wimsatt and Brooks, op. cit., 672 ff.

[3] I am here reminded of I. A. Richards's preference for poems which he would place under the heading of the 'Secondary Imagination', poems which would bear an 'ironical contemplation because they admit the disparate and conflicting elements in experience'.

of 'conflicting' attitudes the way the artist actually reaches his
conclusions without stating them. An ironical structure of this
sort Eliot approves, for irony demands faithfulness to the
complexities, whether they are conflicting or otherwise, of the
experience. Its 'dramatic' nature indicates further justification
for the procedure by which Eliot places his symbols and fragmentary images together in order to express the complexity of
his modernist vision. Irony itself therefore performs a structural
function, by fusing all the images and symbols, making them
chime and clash by their juxtaposition. F. O. Matthiessen, in
quoting from Eliot's 'Dialogue on Dramatic Poetry', comments:

> . . . the dramatic element in poetry lies in its power to communi-
> cate a sense of real life, a sense of *the immediate present*—that is, of the
> full quality of a moment as it is actually felt to consist.[1]

Irony, or Double Mood, heightening the mathematical progression, thus forms the basic method of construction of all the early
poems. 'Prufrock' perhaps offers us the best example. The
'meaning' or articulation is presented by a 'set of objects, a
chain of events', conceived in the way outlined in Chapter II.
If we were forced to make a 'statement' of the poem it could,
perhaps, be paraphrased as follows: 'I am afraid and even
repulsed by the thought of a mature physical relationship with a
woman, but at the same time am aware of the emptiness of life
without it.' Prufrock's attraction for and repulsion from women
are expressed in the rich connotations of the following passage:

> And I have known the arms already, known them all—
> Arms that are braceleted and white and bare
> (But in the lamplight, downed with light brown hair!)
> Is it perfume from a dress
> That makes me so digress?[2]

The essential beauty, set beside the essential ugliness of the
'arms', conveys in a progression—'fixed' by its presentational
accuracy, yet full of suggestiveness—the complex ironical
attitude of Prufrock towards women, in a far more direct and
immediate way than the above paraphrase could have done.

The image which follows this progression is 'of lonely men
in shirt sleeves, leaning out of windows'. This presents a picture

[1] F. O. Matthiessen, *The Achievement of T. S. Eliot* (1935), p. 66.
[2] *Collected Poems*, p. 15.

of the futility and emptiness of life without the fulfilment offered
by the companionship of a woman—an abhorrent prospect which
Prufrock fears as much as the 'presumption' he must assume
to take his chance as it is offered him at various stages throughout the poem. The final image is symbolic. Just as Laforgue in
desperation 'flies to the moon', Eliot's Prufrock wishes he could
escape to the floor of the sea and become a 'pair of ragged claws'.
The image, vividly concrete, suggests escape and is a 'flight of
fancy' in the Laforguian sense. Through such juxtapositions, the
sinister opening, the 'fog' passage and the refrain—

> In the room the women come and go
> Talking of Michelangelo,

fuse into a dramatic, ironical whole, presenting and suggesting
at the same time, Prufrock's general revulsion from life.

The structure here is mathematical. The 'meaning' is the
synthesis which the reader will be able to make, for here Eliot is
working in a complex of associations which, by their vivid and
concrete nature, enable us to see a 'constant' value in each argument. But the *meaning* will not be a constant, for in accord with
the mathematical analogy, it will vary for each reader according
to the 'value' he gives to the connotation—within the boundaries
'fixed' by the poet.

And so we can sum up Eliot's structural form. Articulation is
made up for him, as for the Symbolists, by a series of mathematical-type images, working in a Qualitative Progression, since it
is the most direct and accurate means of communication. An
'emotional structure' of this sort depends for its success upon the
ability or artistic craftsmanship of the poet in 'fixing' the connotations of each of the symbols or images within their context.
Where the images in such progressions are left vague, no
articulation is possible. In Eliot's poetry each symbol has clearly
defined connotations. Each personal symbol is set against a background of myth or religion. Each 'borrowing' from another
author is fixed, both in the context in which Eliot places it and
in its original context. All are Imagist fragments, because all are
consciously concrete and preserved in the immediacy with which
they were perceived or 'found'. Eliot's 'structure of emotions'
thus forms an *ordered* progression. The success of such a method
as this we shall discuss when we examine the poems themselves.

Thus we see Eliot placed at the point where Imagism and Symbolism meet, attracted to those poets in the Symbolist movement, who, while adhering to the useful and vital principles of construction and connotation, have also the qualities associated with the Imagists. 'Suggestion' for its own sake was not enough for Eliot. In his essay on Marvell he compares his poem 'The Nymph and the Faun' and William Morris's 'The Nymph's Song to Hylas':

The effect of Morris's charming poem depends upon the mistiness of the feeling and vagueness of its object; the effect of Marvell's upon its bright, hard precision . . . the verses of Morris, which are nothing if not an attempt to suggest, really suggest nothing; and we are inclined to infer that the suggestiveness is the aura around a bright clear centre, that you cannot have the aura alone.[1]

In his essay on Dryden he says:

Swinburne was also a master of words, but Swinburne's words are all suggestions and no denotation; if they suggest nothing, it is because they suggest too much.[2]

The value of connotation he consistently admits and admires in Baudelaire:

It is not merely in the use of imagery of common life, not merely in the use of imagery of the sordid life of a great metropolis, but in the elevation of such imagery *to the first intensity*—presenting it as it is, and yet making it represent something much more than itself—that Baudelaire has created a mode of release and expression for other men.[3]

It is vital for his own 'formation en structures'[4] and is the reason why he has little to say in favour of Imagist poets, with the exception of H.D. His 'objective correlatives' are clearly formed in the Imagist manner, however, but the connotative structures which Eliot makes of them in the Symbolist manner provide the more complex and vital poetry demanded by Imagist critics. The combination of the two influences on Eliot can be best summed up by Taupin:

[1] T. S. Eliot, *Selected Essays*, pp. 299–300, quoted also by F. O. Matthiessen, op. cit., p. 63.
[2] T. S. Eliot, op. cit., pp. 314, 315.
[3] ibid., p. 426.
[4] René Taupin, op. cit., p. 214.

Il a enrichi l'imagisme, a rendu la formule apte à exprimer plus de choses. On avait reproché aux imagistes leur étroitesse de vision; sans rien perdre de leur précision, de la réalité de leurs images, il a donné au corps du poème la force de soutenir des objets plus variés, des observations plus diverses. En faisant cela, il s'est rapproché du symbolisme français, non du symbolisme vague d'un Samain, ni du symbolisme de formes et de couleurs de Henri de Régnier, mais de celui de Baudelaire, quand il exprime par des images très concrètes un tourment, de celui de Corbière quand il fait voir un objet, de celui de Laforgue, quand il habille d'ironie une émotion pliée aux tortures des bienséances et du monde.[1]

It is the coexistence of the Image and Symbol in Eliot's poetry which explains the complexity of his method, and it is out of the pattern which he makes of the two that he creates a new symbolic language of concrete, visually precise images. Language and what the poet could do with it was his preoccupation up to 1930. Perhaps Eliot himself best expresses his own achievement in this field in a lecture he gave on Dante at the Italian Institute, London, on 4 July 1950:

. . . in developing the language, enriching the meaning of words and showing how much words can do, he is making possible a much greater range of emotion and perception for other men, because he gives them the speech in which more can be expressed.[2]

[1] René Taupin, op. cit., p. 240.
[2] T. S. Eliot, *To Criticize the Critic*, p. 134.

# IV Ezra Pound: fragments into action

T. S. Eliot begins his little-known article 'Ezra Pound: His Metric and Poetry'[1] with a quotation by Carl Sandburg from *Poetry*:

All talk on modern poetry, by people who know, ends with dragging in Ezra Pound somewhere. He may be named only to be cursed as wanton and mocker, poseur, trifler and vagrant. Or he may be classed as filling a niche today like that of Keats in a preceding epoch. The point is, he will be mentioned.

The time now seems appropriate to 'drag in' the name Ezra Pound in connection with Eliot. The present chapter is not, however, an essay in establishing the 'influence' of Ezra Pound on Eliot—the fact that he had a decisive influence on the literary career of the poet is a fact which, in Noel Stock's words, 'does not bear repeating merely for its own sake'.[2] Eliot's debt to Pound he himself has readily acknowledged as his 'greatest personal debt',[3] and we know that, but for him, Eliot's early poems would not have been published when they were—an indication of what was perhaps Pound's most valuable work at this time, discovering and promoting new poetry. Pound waged a relentless war with Harriet Monroe, in correspondence lasting for six months, before 'Prufrock' appeared in *Poetry*, 1915, and it was as a result of his continued effort that 'Prufrock and other Observations' reached the Egoist Press in 1917.[4] Nevertheless, having said this, I feel that there is a necessity to 'place' Pound in the literary movements of his time, for I feel that it is too strong a claim which Alvarez makes for him when he says that he is 'literally the inventor of the accepted medium of modern poetry'.[5] He could perhaps be described more accurately as a

[1] Issued anonymously 12 November 1917, reproduced in T. S. Eliot: *To Criticize the Critic* (1965), p. 162.
[2] Noel Stock, *Poet in Exile, Ezra Pound* (1964), p. 81.
[3] T. S. Eliot, 'Ezra Pound' from *Poetry LXVII*, September 1946, p. 326.
[4] See Noel Stock, op. cit., p. 81.
[5] A. Alvarez, *The Shaping Spirit: Studies in Modern English and American Poets* (1958), p. 49.

crystallizing agent in bringing together a number of the heterogeneous ideas on poetics circulating between France and
England, rather than the literal *inventor* of them. Adequate
testimony of this is given by Pound himself in an obituary notice
which he wrote on Ford Madox Ford, published in August 1939
in *The Nineteenth Century and After*. In it he recalls the reaction
of Ford to a volume of 'soft' poems which he submitted to him
for criticism in Germany 1911:

And he [Ford] felt the errors of contemporary style to the point of
rolling (physically, and if you look at it as a mere superficial snob,
ridiculously) on the floor of his temporary quarters in Giessen when
my third volume displayed me trapped, fly-papered, gummed and
strapped down in a jejune provincial effort to learn *mehercule,* the stilted
language that then passed for 'good english', in the arthritic milieu
that held control of the respected British critical circles. Newbolt, and
the backwash of Lionel Johnson, Fred Manning, the Quarterlies and
the rest of 'em. And that roll saved me at least two years, perhaps
more.

Ford, along with several of his contemporaries, had recognized
*before* Pound's arrival in England the need 'to register my own
times in terms of my own time', and more fully:

I prefer personally the language of my own day, a language clear
enough for certain matters, employing slang where slang is felicitous
and vulgarity where it seems to me that vulgarity is the only weapon
against dullness.[1]

The poets who were later to form the Imagist 'School' had
already seen the value of acquiring a thorough knowledge of the
traditional literature of as many countries as possible, with the
aim of widening and sharpening their perceptions of the world
around them. But Ford, although he had borne these principles
in mind for 'at least a quarter of a century', as he tells us in the
Preface to his own *Collected Poems* (1914), felt a personal inability to fulfil them in the face of the 'breathless' challenge of the
modern world. Consequently the challenge, already articulated,
was handed over to Pound, whose talent was more adequate to
the task. Noel Stock defines this ability as

. . . an instrument of unusual genius; not one that would be content
to tag on to the nineties indefinitely, producing beautiful poems, just

[1] Quoted by Noel Stock, op. cit., pp. 45, 47.

a little more beautiful, a little sharper, a little more graceful perhaps than those of his contemporaries, but one who would quickly take the literary language away from those who held it in their keeping and refashion it according to the cadence of the living tongue.[1]

But this is to anticipate remarks to be made later on in the chapter. For present purposes, I wish to assert that the present chapter will, to a certain extent, simply underline and reiterate what I have already said in the two previous chapters, showing how Pound pushed forward an idea here and there, re-defined and re-articulated principles already in embryo among poetic theorists in England. Certain additions must be acknowledged as Pound's personal contribution to Eliot's poetic method, but I view the 'influence' of Pound on Eliot mainly as a quickening and crystallizing force, rather than a purely formative one.

At the outset, it must be stated that the poetic interests of the two poets were running parallel at this time—each was pre-occupied above all else with the perfection of craft, intent on exploring the possibilities of the language of poetry, in order to render it a more exact, more precise medium for the communication of a comprehensive vision of modern life; since contemporary poetry was useless, 'the only recourse was to poetry of another age and to poetry of another language'.[2] Eliot saw in his fellow poet 'a steady effort towards the construction of a style of speech',[3] an effort to which he gave his entire energy in the aspiration towards becoming, in Pound's words, a 'flawless artist'.[4] Perhaps the best summary of the identical attitudes of the two poets to their medium is provided for us by Eliot at the end of the article from which I have already quoted. The passage is worth quoting in full:

I think that Pound was original in insisting that poetry is an art, an art which demands the most arduous application and study; and in seeing that in our time it had to be a highly conscious art. He also saw that a poet who knows only the poetry of his own language is as poorly equipped as the painter or musician who knows only the painting or the music of his own country. The business of the poet is to be more conscious of his own language than other men, to be more sensitive to

[1] ibid., p. 31.
[2] T. S. Eliot, 'Ezra Pound', op. cit., p. 326.
[3] T. S. Eliot, Introduction to *Selected Poems* (1928 Introduction), p. 12.
[4] 'How I began', *T.P.'s Weekly*, 10 June 1913.

the feeling, more aware of the meaning of every word he uses than other men. He needs, however, to know as much as he can of several languages: because one advantage of a knowledge of other languages is that it makes us understand our own better . . . Pound's great contribution to the work of other poets (if they choose to accept what he offers) is his insistence upon the immense amount of *conscious* labour to be performed by the poet; and his invaluable suggestions for the kind of training the poet should give himself—study of form, metric and vocabulary in the poetry of divers literatures and study of good prose.[1]

Like Eliot, Pound found Dante his most useful literary ancestor. He calls Dante's *De Vulgari Eloquio* his 'Baedeker in Provence' and Noel Stock tells us that he began to study it before he wrote *The Spirit of Romance* and was still looking into it in 1933 when he wrote the essay 'Immediate Need of Confucius'.[2]

I have noted already the similarities in procedure which Eliot shared with the Imagists and implied that the ideals for which they strove would have been achieved by him without the intervention of Pound. (Eliot himself is hazy as to whether Imagist principles were Hulme's or Pound's and does not seem to care much either way.) Such an implication requires certain modification. It was, of course, largely due to Pound that Imagist principles were made known to anyone in any systematic form, for it was he, along with Flint, as has been shown in Chapter II, who drew up the famous Manifesto of 1913. It is not necessary to restate these principles in full here, but to summarize them as the aim to present in a poem something concrete, in language which observes absolute economy and accuracy in the choice of words, and in rhythm which does not require the use of 'loose' epithets in order to fill up 'the sequence of the metronome'. The enduring attraction which Imagism held for Pound was twofold. In *Poetry*, 1913, Pound was to write:

Space forbids to set forth the program of the Imagistes at length, but one of their watchwords is Precision, and they are in opposition to the numerous and unassembled writers who busy themselves with dull and interminable effusions and who seem to think that a man can write a good long poem before he learns to write a good short one, or even before he learns to produce a good single line.

[1] T. S. Eliot, 'Ezra Pound', op. cit., p. 338.
[2] Noel Stock, op. cit., p. 11.

And of equal importance was the Image, formed in the manner
outlined in Chapter II: '. . . a presented image' is 'the
perfectly adequate expression or exposition of *any* urge whatsoever its nature'.[1]

Holding firm to these two vital principles, Pound produced
what may well be, along with 'Cathay', his best one-image
'poems'—the delicate fragments which go to make up the
*Lustra* Collection. The most famous of these is 'In a Station
of the *Métro*':

> The apparition of these faces in the crowd;
> Petals on a wet black bough.[2]

Here is initial observation of a 'thing'—the faces of the people
in the *Métro*—which strikes the poet with such force that it
seeks articulation. An analogy is found, itself a separate,
concretely observed 'thing', and the two are juxtaposed. The
poem is, in Herbert Read's terms, what 'happens'.[3] Something
like the shock of an electric current runs between the two
observations, rendered without connecting prose statement, and
the initial emotion of the poet is immediately aroused in the
reader. The *Lustra* poems are, for the most part, tiny brilliant
poems, but as G. S. Fraser in his interesting study on Pound
points out:

> William Empson once said to me that the poems in *Lustra* would be
> good little observations to put into a novel but were too slight to
> stand by themselves.[4]

Pound's little pieces are as liable to undergo the same sort of
criticism as similar poetic attempts by fellow Imagists. There is
among them the kind of *naïveté* that Lewis Worthington Smith
identifies with that of the child

> . . . picking up pebbles on the beach and running to some other child
> with yellow hair in happy wonder at finding the pebble and the hair of
> like colour.[5]

Perhaps Pound was at this time unable to face the complex

[1] Ezra Pound, *Polite Essays* (1937), p. 13.
[2] Ezra Pound, *Selected Poems* (1928), p. 89.
[3] See Chapter II, p. 31.
[4] G. S. Fraser, *Ezra Pound* (1960), p. 42.
[5] See Chapter II, p. 34.

world that confronted him, and so, like the Imagists, 'relaxed and took his experiences one at a time'.[1] Clearly this is how Alvarez views his early poems, criticizing them not for lack of skill but because Pound often seemed to have 'so little to say'.[2] Nevertheless, the practice which these poems offered him in perfecting a technique was of inestimable value. Pound was as ready to sense the limitations of the Image as rendered by the Imagists, as were the vociferous critics I have quoted.

It was Pound's realization of the limitations of the single Image, along with his personal inability to remain with any one movement for long after it had become 'established', which led him to Vorticism and the valuable poetic principles of Fenollosa's 'The Chinese Written Character as a Medium for Poetry', i.e. the ideogrammic method. Vorticism implies, in effect, the same basic principles as Imagism, but is a more sophisticated attempt at defining the Image, seeking to make a correlation between it and the articulation of the other arts, i.e. painting, sculpture and music. Its principles are set out by Pound in a long and difficult study of a contemporary sculptor, Gaudier-Brzeska.[3] The analogy between poetry and art which he makes is an interesting one to examine, but our present interest lies in the addition Pound made to the Image as a result of his study of Fenollosa. This 'new' interest in Fenollosa has been regarded as a breakaway from Imagism on Pound's part, although he himself rightly sees it as complementary. In an article called 'Imagisme and England',[4] Pound writes:

There are two sorts of poetry which are to me the most interesting, the most *poetic*. The one is that sort of poetry where music, sheer melody, seems as if it were *just coming over into speech*; the other, where painting or sculpture seems as if it were just forcing itself to words. The first has long been called lyric. You are able to discern a lyric passage in a drama or in a long poem not lyric in its entirety. The second sort of poetry is as old and as distinct, but until recently no one had named it. We now call it *Imagist*, it is not a new invention, it is a critical discrimination.

Apart from this new and more articulate designation of 'The Image'

---

[1] See Chapter II, p. 33.          [2] A. Alvarez, op. cit., p. 57.
[3] Ezra Pound, *Gaudier-Brzeska, A Memoir* (1916).
[4] 'Imagisme and England', *T.P.'s Weekly*, 20 February 1915, quoted also by Noel Stock, op. cit., pp. 76, 77.

certain writers have dared to say openly that poetry ought to be written 'at least as well as prose', and if possible with greater concentration and pertinence . . .

The English Language is composed, roughly speaking, of Anglo-Saxon, Latin and French. Imagisme exists in all three of these languages; in the Anglo-Saxon 'Seafarer', in Catullus' 'Collis o Heliconii', and in 'Charles d'Orléans'. It is ridiculous to say that a form of poetry, a form of beauty, which is possible in each of these three main components, is *impossible* in the language which results from picking the best and the strongest elements from each of the others.

As for Chinese, it is quite true that we have sought the force of Chinese ideographs *without knowing it*. As for the unsuitability of English for that purpose, I have now by me the papers of the late Ernest Fenollosa, sometime Imperial Commissioner of Art in Tokyo. He certainly knew more about this matter than anyone else whose opinion we are likely to get at.

In his essay on the Chinese written character he expressly contends that English, being the strongest and least inflected of the European languages, is precisely the one language best suited to render the force and concision of the uninflected Chinese.

Noel Stock points out that Fenollosa acted as

a sort of chemical agent who helped to bring together, relate and solidify a number of elements individually present in Pound's work or thought.[1]

These elements are clearly the basic principles of Imagism.

The implications of 'The Chinese Written Character' essay have been studied in detail by Donald Davie in *Articulate Energy*[2] and also by Hugh Kenner in *The Poetry of Ezra Pound*.[3] It is generally agreed that Pound's was an imperfect reading of Fenollosa and that his knowledge of Chinese was far from sound; nevertheless, he did indicate the right direction which English poetic style was to take by placing such emphasis on a treatise which Donald Davie calls 'the only English document of our time fit to rank with Sidney's *Apologie* and the Preface to

---

[1] Noel Stock, op. cit., p. 77.
[2] Donald Davie, *Articulate Energy, An Enquiry into the Syntax of English Poetry* (1955).
[3] Hugh Kenner, *The Poetry of Ezra Pound* (1951).

*Lyrical Ballads*, and Shelley's *Defence*—the great poetic mani-
festos of the past.'[1]

The Chinese Ideogram, I have said, is in essence a complement
of the Image. Hugh Kenner summarizes the case for us in
'Ideogram: Seeing':

> The mind lays hold only on particular things. It can NOT know an
> abstraction it has not itself made. Hence the fundamental scholastic
> principle, 'Nothing is in the intellect that is not first in the senses.'[2]

(This seems very close to the 'direct sensuous apprehension of
thought', which Eliot finds to praise in Chapman, etc.)[3] Kenner
goes on:

> Looking about the world we know *things*. On a page of poetry there
> are set in motion the intelligible species of things. Words are solid,
> they are not ghosts or pointers. The poet connects, arranges, defines
> *things*: pearls and eyes; garlic, sapphires, and mud.[4]

'Things' and the observation of them articulated in poetry as
opposed to abstract 'thought' was what the Imagists and Eliot
demanded of poetry. 'The method of poetry' as opposed to
'philosophic discussion' is therefore implied in the way Chinese
defines abstractions. When a European is asked to define 'red',
he says that it is a 'colour'. 'If you ask him', Pound goes on,
'what a colour is, he tells you it is a vibration or a refraction of
light, or a division of the spectrum.'[5] Ask a Chinese on the
other hand to define 'red' and he will put together the abbreviated
pictures of

| ROSE | CHERRY |
|---|---|
| IRON RUST | FLAMINGO |

That, you see, is very much the kind of thing a biologist does (in a
very much more complicated way) when he gets together a few
hundred or thousand slides, and picks out what is necessary for his
general statement. Something that fits the case, that applies in all of
the cases.[6]

This process will surely take us away from abstraction, away
from statements about things, to things themselves. But Fenollosa requires a more accurate definition of 'things':

---

[1] Donald Davie, op. cit., p. 33.     [2] Hugh Kenner, op. cit., p. 76.
[3] See Chapter II, p. 29.                   [4] Hugh Kenner, op. cit., p. 77.
[5] Ezra Pound, *A.B.C. of Reading* (1934), p. 3.     [6] ibid., p. 6.

A true noun, an isolated thing, does not exist in nature. Things are only the terminal points, or rather the meeting points, of actions, cross-sections cut through actions, snapshots. Neither can a pure verb, an abstract motion, be possible in nature. The eye sees noun and verb as one: things in motion, motion in things, and so the Chinese conception tends to represent them.

The sun underlying the bursting forth of plants = spring.
The sun sign tangled in the branches of the tree sign = east.
'Rice-field' plus 'struggle' = male.
'Boat' plus 'water' = boat-water, a ripple.[1]

Donald Davie, pursuing the valuable implications that such observations can have for poetry written in English, goes on to quote Fenollosa on the way 'the sentence form' came about. The passage is worth quoting in full:

The sentence form was forced upon primitive men by nature itself. It was not we who made it; it was a reflection of the temporal order in causation. All truth has to be expressed in sentences because all truth is the *transference of power*. The type of sentence in nature is a flash of lightning. It passes between two terms, a cloud and the earth. No unit of natural process can be less than this. All natural processes are, in their units, as much as this. Light, heat, gravity, chemical affinity, human will, have this in common, that they redistribute force. Their unit of process can be represented as:

| term from which | $\longrightarrow$ | transference of force | $\longrightarrow$ | term to which |
|---|---|---|---|---|

If we regard this transference as the conscious or unconscious act of an agent, we can translate the diagram into:

| agent | $\longrightarrow$ | act | $\longrightarrow$ | object |
|---|---|---|---|---|

. . . It seems to me that the normal and typical sentence in English as well as in Chinese expresses just this unit of natural process. . . . Thus:

| Farmer | pounds | rice |
|---|---|---|

the form of the Chinese transitive sentence, and of the English (omitting particles), exactly corresponds to this universal form of action in nature. This brings language close to *things*, and in its strong reliance upon verbs it erects all speech into a kind of dramatic poetry.[2]

[1] Ernest Fenollosa, *The Chinese Written Character as a Medium for Poetry*, quoted by Donald Davie, op. cit., p. 35.
[2] ibid., pp. 35, 36.

Since the Chinese written character is pictorial, the ideograph
has the unique quality of being able to depict verb and noun as
one and thus becomes the picture of an action. English can
nevertheless attain the precision and conciseness of the Chinese
sentence by showing a thing in action through a picturesque and
transitive verb, wherever possible. While the ideograph re-
articulates so much of what is implied in the Image, it enables it
to become more precise by becoming more *alive*. The most
accurate Images, of whatever the 'urge', to use Pound's term,
imply the juxtaposition of two things in action. The best
analogies present, or at least imply, actions. The Image in these
terms is thus extended in definition and becomes the presentation
of a visual, concrete picture o*f action*.

Poetry, especially the type with which we are dealing, is not
always a simple representational rendering of a single abstract
thing, like 'spring', or 'east', or 'male'. It is often, as Fenollosa
recognizes, concerned with the articulation of 'lofty thoughts,
spiritual suggestions, and obscure relations'.[1] The only way the
poet can articulate these in poetry is by metaphor. Fenollosa, in
terms reminiscent of Hulme, concluded that

Metaphor, the revealer of nature, is the very substance of poetry.[2]

Pound too acknowledges that at the basis of the ideographic
process is metaphor, '. . . the use of material images to suggest
immaterial relations',[3] and views metaphor in Fenollosa's terms:

The whole delicate substance of speech is built upon the substrata of
metaphor. Abstract terms, pressed by etymology, reveal their ancient
roots still embedded in direct action. But the primitive metaphors do
not spring from arbitrary *subjective* processes. They are possible
because they follow objective lines of relation in nature herself.[4]

How many of Fenollosa's ideas reached Eliot through Pound
we do not know. Eliot, it is generally agreed, does not do his
best work when he writes on Pound, and he tends to play down
the influence of the Chinese language on the formation of

[1] Ernest Fenollosa, *The Chinese Written Character as a Medium for Poetry*, quoted by
Donald Davie, op. cit., p. 35.
[2] Fenollosa, quoted by Herbert Read, *The True Voice of Feeling* (1953), p. 125.
[3] Ezra Pound, *Instigations* (1920), p. 376.
[4] Fenollosa, quoted by Herbert Read, op. cit., pp. 124, 125.

Pound's style when he writes of it.[1] Pound came across the papers of Fenollosa in 1913 and it therefore seems unlikely that, when Pound himself lays such stress on their importance, Eliot remained unaffected by the ideas they contain. The germ of metaphorical action-images was, however, present in Pound's thought as early as the 1910 *Spirit of Romance*. In it he praises Arnaut Daniel for his contribution to Dante's style and, dealing with one particular stanza of a Daniel poem, he writes:

Three times in this stanza the Provençal makes his picture, neither by simile nor by metaphor, but in the language beyond metaphor, by the use of the picturesque verb with an exact meaning. Firstly, 'pools himself'—the natural picture. Secondly, after the comparison of gold and lead, the metal workers' shop gives tribute, and is present to the vision in the technical word 'refine'. Thirdly, the feudal ceremony and the suggestion of its pageantry are in the verb 'invest'.[2]

It seems possible, therefore, that Pound's emphasis on the importance of the action-image may have come to Eliot through comment such as this, but however it reached him, it is interesting to note the very technique advocated by Fenollosa appearing again and again in Eliot's concrete images. One of the most obvious examples is an image which has already been examined in an earlier chapter:

I have measured out my life with coffee spoons;[3]

Let us now examine it with regard to Fenollosa's remarks. There is the 'urge' to express the empty, futile, smallness of bourgeois life coupled with Prufrock's self-regarding disgust at his participation [in it. It can be expressed only by analogy and Eliot finds a concrete visual image through the action of the transitive verb 'measured'. Prufrock has 'measured' out his life in the small quantities afforded by the use of a coffee spoon. A further example is offered by the image of fog in the same poem:

The yellow fog that rubs its back upon the window-panes,
The yellow smoke that rubs its muzzle on the window-panes,
Licked its tongue into the corners of the evening,
Lingered upon the pools that stand in drains,

[1] See correspondence between Eliot and Pound which resulted from Eliot's article 'The Method of Mr. Pound', *Athen.*, 24 October 1919.
[2] Ezra Pound, *The Spirit of Romance* (1910), quoted by Noel Stock, op. cit., p. 77.
[3] 'The Love Song of J. Alfred Prufrock', *Collected Poems*, p. 14.

Here two things are juxtaposed, the 'fog' and the implied cat, and the uneasy atmosphere of the evening is articulated in an image which shows 'transference of power' in a compressed metaphor. In 'Morning at the Window', housemaids' 'souls' are seen in a state of degradation and defined:

*Sprouting* despondently at area gates.[1]

Vegetables in a state of decay 'sprout', the opposite of the action of 'blossoming'. Here a precise image of waste and decay is carved out through the use of a concrete verb, transitive by implication. One of the most vivid series of images of this sort is found in 'Gerontion':

What will the spider do,
Suspend its operations, will the weevil
Delay? De Bailhache, Fresca, Mrs. Cammel, whirled
Beyond the circuit of the shuddering Bear
In fractured atoms. Gull against the wind, in the windy straits

Of Belle Isle, or running on the Horn.
White feathers in the snow, the Gulf claims,
And an old man driven by the Trades
To a sleepy corner.[2]

We note here the avoidance of the 'copula' altogether in 'white feathers in the snow'. Here the action of 'blown' or 'driven' is implied in pure Imagistic fashion by the simple juxtaposition of two objects. 'Helplessness' and the resultant inactivity of the old man are articulated in the most precise language possible in:

Vacant shuttles
Weave the wind.[3]

The 'timidity' of Prufrock is expressed in:

Shall I part my hair behind? Do I dare to eat a peach?[4]

Here Eliot is reaching the essential action implied by all 'abstract' words. His language is precise, and what is most important, it raises emotions into a kind of dramatic poetry. One

[1] *Collected Poems*, p. 29.    [2] 'Gerontion', ibid., p. 41.
[3] ibid., p. 40.                [4] ibid., p. 17.

final example will illustrate this quality. The following lines from 'The Waste Land' are well known as a parody of a song from Goldsmith's *A Vicar of Wakefield*:

> When lovely woman stoops to folly and
> Paces about her room again, alone,
> She smoothes her hair with automatic hand,
> And puts a record on the gramophone.[1]

The Goldsmith lines are referred to in the notes at the end of the poem:

> When lovely woman stoops to folly
> And finds too late that men betray,
> What charm can soothe her melancholy?
> What art can wash her tears away?[2]

It is interesting to contrast the means whereby each poet expresses the same emotion. Goldsmith makes the abstract statement:

> And finds too late that men betray,

Eliot presents the woman's uneasy state of mind, resulting from the realization that she has been deserted, in a visually concrete image:

> Paces about her room again, alone.

'Paces about the room' is a visible action and replaces the 'finds' of Goldsmith's song. It connotes immediately the anguish and frustration of the woman and achieves a poignancy lacking in the Goldsmith line. Instead of asking the questions—

> What charm can soothe . . . ?
> What art can wash . . . ?

Eliot implies the negative which must answer them, in two positive, concrete action-images:

> She smoothes her hair with automatic hand,
> And puts a record on the gramophone.

The turning motion of the gramophone record along with the

---

[1] See Notes on 'The Waste Land', *Collected Poems*, p. 83.
[2] Quoted by Kenneth Muir, 'A Brief introduction to the method of T. S. Eliot,' *Durham University Journal*, V, June 1944.

futile gesture of smoothing her hair, suggest simply and directly that life, the daily round, will go on. There is no answer to the woman's dilemma. Whether or not Eliot was aware of it, many of his images, by hewing close to 'things' as Fenollosa sees them, illustrate language used to its truest and fullest advantage.

The study of Fenollosa offers indeed a rich field for exploration, for, in his analysis of words, he leads us into the field of semantics in general—outside the scope of this chapter. It is interesting, nevertheless, in passing, to make reference to a useful study by R. P. Blackmur who, in terms reminiscent of Fenollosa, writes:

Language is made of words and gesture is made of motion . . . Words are made of motion, made of action or response, at whatever remove; and gesture is made of language—made of the language beneath or beyond or alongside of the language of words . . . when the language of words most succeeds it *becomes* gesture in its words . . . the language of poetry may be regarded as symbolic action.[1]

Blackmur sees 'movement' or 'gesture' in all the art forms; '. . . a bridge spans or leaps', 'a dome covers us', 'a crypt appals us'.[2] He quotes, as successful poetic articulation, words of Isaiah:

'Behold, all ye that kindle a fire, that compass yourselves about with sparks: walk in the light of your fire, and the sparks that ye have kindled.' In these words of Isaiah there is a motto for poetry, a judgement of poetry, and a poetic gesture which carries the prophetic meaning of poetry. The words sound with music, make images which are visual, seem solid like sculpture and spacious like architecture, repeat themselves like the movements in a dance, call for a kind of mummery in the voice when read, and turn upon themselves like nothing but the written word.[3]

And Blackmur recalls two lines from *Othello* which he has quoted earlier and which apply to these lines. While he appreciates the qualities set out above, Blackmur admits with Desdemona:

I understand a fury in your words
But not the words.[4]

[1] R. P. Blackmur, *Language as Gesture* (1954), p. 3.
[2] ibid., p. 7.
[3] ibid., p. 12.
[4] (Quarto ed.) *Othello* Act iv Sc. ii, ll. 32–3, quoted by Blackmur, p. 4.

This seems to indicate the initial, but one of the most significant pleasures to be had from the poems of Eliot, made up of complex fragments which articulate so much of the 'gesture' and 'action' of speech. We know the fury of:

Then how should I begin
To spit out all the butt-ends of my days and ways?[1]

or the poetic 'gesture' of:

Son of man
You cannot say, or guess, for you know only
A heap of broken images, where the sun beats,
And the dead tree gives no shelter, the cricket no relief,
And the dry stone no sound of water. Only
There is shadow under this red rock,
(Come in under the shadow of this red rock),
And I will show you something different from either
Your shadow at morning striding behind you
Or your shadow at evening rising to meet you;[2]

long before we understand the 'meaning' of them. While we cannot place too strong an emphasis on this level of apprehension of the poems, we must agree with Rosenthal who writes:

. . . the force and emotion of the poems is largely derived from the more elementary nature of their first impact.[3]

This impact is made largely through Eliot's choice of verbs.

But this is to depart from the immediate study in hand. The fault which Pound found in the early Imagist propaganda he summed up as being 'incomplete statement' rather than 'misstatement'. A move had to be made from the 'stationary' image, which we remember was a 'drifting, homeless, expatriated thing', having 'no history, no prospects, no causes, no sequels, no association, no allies'.[4]

If you can't think of imagism or phanopoeia as including the moving image, you will have to make a really needless division of fixed image and praxis or action.[5]

[1] *Collected Poems*, p. 15.
[2] ibid., pp. 63, 64.
[3] M. L. Rosenthal, *The Modern Poets* (1960), p. 78.
[4] See Chapter II, pp. 32–3.
[5] Ezra Pound, *A.B.C. of Reading*, p. 36.

Hugh Kenner sees a deliberate use of Aristotle's term 'praxis' for 'actions'.[1] In a footnote he quotes what Aristotle has to say on 'praxis':

All human happiness or misery takes the form of action; the end for which we live is a certain kind of activity, not a quality. Character gives us qualities but it is in our actions—what we do—that we are happy or the reverse.[2]

Kenner adds:

When it is recalled that action (praxis) includes deeds, fortunes, and mental and emotional happenings, 'plot' will be seen to be applicable to a lyric as well as a tragedy.[3]

Eliot has consistently maintained along with Aristotle, that even the simplest lyric is dramatic.[4] Thus, if a poet chooses to embody 'emotions' in 'personae' as Eliot, like Pound, often does in his early poems, he is being most 'dramatic' when he shows us ennui, frustration, disgust or pleasure, in images which embody actions. Like Pound, however, he will only show us the character in moments and not in any continuous narrative of action. Eliot's method is close to Pound's definition of his own technique which he outlined in a letter to William Carlos Williams dated October 1908:

To me the short so-called dramatic lyric—at any rate the sort of thing I do—is the poetic part of a drama the rest of which (to me, the prose part) is left to the reader's imagination or implied or set in a short note. I catch the character I happen to be interested in at the moment he interests me, usually a moment of song, self-analysis, or sudden understanding or revelation.[5]

The sudden transition from image to image, scene to scene, in what Winters called a Qualitative Progression, Pound called the process of 'cut'; Davie, like Kenner, sees it as the method whereby a film director like Eisenstein shifts from scene to scene to form something like a cinematic montage but claims, in his examination of Pound in *Ezra Pound: Poet as Sculptor*,

[1] Hugh Kenner, op. cit., p. 57.
[2] Aristotle, *Poetics* VI, 2, quoted by Hugh Kenner, ibid., p. 37.
[3] ibid., p. 57.
[4] T. S. Eliot, 'Essay on Dramatic Poetry', *Selected Essays* (1951 edition), p. 51.
[5] Quoted by Noel Stock, op. cit., p. 32.

that this was a 'context which Pound overlooks'.[1] However, Herbert Howarth, in his study on Eliot, quotes a passage from an article which Pound contributed to *The Dial* in 1921, which refutes Davie's argument. 'Pound', Howarth writes, 'claimed that Cocteau, inheriting from the "École de Laforgue", wrote the poetry of the city intellect, a poetry which reflected the intersecting pluralities of the city.' He goes on to quote from the article :

> The life of the village is narrative; you have not been there three weeks before you know that in the revolution et cetera, and when M. le Comte et cetera, and so forth. In a city the visual impressions succeed each other, overlap, overcross, they are 'cinematographic'.[2]

Howarth claims that this 'cinematographic' technique appealed to Eliot long before Pound came to 'cut' 'The Waste Land', because 'with the help of Pound's sentence in *The Dial* he perceived that the technique was right for communicating the rhythm of London where the eye passes moment by moment from green to drab, from grim to nostalgic'.[3]

The succession of scenes and images built up into a concatenation therefore adds up to Aristotle's praxis. Each image is separate, rendered in the immediacy with which it was observed, and there is no connecting prosaic comment. Donald Davie makes further comment on such a technique by rearranging 'Provincia Deserta' from Pound's lineation to one of rigid blank verse. For the sake of brevity I shall quote only two lines. Pound's lineation is as follows:

> I have crept over old rafters,
>     peering down
> Over the Dronne,
>     over a stream full of lilies.

Rewritten in blank verse, this becomes in Davie's rendering of it:

> I have crept along old rafters, peering down
> Over the Dronne, a stream there full of lilies.

Davie points out that '. . . everything is lost by such a rearrangement':

[1] Donald Davie, *Ezra Pound: Poet as Sculptor* (1965), p. 122.
[2] Herbert Howarth, *Some Figures Behind T. S. Eliot* (1965), p. 236.
[3] ibid.

Pound's lineation points up the distinction of each image or action as it occurs, and thus insists on the sequence they occur in, whereas blank verse, by speeding up the sequence, blurs them together.[1]

In Pound's lineation, as Davie points out, 'the eye *discovers* that the Dronne is a stream full of lilies',[2] in the way that the camera would move with the eye of the observer. Davie has given a valuable examination and justification of Pound's intention in this and it serves a dual purpose when we apply it to the identical method of Eliot in 'Preludes'; to take the most obvious example:

> The winter evening settles down
> With smell of steaks in passageways.
> Six o'clock.
> The burnt-out ends of smoky days.
> And now a gusty shower wraps
> The grimy scraps
> Of withered leaves about your feet
> And newspapers from vacant lots;
> The showers beat
> On broken blinds and chimney-pots,
> And at the corner of the street
> A lonely cab-horse steams and stamps.[3]

Davie quotes William Carlos Williams in justification of such a method:

The virtue of strength lies not in the grossness of the fiber but in the fiber itself. Thus a poem is tough by no quality it borrows from a logical recital of events nor from the events themselves but solely from the attenuated power which draws perhaps many broken things into a dance by giving them thus a full being.[4]

By adding the 'moving' image, i.e. the image which implies movement within itself, and by building up images into a 'movement', such as we have examined above, we can appreciate the full implications of what Eliot meant when he wrote his definition of the 'objective correlative'. He does not emphasize one object, but a 'set' of them; not one event but a 'chain' of events. Some-

[1] Donald Davie, op. cit., pp. 61, 62.
[2] ibid., p. 62.
[3] T. S. Eliot, *Collected Poems*, p. 23.
[4] Prologue to 'Kora in Hell', in *Selected Essays of William Carlos Williams* (1954), quoted by Davie, op. cit., p. 62.

thing like a progression, like Pound's cinematic montage, is necessary to communicate emotion in its totality.

I have stressed at the beginning of this chapter that my purpose in bringing in Pound at this juncture is largely to emphasize what I have already stated—that talk of the 'influence' of Pound simply underlines the observations already made. My remarks on the Image and Fenollosa's contribution to its further definition by drawing Pound's notice to the 'action' inherent in things, show the most important addition which Pound made to the theory of Imagism: he indicated the way that groups of images could be built up into an Aristotelian 'praxis' or 'cinema' to counteract the basic weakness of the typical Imagist structure.

We must now turn briefly to Pound's association with French Symbolism and the structural principles which it emphasizes. A reading of Pound's *Gaudier-Brzeska* would seem to reveal that Pound wished to separate himself from the Symbolists; and Donald Davie in his chapter 'Gaudier-Brzeska—Vorticism— *Lustra*' would seem to endorse Pound's insistence. It is not as simple as Davie would have us suppose. Taupin, for example, writes of Pound in *L'Influence du Symbolisme Français sur la Poésie Américaine* as one who has closely observed Pound's associations with the French movement. The articles written by Pound appearing in *Poetry*—'New Age—The Approach to Paris'—'. . . sont d'un homne qui vient de découvrir une terre nouvelle, et qui y va à l'aventure . . .'.[1] Taupin quotes from one of these articles:

Il me semble que si nos écrivains fixaient leurs yeux sur Paris au lieu de Londres . . . peut-être auraient-ils quelque chance de faire un travail qui ne serait pas démodé avant d'arriver chez l'imprimeur.

and more specifically:

Je crois que si nos chantres américains étudiaient Kémy de Gourmont pour le rythme, Laurent Tailhade pour le dessin, Henri de Régnier pour la simplicité d'expression syntaxique, Francis Jammes pour l'intérêt humain et le don de rendre sa propre époque; et, s'ils voulaient se faire une idée de ce qui est l'intensité chez Corbière, puisqu'ils ne prendront jamais leur Villon dans l'original, peut-être y auraient-ils quelque espoir pour la poésie américaine.[2]

[1] 'Paris', *Poetry*, October 1913, quoted by R. Taupin, pp. 91–2.     [2] ibid.

Pound may reject some Symbolists, but as the above comment shows, he identifies himself with the group within the movement which I called Imagist-Symbolists. Davie implies the same sort of separation as I made when he comes to deal with Pound and de Gourmont, and quotes Pound's famous dictum:

From Rémy de Gourmont alone there proceeded a personal living force. 'Force' is almost a misnomer; let us call it a personal light.[1]

De Gourmont, we remember, spoke of an 'idea' as 'une sensation défraîchie, une image effacée'.[2] He, like Fenollosa, was anxious for the employment of the exact image—an image created from scrupulously close and disciplined observation of objects. Images of this sort Pound does allow in poetry, but believes

that the proper and perfect symbol is the natural object, that if a man use 'symbols' he must so use them that their symbolic function does not obtrude; so that *a* sense, and the poetic quality of the passage, is not lost to those who do not understand the symbol as such, to whom, for instance, a hawk is a hawk.[3]

Here he is on common ground with those Symbolists who wished to 's'inspirer directement de la vie'. He would, like them, object to purely personal symbols, depending *entirely* on their connotative value for any communication. When the reader is unable to perceive the associations which led the poet to use them, such symbols, he says, must retain their absolute, i.e. their literal or denotative value. In other words, for them, 'the hawk is simply a hawk'. It is perhaps with these ideas in mind that he writes in the Gaudier-Brzeska study:

The Symbolist's *symbols* have a fixed value, like numbers in arithmetic, like 1, 2, and 7.[4]

His images on the other hand *have* associative variable qualities, like algebraic symbols. I believe that Pound may well confuse symbol and sign in this context (where he writes, 'One can be grossly "symbolic", for example, by using the term "cross" to mean "trial"'). Genesius Jones distinguishes between the two:

[1] Ezra Pound, quoted by Donald Davie, op. cit., p. 71.
[2] R. de Gourmont, *Le Problème du Style*, quoted by Davie, ibid., p. 66.
[3] Ezra Pound, *Literary Essays* (1954) (ed. T. S. Eliot), p. 9.
[4] Ezra Pound, *Gaudier-Brzeska*, p. 97.

. . . a sign and its object, stand in a very simple one-to-one correlation. Given the sign, the existence of the object is at once presumed.[1]

He quotes Susanne Langer in distinguishing the symbol from
this:

Symbols are not proxy for their objects, but are *vehicles for the conceptions of objects* . . . and it is the conception not the things that
symbols directly mean.[2]

Despite this possible confusion, it would appear that, while
Pound advocates the associative qualities of symbols, he wishes
to defend poetry from the 'undelimited' symbols of which the
pure Symbolists were guilty. Like the Symbolist-Imagists
whom he praises:

An *image*, in our sense, is real because we know it directly . . . It is
our affair to render the *image* as we have perceived or conceived it.[3]

Pound is, nevertheless, bound to allow connotation—his communication ultimately depends on it. A few examples will suffice
to show this. He frequently alludes to other authors, for
example, and by simply citing a name, he expects us to call to
mind all the historical associations of that name. G. S. Fraser
calls this connotative use of names 'cluster evocations'.[4] He
gives as example a few lines from 'Yeux Glauques':

> Gladstone was still respected
> When John Ruskin produced
> 'King's Treasures'; Swinburne
> And Rossetti still abused.

The effect of the lines, as Fraser points out, depends on our sharing Pound's particular associations with Gladstone; not, that is,
that 'he was an eminent Victorian, notable for the high principles
of morality held by Victorians', as Lytton Strachey viewed him,
but that he represented for Pound, in Fraser's terms, 'pompous-
ness and humbug':[5]

It is the use of an historical proper name, or more rarely one out of
myth or legend, to stand not for one abstract idea but for a cluster of

[1] Genesius Jones, *Approach to the Purpose* (1964), p. 31.
[2] Susanne Langer, *Philosophy in a New Key* (1951), quoted by Jones, ibid., p. 57.
[3] Ezra Pound, *Gaudier-Brzeska*, p. 99.
[4] G. S. Fraser, op. cit., pp. 56–7.
[5] ibid.

attitudes. It depends very much, of course, on the reader sharing
Pound's historical knowledge and either intuitively sympathizing with,
or guessing and adjusting himself to, Pound's attitudes.[1]

Eliot makes use of 'cluster evocations' of this sort as we shall see
in the following chapters, whose efficacy in the poems in which
they occur depends on the way they are introduced into the
poet's structure.

Eliot has himself pointed out 'deliberately arbitrary images'
or symbols in Pound's poetry 'having their place in the total
effect of the poem', and he quotes among others:

> Red leaf that art blown upward and out and over
> The green sheaf of the world . . .

and 'Black lightning' as examples.[2] Such images as these
depend on their connotational value for communication of the
poet's emotions. It is interesting to note how Eliot praises them,
by comparing them with symbols of Mallarmé, which are often
vague and not clearly enough defined:

> . . . each has always its part in producing an impression which is
> produced always through language. Words are perhaps the hardest of
> all material of art: for they must be used to express both visual beauty
> and beauty of sound, as well as communicating a grammatical state-
> ment. It would be interesting to compare Pound's use of images with
> Mallarmé's; I think it will be found that the former's, by the contrast,
> will appear always sharp in outline, even if arbitrary and not photo-
> graphic.[3]

Davie compares Pound's use of images with Eliot's 'objective
correlatives'. Eliot, he says, like the Symbolists, was interested
in Images 'only to the extent that they may *stand in for* the subjective phenomena (such as states of mind or of feeling) which
can thus be objectified through them',[4] but also recognizes that
Pound's quarrel with Symbolism is 'blurred' because

> . . . Pound, insisting on how his poetry, unlike symboliste poetry,
> hews close to the contours of the perceivable world, is forced to insist
> that on the other hand the art he is promoting is not simply representa-
> tional.[5]

---

[1] G. S. Fraser, op. cit., p. 56.
[2] T. S. Eliot, *To Criticize the Critic*, p. 171.     [3] ibid.
[4] Donald Davie, op. cit., p. 74.     [5] ibid., p. 57.

It is indeed a 'blurred' quarrel, for Pound, as Graham Hough has also pointed out, was unable to maintain consistently that 'clear presentation of the object' was the sole aim of poetry.[1] Several years before the 'Hamlet' essay was written, Pound spoke of poetry in terms that anticipated the 'objective correlative' passage. Poetry, he wrote, was

> a sort of inspired mathematics which gives equations not for abstract figures, triangles, spheres and the like, but equations for human emotions.[2]

The image, for him, remaining close to perceivable and concrete experiences, therefore takes on the connotative qualities of the symbol in making articulations of emotions. Davie seeks for a label by which to identify him. Pound is not 'post-symboliste', Davie says, and finally ascribes to him the 'lame' title of 'realist'.[3] Perhaps the title Imagist-Symbolist, though clumsy, would more accurately describe him, since it is interesting to note that the group of Symbolist poets which we identified with the Symbolist-Imagist practice appealed to both Pound and Eliot.

And so we are led to our remarks which were made in the previous chapter regarding structure. It is generally agreed that apart from the translations where form is given, Pound's poetry is 'structureless'. This may be somewhat unfair, for apart from the *Cathay* poems, we can find numerous examples which illustrate Pound's adherence to the structural principles which I have defined in the previous chapter. Donald Davie quotes 'South Folk in Cold Country' as one of Pound's most successful poems:

> Flying snow bewilders the barbarian heaven.
> Lice swarm like ants over our accoutrements.
> Mind and spirit drive on the feathery banners.
> Hard fight gets no reward.
> Loyalty is hard to explain.[4]

Davie commends it in these words:

[1] Graham Hough, *Image and Experience* (1960), p. 13.
[2] Ezra Pound, *The Spirit of Romance* (1910), p. 5, quoted by Hugh Kenner, p. 61. It is interesting to note that he still speaks of it in terms of mathematical equations in the Gaudier-Brzeska study in a complicated analogy which he makes with the equations made by co-ordinating geometry.
[3] Donald Davie, op. cit., p. 66.
[4] Ezra Pound, *Selected Poems*, p. 117.

The poem establishes a convention by which the gauge of a poetic line
is not the number of syllables or of stressed syllables or of metrical feet,
but the fulfilment of the simple grammatical unit, the sentence; and,
the convention thus established, we conspire in giving to naïvely
abstract sentences like 'Hard fight gets no reward' and 'Loyalty is
hard to explain' as much weight as to the longer sentences which make
vivid images about lice on armour, and flying snow in the skies. This
seems to be a wholly original and brilliant way of embodying abstractions in English poetry.[1]

The structural principle involved seems the same in:

> Particularly I remark
> An English countess goes upon the stage.
> A Greek was murdered at a Polish dance,
> Another bank defaulter has confessed.
> I keep my countenance,
> I remain self-possessed
> Except when a street-piano, mechanical and tired
> Reiterates some worn-out common song
> With the smell of hyacinths across the garden
> Recalling things that other people have desired.
> Are these ideas right or wrong?[2]

Or again:

> But though I have wept and fasted, wept and prayed,
> Though I have seen my head (grown slightly bald) brought in upon
>     a platter,
> I am no prophet—and here's no great matter;
> I have seen the moment of my greatness flicker,
> And I have seen the eternal Footman hold my coat, and snicker,
> And in short, I was afraid.[3]

Davie notes variations on this structure in, for example, 'The
River Merchant's Wife: A Letter', where many sentences are
strung over two lines. I quote only a short passage:

> The leaves fall early this autumn, in wind.
> The paired butterflies are already yellow with August
> Over the grass in the west garden;
> They hurt me. I grow older.[4]

[1] Donald Davie, op. cit., p. 42.
[2] 'Portrait of a Lady', *Collected Poems*, pp. 20, 21.
[3] 'The Love Song of J. Alfred Prufrock', ibid., p. 16.
[4] Ezra Pound, *Selected Poems*, p. 109.

There is, he goes on to say, 'an exceptional poignancy about the one short line which comprehends two complete sentences'.[1] The same sort of poignancy, by precisely the same means (if we allow Eliot's substitution of the semicolon for the full stop), is achieved in 'Portrait of a Lady':

> 'I have been wondering frequently of late
> (But our beginnings never know our ends!)
> Why we have not developed into friends.'
> I feel like one who smiles, and turning shall remark
> Suddenly, his expression in a glass.
> My self-possession gutters; we are really in the dark.[2]

This 'breaking of the pentameter', as Pound calls it in Canto 81, (which Davie also notes), indicates *vers libre* as he understood it and it is the type which Eliot obviously appreciates by his frequent use of it.

We can commend this device of Pound's for structural qualities other than the metrical ones which Davie praises. They make progressions in the Imagist-Symbolist manner (although admittedly in a much simpler form). Each image is a separate, concrete, perceived experience presented to the reader without comment. The lines, however, although denotatively clear, depend on their connotational value for the effect which they produce. Each image has to be set against the statements 'Hard fight gets no reward' and 'Loyalty is hard to explain', before we can fully appreciate their function in the poem. Poems such as these may well have pointed out the way whereby Eliot could fix the connotations of his more complex images. They seem close to the method of the Symbolist poem which has already been mentioned in Chapter III, where something like the 'answer' to the mathematical progression is contained within the framework of the poem and against which we set the 'terms' which go to make up the other side of the equation.

This is a relatively simple type of structure. There is one further type, which represents a more comprehensive structure of images and which we have already mentioned in connection with Eliot: the Qualitative Progression, heightened by Double Mood, or irony which fuses the poem into structural unity. We saw that it was essentially a dramatic construction, where the

---

[1] Donald Davie, op. cit., pp. 43–4.          [2] *Collected Poems*, p. 21.

poet gives us a succession of images which allow for and articulate 'conflicting' attitudes. 'Hugh Selwyn Mauberley' is the obvious example, but there is among the *Lustra* collection a little poem, 'The Garden',[1] which is a perfect example of the procedure which Eliot adopts in 'Prufrock' and 'Portrait of a Lady'. The 'heroine' shares something of the self-consciousness and emotional ennui of both Prufrock and the Lady of Eliot's poems. An image of the woman, whose 'boredom is exquisite and excessive' and who walks

> Like a skein of loose silk blown against a wall

is set beside an image of 'emotional anaemia'. The 'sickness' of her soul, articulated by 'anaemia', could be compared with the 'etherized patient' image in 'The Love Song of J. Alfred Prufrock'. Pound sets beside this image an image

> Of the filthy, sturdy, unkillable infants of the very poor

who will nevertheless 'inherit the earth'—the implication being that the lady will not. Her 'breeding', the social circumstances of her life, prevent her from accepting the challenge offered her by the 'I' of the poem. She senses the opportunity:

> She would like someone to speak to her.

She feels the emptiness of her life, however 'self-assured' she appears on the surface. Following the simply articulated desire, the 'lofty' language of the last two lines implies that the challenge remains unaccepted:

> She would like someone to speak to her
> And is almost afraid that I will commit that indiscretion.

The formality of tone associated with 'commit that indiscretion', set against the simplicity of 'She would like someone to speak to her', is exquisite irony. Her situation, like Prufrock's, is one from which there is no escape. The structure here is complete or 'sphere-like' to use Yeats's term for good 'form' in verse.[2] Pound has circled the emotions of the lady and returned to his starting point with a full comprehension of them. This comprehensive vision is given coherence by the ironical juxtaposing of the images which go to make it up.

[1] Ezra Pound, *Selected Poems*, p. 67.
[2] *Oxford Book of Modern Verse*, Introduction by W. B. Yeats, p. xxiv.

We could go on to examine the longer and more difficult 'Mauberley', where 'conflict' is again presented by a series of fragment images. The 'opposites' here are the aspirations of a poet to create a great work of art comparable to that of the great Renaissance artists, and the inability to achieve such a 'lofty' task because of the depraved civilization in which he finds himself. F. R. Leavis describes the 'wholeness' of construction which the poem achieves:

The poems together form one poem, a representative experience of life —a tragedy, comedy, pathos and irony. And throughout there is a subtlety of tone, a complexity of attitude, such as we associate with seventeenth-century wit.[1]

The success of a short poem like 'The Garden' is obvious. What is not so obvious, however, is the success of a poem of the magnitude and scope of *The Cantos*. After 'Mauberley', Pound's quest for exact articulation took on political connotations, which led him away from purely poetic aims towards participation in anti-semitic and Fascist activities. How this came about, and the implications which it held for his poetry, have been the result of his reading of the Confucian *Ta Hio*:

The men of old wanting to clarify and diffuse throughout the empire that light which comes from looking straight into the heart and then acting, first set up good government in their own states; wanting good government in their own states, they first established order in their own families; wanting order in the home, they first disciplined themselves; desiring self-discipline, they rectified their own hearts; and wanting to rectify their hearts, they sought precise verbal definitions of their inarticulate thoughts . . . wishing to attain precise verbal definitions, they set to extend their knowledge to the utmost. The completion of knowledge is rooted in sorting things into organic categories.[2]

It is the 'sorting of things into organic categories' in Pound's sailing after complete knowledge,[3] which stands as the ultimate aim for and justification of the method of *The Cantos*. He believes that it is this same sorting and arranging of material which is the

[1] F. R. Leavis, *New Bearings in English Poetry* (1932 edition), p. 141.
[2] Quoted by Hugh Kenner, op. cit., p. 37.
[3] I borrow the phrase from George Dekker's book on Pound's *Cantos, Sailing After Knowledge* (1963).

method of scientists. William Carlos Williams, himself a
scientist, values the method on one condition:

Given many things of nearly totally divergent natures but possessing
one thousandth part of a quality in common, provided that be new,
distinguished, these things belong to an imaginative category and not
in a gross natural array. To me this is the gist of the whole matter.[1]

Williams rightly demands an *imaginative* category which critics
like Matthiessen have said depends on the 'unified sensibility' of
the poet.[2] In *The Cantos* we are asked to see the connection between such diverse items as lynxes, little boys on bicycles and a
précis of the history of the Chinese dynasty. The relationship is
not so easily imagined as 'Red: Cherry, rust, flamingo, etc.'.
Such scientific procedure reaches Eliot in 'The Waste Land'
where bits and pieces of literature in the 'scissors-and-paste like
manner'[3] (to use Davie's term) of the collage artist are incorporated, undigested, into the pattern of the poem. Davie
attempts to justify them in Pound's case on the grounds that
'the specimens to be examined must not be tampered with
before being offered for inspection'.[4]

It is doubtful if such a method can be justified even on scientific
grounds. It is surely the object of the scientist to perceive the
general relationships existing among his specimens and to cor-
relate his data in such a way that the observer is also aware of
'the thousandth part of a quality' that they have in common.
Although the 'generality' or 'universality' of all modern art,
as we have emphasized from the beginning of this study, is not
to be confused with the general concepts which the scientist
deduces from his analyses, the same basic principle, nevertheless,
holds for both. The particular aspects of the object of a modern
Cubist painting, for example, must be so arranged that we are
aware all the time that we are looking at the same object, no
matter how many views of it the artist incorporates in his picture.
Similarly, the particular 'appearances' or images which articulate an emotion, should be so arranged in a poem that we should
be aware that it is a comprehensive or universal presentation of
that emotion. In *The Cantos* the poet rarely achieves this uni-

[1] William Carlos Williams, *Selected Essays* (1954), quoted by Davie, op. cit.,
p. 121.
[2] F. O. Matthiessen, *The Achievement of T. S. Eliot* (1935), p. 68.
[3] Donald Davie, op. cit., p. 125.        [4] ibid.

versality, which should transcend the particularity of the items he presents. Warren Ramsey sums up this structural failure in a short article: 'Pound, Laforgue and the Dramatic Structure':

The larger problems of structural order would seem to arise with particular force when a poet who has first written verse suffused with Celtic twilight, then poems turning around a pointed intellectual remark, finally undertakes a poem of some length, 'The Cantos'. In the long run he is faced with the necessity of rising from image and remark to some kind of general design. The unsuccessful Cantos will be those in which Pound fails to rise from the particular to the general, those in which he follows most faithfully his so-called 'ideograph' or Chinese-picture-writing method of heaping disconnected particulars together.[1]

In the terms of this study, structural coherence depends on the harmonizing vision of the poet, which connects the fragments of the poem together in such a way that the reader is aware of the connotations of each particular image, for it is these connotative 'fields of force'[2] which raise the poem-equation from the level of the heap of disconnected particulars to the level where it will have some general or universal significance. What we are given in *The Cantos* is often a gross array of images, images as 'absolute' as the personal symbols chosen by the pure symbolists. We are aware all the time that they have a 'symbolic' value which we cannot grasp, since the poet has not attempted to fix them in a 'convenientia'.[3] It is a strange paradox that Pound, in his demand for greater and greater exactitude, has become as obscure as the purest of mystic symbolists, each as guilty as the other of over-connotative, over-personal and hence undefined symbols.

The Cantos are, of course, historically and every other way, outside the scope of this study. The only reason for bringing to notice the sort of criticism that is levelled at them is to stress the need for 'the scaffold' or structural unity which Eliot demanded, and to restate his remarks on Dante's construction in *The Divine Comedy*:

The significance of any single passage, of any of the passages that are selected as 'poetry' is incomplete unless we ourselves apprehend the whole.[4]

[1] *Comparative Literature* (1951), III.          [2] Hugh Kenner, op. cit., p. 233.
[3] Genesius Jones, op. cit, p. 39.
[4] T. S. Eliot, *The Sacred Wood* (1950 edition), p. 168.

We might also remind ourselves here of Herbert Read's words, quoted in the previous chapter:

The projection of a symbol or image from the unconscious is not an act of creation . . . it is merely the transfer of an existing object from one sphere to another . . .

The essential function of art is revealed in a co-ordination of images . . . into an effective pattern. The art is in the pattern which is a personal intuition of the artist and not in the imagery.[1]

We are bound to conclude, therefore, that Pound's best poems are those written before he entered the 'structureless' world of *The Cantos*, lawless because he is unable to discipline himself into forming 'patterns' of the items he produces.

The question to be raised concerning the ultimate success of Eliot's art, or Pound's, or indeed any art, could, perhaps, best be summed up in the words of Paul Klee, writing on the procedure of the modern painter:

The artist has studied this world of variety and has, we may suppose, unobtrusively found his way in it. His sense of direction has brought order into the passing stream of image and experience.[2]

The poets with whom we have dealt have studied vigorously and scrupulously the 'world of variety', both in its natural manifestations and in the art and literature of the vast tradition of the past. The images they have perceived in this world are often fine and masterful. What is doubtful in Pound's case and in the case of many of the pure symbolists is their 'sense of direction' and the consequent lack of order which they have brought to bear on 'the passing stream of image and experience'. It remains for us to make an evaluation of Eliot's early poems, bearing in mind the structural demands made on the procedures already outlined, along with the failure of Pound, and many Symbolists and Imagists to meet up to them. Their structural failing could be summed up, again in the words of Paul Klee:

We have found the parts but not the whole.[3]

[1] See Chapter III, pp. 38–9.
[2] Paul Klee, *On Modern Art* (1959), p. 13.
[3] ibid., p. 55.

# V    Fragments into poems

It is necessary before discussing the poems themselves to make a brief summary of what we have described as the 'method' of the early poetry. A poem, according to Eliot's implications, is the 'formula' which a poet makes of emotions, that is, the 'objective correlative' of an emotional complex. For the early Eliot, language, and the rendering of it more concrete for the expression of the 'sets of objects' or 'chains of events' which made up the 'objective correlative', were of the utmost importance, and our concern so far has been in showing the ways in which Eliot made the poetic language of his own day more precise for the articulation of those 'parts'. In terms similar to those of the Imagists, he stressed the importance of visual or sensuously apprehended images of 'things' as the basic units of poetry. Language, however, has by the syntactical forms in which we employ it a tendency towards a generalizing 'abstractness'. Donald Davie, in examining Hulme's concern for the concrete presentation of 'intensive manifolds' in poetry, saw an *implied* denial of syntax altogether. He writes:

Syntax assists explanation, but explanation is unfolding, and intensive manifolds, which should be poetry's main concern, cannot be unfolded; hence it appears that syntax is out of place in poetry.[1]

The point which Davie made has been taken up more recently by Genesius Jones, who writes that the rules of grammar are the result of 'the generalizing tendency of language':

These rules are no doubt the highest achievement of the semantic of language and one of the finest achievements of the human spirit. But for the poet who works in language as a medium, they are not without dangers. Because of the generalizing tendency they embody, they are inclined to make meaning less and less immediate and to rob it of nuance.[2]

The remarkable achievement of Eliot regarding language is that he has been able to preserve both nuance of meaning and

[1] Donald Davie, *Articulate Energy* (1955), p. 9.
[2] Genesius Jones, *Approach to the Purpose* (1964), p. 182.

verbal exactitude by making use of the normal syntactical structures, as we have seen in the previous chapter, by his careful selection of visually precise yet connotatively rich transitive and intransitive 'action-images', especially where he chose to articulate emotion through 'personae'.

His structure was therefore defined as a connotative, sensuous form comparable to that of the Symbolist-Imagists, and I borrowed from the language of mathematics terms by which to describe a poem. A comprehensive poetic articulation was the sum of a series of mathematical-type 'arguments' fused into unity by shared connotation. The previous chapters have thus been an attempt to provide a full definition of what Eliot meant when he wrote:

The only way of expressing emotion in the form of art is by finding an 'objective correlative'; in other words, a set of objects, a situation, a chain of events which shall be the formula of that *particular* emotion; such that when the external facts, which must terminate in sensory experience, are given, the emotion is immediately evoked.[1]

However tired critics like Graham Hough may be with the 'objective correlative', it is the best, if not the only, way to describe the method of the early poems.

So far, however, we have looked mainly at one side of the equation, the way by which articulation of the 'arguments' comes about. We must now look at the other side, the 'value' of the equation, and consider once again the materials out of which Eliot constructs his poem. From the 1917 'Tradition and the Individual Talent' until the 1927 essay on 'Shakespeare and the Stoicism of Seneca', Eliot has consistently maintained that poetry is the presentation, in concrete form, of emotion, and that it is from his own emotion that the poet must start. He asserts, nevertheless, and this is most important for our study of the poems, that these emotions are *not* the most important part of the poetic process. The emotions of the poet may in fact be 'simple, or crude, or flat'.[2] The emotion of the poem on the other hand will be 'a very complex thing, but not with the complexity of the emotions of people who have very complex or unusual emotions in life'.[3] The task of the poet is, therefore,

[1] *Selected Essays* (1951 edition), p. 145.
[2] *The Sacred Wood* (1950 edition), p. 57.          [3] ibid.

. . . not to find new emotions but to use the ordinary ones, and, in working them up into poetry, to express feelings which are not in actual emotions at all. And emotions which he has never experienced will serve his turn as well as those familiar to him.[1]

The way in which emotions, whether 'ordinary' emotions which the poet has himself experienced or those from the emotional range of experience offered him by a thorough knowledge of as much past and present European literature as possible, are 'worked up' into poetry seems, clearly, in Eliot's terms, to be the result of deliberate and conscious workmanship. Eliot has expressed this effort in 'The Function of Criticism' where he writes that the task of the artist is as much critical as creative. It is 'the labour of sifting, combining, constructing, expunging, correcting, testing'.[2] He has consistently maintained that the poet should regard his emotions simply as the *starting point* of poetry, the material from which he can begin to construct a poem. Only when he is prepared to use his material objectively is he fit to become an artist. The process of the depersonalization of the artist to this end has already been examined in Chapter I. It is sufficient to remind ourselves here of Eliot's definition of the mature artist in 'Tradition and the Individual Talent':

. . . the mind of the mature poet differs from that of the immature one, not precisely in any valuation of 'personality', not being necessarily more interesting, or having 'more to say', but rather by being a more finely perfected medium in which special, or very varied feelings are at liberty to enter into new combinations.[3]

The poet therefore does not have to be an inspired thinker or philosopher, he does not have to 'believe' or 'think' anything. Applying this idea to his criticism of other poets, Eliot writes:

Donne, Poe, Mallarmé ont la passion de la spéculation métaphysique, mais il est évident qu'ils ne croient pas aux théories auxquelles ils s'intéressent ou qu'ils imitent à la façon Ovide et Lucrèce affirmaient les leurs. Ils se servent de leurs théories pour attendre un but plus limité et plus exclusif: pour raffiner, pour développer leur puissance de sensibilité de l'émotion. Leur oeuvre était une expansion de leur sensibilité au delà des limites du monde normal, la découverte d'une

[1] ibid., p. 58.  [2] *Selected Essays*, p. 30.
[3] ibid., p. 18.

nouvelle combinaison propre à susciter de nouvelles émotions—
transmutations de l'accidentel en réel.[1]

Whether or not Eliot is right about Donne, Poe or Mallarmé,
is not relevant to our study. What is relevant, however, is the
light comment like this throws on Eliot's own fragmentary
method. Phrases like 'working up' emotions in themselves
'ordinary and flat', in order to achieve 'une nouvelle combinaison' 'au delà des limites du monde normal', illustrate very well
that Eliot's early approach to his material placed strong emphasis
on the 'art' rather than the 'thought', that the principles which
were foremost in his mind were those of an 'artist', not those of
a 'thinker'. It is this view of the function of poetry which I have
identified as synonymous with the movement of modern art in
general in this century. All artists, in whatever medium they
work, attempt to present us with 'une nouvelle combinaison', 'au
delà des limites du monde normal', which involves, first of all,
transcending the limits of their own personal vision. The
technique which Eliot shares with these artists is one of assemblage. Each brings together various 'appearances' of the same
object or emotion, various aspects which the same 'scene'
presents at different times, and attempts to 'fix them on the
canvas with precision'.[2] The resultant 'assembled' emotion of
the poem will be a new complex art-emotion, *'significant'*
because it has its 'life in the poem and not in the history of the
poet'.[3]

From another viewpoint, however, expressed in his essay on
*Hamlet*, Eliot suggests that what the poet starts off from is an
extremely complex emotion, too complex for conventional
means of expression. This emotion,

The intense feeling, ecstatic or terrible, without an object or exceeding
an object, is something which every person of sensibility has known;[4]

Emotions such as these the ordinary man 'turns down', burdened
as he is by something which has no exact referent in his experience. The job of the poet in such circumstances is to keep such
complex emotions 'alive', and he must therefore make a deliberate
effort to avoid the surface logic and reasoning which the 'thinker'

[1] T. S. Eliot, 'Note sur Mallarmé et Poe', *Nouvelle Revue Française*, November
1926.
[2] See Chapter I, p. 4.       [3] *The Sacred Wood*, p. 59.       [4] ibid., p. 102.

would impose on them. In order to convey this emotional complex exactly, and to present it directly to the reader, the poet can only attempt to 'intensify the world to his emotions'[1] by finding images, symbols, 'series of events' from the world of experience, by which to formulate it. Emotion like this is conflicting, 'dramatic' emotion and it is the poet's task in making art of it to

. . . purge it of its murky turbulence and bring it into some ordered calm vision in the clear sunlight.[2]

We can therefore identify two methods of poetic assemblage used by Eliot. The first is where the poet starts off with a simple emotion and assembles various images which articulate it to form a poetic structure which produces a new, significant art-emotion. The second method results from the poet's starting off with complex emotions which he can only attempt to express by assembling images and symbols from the world of ordinary things, to form a comprehensive poetic structure. The two methods are complementary and the resultant poem is the same in each case. The poem *is* an articulation of a complex of emotions. From this we can see that what Eliot wishes to stress is the final structure which is the poem. Taupin sums up this artistic formulation well when he writes:

T. S. Eliot ne reconnaît à l'écrivain que le droit de précipiter le groupe-ment, la 'formation en structures' des émotions, des expériences émotives. Il comprend la poésie comme une organisation vivante des expériences faites à diverses époques et comme 'the living whole of all the poetry that has ever been written.[3]

The poetry, it is no longer necessary to assert, has occasioned, in the words of I. A. Richards, 'an unusual amount of irritated or enthusiastic bewilderment' and he goes on to define the cause of this and its result:

The most formidable is the unobtrusiveness, in some cases the absence, of any coherent intellectual thread upon which the items of the poem are strung. A reader of 'Gerontion', of 'Preludes', or of 'The Waste Land',

[1] ibid.
[2] M. L. Rosenthal, *The Modern Poets* (1960), p. 83.
[3] R. Taupin, *L'Influence du Symbolisme Français sur la Poésie Américaine* (1929), p. 214.

may, if he will, after repeated readings, introduce such a thread. Another reader after much effort may fail to contrive one. But in either case energy will have been misapplied. For the items are united by the accord, contrast, and interaction of their emotional effects, not by an intellectual scheme that analysis must work out. The value lies in the unified response which this interaction creates in the right reader. The only intellectual activity required takes place in the realization of the separate items. We can, of course, make a 'rationalization' of the whole experience, as we can of any experience. If we do, we are adding something which does not belong to the poem. Such a logical scheme is, at best a scaffolding that vanishes when the poem is constructed.[1]

The fragmentary presentation is, however, Eliot's choice as an artist, and this has been acknowledged by all those who have dealt with the poems. It is at the same time a striking 'failure' of many critics, as Hugh Kenner points out, that their 'discussion of the poems . . . still slips off into *ideas* when it doesn't begin there'.[2]

It is perhaps for the reason that it is difficult to avoid introducing a logical thread that the mathematical analogy made in this study is most useful. The equation of an emotion is different from a prose-type definition of it: the definition of an emotion by the use of mathematical-type arguments provides an organized structure—or as Eliot called it an 'emotional systematization'[3]—different from the logic which is imposed on it by making abstract statements about it. It also enables the poet to be more exact, and at the same time 'general', in the sense that it allows the reader to make various 'interpretations' of a poem, according to the 'value' he gives each fragment within the ordered structure imposed by the poet. I therefore look on the early Eliot as an assemblage poet who collects emotions or ideas, in the form of images—vividly precise, denotatively clear fragments with rich connotations—which he presents in a patterned, poetic structure. The poem is the thing we are concerned with, and just as Pound defined the Image as the presentation of 'an emotional complex in an instant of time', so we should view the early poems as an arrangement of such images arrested as instances of art. Eliot would not refute the idea that all poetry

[1] I. A. Richards, *Principles of Literary Criticism* (1926 edition), Appendix B., pp. 289–90.
[2] Hugh Kenner, *T. S. Eliot: The Invisible Poet* (1960), p. ix.
[3] *The Sacred Wood*, p. 9.

articulates a vision of life. In his earliest essay on Dante in *The Sacred Wood* he writes:

The aim of the poet is to state a vision, and no vision of life can be complete which does not include the articulate formulation of life which human minds make.[1]

The poem *includes* a vision but *is* something larger than that. The 'criticism of life' is one thing, but is only part of the greater art form which contains it and transcends it. The emotions embodied in the poem *are* capable of rationalization into an interpretation of life, but rationalization is not a part of the poem. Having 'explained' each unit, which requires the reader to enter the world of connotation, it must then be sent back into the assembled structure which is the poem, and the whole poem viewed as an art form in the way Matthiessen, for example, suggests that we look at the work of painters like Vermeer or Cézanne:

. . . neither of whom was using for his material the representation of any religious or political doctrines whatsoever, but, for the most part, the everyday objects and scenes which surrounded him, and which each transformed into a new realm of space, colour, and design.[2]

In these terms, a poem is 'excellent words in excellent arrangement and excellent metre',[3] arrested in an instance of art.

'Preludes' offers the best way of approaching the poetry. The history of its composition is adequate testimony of the piecemeal method of combining fragments to form an artistic structure. The first two Preludes were written between 1909 and 1910 at Harvard, the third in Paris and the fourth on Eliot's return to London in 1911.[4] Leonard Unger quotes an interesting answer which Eliot gave to an interviewer who asked whether 'Ash Wednesday' had begun as separate poems, and provides Eliot's own acknowledgement of his assembling method:

Yes, like 'The Hollow Men', it originated out of separate poems. . . . Then gradually I came to see it as a sequence. That's one way in which my mind does seem to have worked throughout the years poetically—

[1] ibid., p. 170.
[2] F. O. Matthiessen, *The Achievement of T. S. Eliot* (1935), pp. 112–13.
[3] *The Sacred Wood*, p. ix.
[4] See Grover Smith, *T. S. Eliot's Poetry and Plays* (1956), p. 20.

doing things separately and then seeing the possibility of fusing them together, altering them, and making a kind of whole of them.[1]

We have already noticed in the previous chapter the cine-matic-type images of the first Prelude, where a succession of cinematic-type shots are 'worked up' into a complex montage. Whether or not Eliot was consciously using the technique of cinematic assemblage is perhaps doubtful, but it is perhaps not unreasonable to view the structure of 'Preludes' with this in mind since he makes allusion to the cinema in Prelude III. The woman is seen here, lying on her back, 'watching' the thousand sordid images of her soul as they flicker in cinematic-type projection on the ceiling overhead.[2] Applied to Prelude I we can see how the camera moves with the observer through the dirty littered streets at evening, picking out 'grimy scraps', bits of newspaper, showers beating on chimney-pots, broken blinds and a solitary cab horse, steaming and stamping. Eisenstein spoke of working up a montage from a series of varying shots by which, 'combining these monstrous incongruities, we newly collect the disintegrated event into one whole'.[3]

The first Prelude is fused into unity by the line:

The burnt-out ends of smoky days.[4]

Here we have two distinct images fused into one in typical Imagist manner. We see a dark evening. We see perhaps a cigarette end finished, burnt out. The two act together and the poetic image 'happens'.[5] The connotations of the fragments are clearly defined. Night is the burnt-out end of a day which smouldered, a 'smoky day' which never burst forth into living flame. A useless end to a useless day is suggested, and an emotion of despondency is worked up.

In the second Prelude the camera moves to day and picks out the 'masquerade' which people resume in a typical, 'smoulder-ing', damp day. With the mention of the 'furnished rooms'— which connotatively suggest all the loneliness and dinginess not

---

[1] Leonard Unger, *T. S. Eliot* (1960), p. 29.
[2] It is interesting to note that 'Prufrock' also contains a similar allusion:
   It is impossible to say just what I mean!
   But as if a magic lantern threw the nerves in patterns on a screen:
[3] Wylie Sypher, *Rococo to Cubism in Art and Literature* (1960), p. 283.
[4] *Collected Poems* (1963 edition), p. 23.
[5] Herbert Read, *The True Voice of Feeling* (1953), p. 115.

associated with 'home'—the camera moves inside and gives a 'close-up' of a Berthe-type creature of Charles-Louis Philippe's novel *Bubu de Montparnasse*,[1] alone, 'clasping' her yellow feet, and then 'curling' the papers from her hair, after the 'masquerades' of the night before—presumably these are the images which 'flickered against the ceiling'. This woman knows the life of the 'inside' as the street comprehends the sordid life of outside. The images which she sees flickering overhead do not form any revitalizing vision. 'Clasping' and 'curling' are verbs which suggest no action.

And here the camera comes to rest. So far we have fragments. In Prelude IV they act together and add up to form something like artistic 'empathy'. The soul of the street and the souls of the passers-by are fused into a single dominant image. Eliot, we remember, was concerned with the Bradleyan philosophy of 'finite centres' at this time, which stated that the private feeling is continuous with, even identical to, the objective material that has provoked it. Subject and object become one in a pure contemplation. Here we have artistic presentation of it. Vital art is opposed to abstract art, as Worringer puts it, where there is a 'feeling of separation in the face of outside nature':[2]

In empathizing . . . into another object, however, we *are* in the other object. We are delivered from our individual being as long as we are absorbed into an external object, an external form, with our inner urge to experience.[3]

In Prelude IV, the previous Preludes are fused into a whole to become an instance of art. In this Prelude, associations of despondency, suffering, along with the grim impatience of the passers-by to assume the daily 'round', are identified with the soul of the suffering, 'trampled' street. Written after Eliot's return from Paris where he heard Bergson's lectures on art, it is not surprising that we have here an illustration of his idea— the idea of the later Imagists—that

. . . many diverse images borrowed from very different orders of things may, by the convergence of their action, direct the consciousness to the precise point where there is a certain intuition to be seized.

[1] See Grover Smith, op. cit., pp. 20–1.
[2] See Herbert Read, *The Philosophy of Modern Art* (1951), p. 218.
[3] F. Worringer, *Abstraction and Empathy* (1953), p. 24.

By choosing images as dissimilar as possible, we shall prevent any one of them from usurping the place of the intuition it is intended to call up.[1]

The intuition is obvious, but Eliot expresses it:

> I am moved by fancies that are curled
> Around these images, and cling:
> The notion of some infinitely gentle
> Infinitely suffering thing.[2]

The emotion of pity in the face of suffering humanity is not allowed to dominate, however. This feeling may be the personal reaction of the poet, but to conclude the poem here would be to indicate a singleness of attitude which is not compatible with the impersonal, comprehensive art which Eliot advocates. Hence he goes on:

> Wipe your hand across your mouth, and laugh;
> The worlds revolve like ancient women
> Gathering fuel in vacant lots.[3]

Here we have two clear-cut reactions to the same scene, two ways that the reader might look at it. The emotion which the poem evokes is therefore comprehensive and not single. The end of the poem thus completes a circle. The poet has circled an object, a single scene of degradation and misery, and 'worked up' a comprehensive emotion in the reader from it.

Gertrude Stein perhaps sums up the structure of the poem best. She sees that art must 'live in the actual present' and describes all modern art as a cinematic 'series production'. In describing her own work, she describes Eliot's:

I was doing, what the cinema was doing, I was making a continuous succession of the statement of what that person was until I had not many things but one thing.[4]

The poem is an excellent example of how a new art-emotion is worked up from a series of images articulating the simple, un-dramatic emotion of disgust, an 'ordinary' emotion which the poet experiences, or in the case of Prelude III—where Grover Smith points out an obvious source in a passage from Charles-

---

[1] Henri Bergson, *Introduction to Metaphysics*, quoted by William Seitz, *The Art of Assemblage* (New York, 1961), p. 83.
[2] *Collected Poems*, pp. 24–5.      [3] ibid., p. 25.
[4] Quoted by Wylie Sypher, op. cit., p. 267.

Louis Philippe's novel *Bubu de Montparnasse*[1]—an objective
equivalent of it which he has found. The group assembled forms
a connotative structure. If we applied the mathematical formula
to it: I + II + III = IV. The comprehensive art-emotion of
Prelude IV is worked up from the individual emotions of the
first three.

'Rhapsody on a Windy Night', belonging to the same period
as 'Preludes', has been variously described as a 'sick version of
life'[2] or, in Maxwell's terms, a poem which 'does not mean
"anything"', anything more, that is, than 'the translation of a
mood':

. . . a conscious attempt to do in English what the symbolists had
done in French to mirror a mood by a selection of images which have in
common subservience to that mood, and hence act as symbols for it.[3]

Grover Smith speaks in more specific terms of its connotational
structure whereby

. . . the dissolution of orderly thought into an irrational, almost
surrealistic collage of discontinuous mental impressions obeys the laws
of instinctive consciousness according to Bergson. Mingling as fluid
perceptions, kaleidoscopic images pour into memory, the organ of
time, the 'floors' of which break down to enable their total synthesis.
This dreamlike process, the quintessence of the non-intellectual, works
by free association rather than by logic.[4]

The analogy which Grover Smith makes to painting is perhaps
a more useful one to examine than the musical, rhapsodic
structure which he himself goes on to describe in his examination of the poem. 'Free association' was the battle-cry of the
Collage group of painters, working at the same time as Eliot
was writing 'Rhapsody'. These painters introduced into the
texture of their 'painting', objects and materials which they
found in the world of their immediate experience, rather than use
the 'pure' colours of more traditionalist media. Found objects
were presented in the Collage structure in the recognisable and
concrete form in which the artist found them, retaining 'marks of
their previous form and history':[5]

1 Grover Smith, op. cit., pp. 20–1.
2 M. L. Rosenthal, op. cit., p. 7.
3 D. E. S. Maxwell, *The Poetry of T. S. Eliot* (1952), pp. 65–6.
4 Grover Smith, op. cit., p. 24.
5 W. Seitz, op. cit., p. 17.

When paper is soiled or lacerated, when cloth is worn, stained, or torn, when wood is split, weathered, or patterned with peeling coats of paint, when metal is bent or rusted, they gain connotations which unmarked materials lack. More specific associations are denoted when an object can be identified as the sleeve of a shirt, a dinner fork, . . . In both situations meaning and material merge.[1]

Perspective is abandoned in this type of art and its 'communication' depends on the imaginative sensibility of the spectator, that is, on his ability to perceive the same areas of connotation as those which the found objects held for the artist. The success of these structures demanded from the artist the task of defining these connotations in the same way that we outlined the Symbolist 'convenientia' in Chapter III.

What we are presented with in 'Rhapsody on a Windy Night' is the observer's (the 'I' of the poem) immediate experience of the real world, the immediacy of which is emphasized by a clock-time progression from midnight until four o'clock. Juxtaposed with it is the world of the past, a Bergsonian 'durée', a subjective time, measured out here by street lamps which illuminate visually the 'memories' which are the assembled subconscious 'self' of the observer. Kristian Smidt in *Poetry and Belief in the Work of T. S. Eliot* quotes Bergson's own definition of 'durée' from 'Essai sur les données immédiates':

La durée toute pure est la forme que prend la succession de nos états de conscience quand notre moi se laisse vivre, quand il s'abstient d'établir une séparation entre l'état présent et les états antérieurs . . . il suffit qu'en se rappelant ces états il ne les juxtapose à l'état actuel comme un point à un autre point, mais les organise avec lui, comme il arrive quand nous nous rappelons, fondues pour ainsi dire ensemble, les notes d'une mélodie.[2]

The remembered things of this poem are as real as the immediate things, and are pressed into the foreground, so that what we are confronted with is a perspective-less collage structure. Writing of Picasso and Braque, Seitz says:

The objects they depicted no longer diminished in size or disappeared in light and atmosphere. Immediate and tangible, their subjects were pressed forward by the advancing rear wall of the picture, so that

[1] W. Seitz, op. cit., pp. 84–5.
[2] Kristian Smidt, *Poetry and Belief in The Work of T. S. Eliot* (1961), p. 166.

cubism became an art of the close-up, that dealt with what was, literally as well as figuratively, 'close at hand'.[1]

This simultaneous existence of past and present becomes an increasingly important element in Eliot's poetry. Its implications are obvious here: Eliot does away with 'perspective' in this poem, in the sense that for the observer past and present coexist. Both worlds present equally abhorrent, equally useless images of life. Hence Rosenthal can say of the poem:

. . . we cannot ignore the possibility . . . that the night-time world may be the real world.[2]

A passage from Conrad's *Heart of Darkness* provides an interesting background against which we may view the connotations of the fragments of the poem. It is the passage where Marlowe sits brooding in the darkness falling over the Thames and remembers that his experiences with Kurtz are like a dream:

To him the meaning of an episode was not inside, like a kernel, but outside, enveloping the tale which brought it out only as a glow brings out a haze, in the likeness of those misty haloes that sometimes are made visible by the spectral illumination of moonshine.[3]

When we remember how the wilderness whispered things to Kurtz in 'the heart of darkness' and that Marlowe listened to drums beating in the night, we may well here have found one possible source of 'Rhapsody'. In Eliot's poem too, the moonlight and the misty haloes of the lamplight throw up images and objects from the world of memory, which likewise illuminate the present:

> Every street lamp that I pass
> Beats like a fatalistic drum,
> And through the spaces of the dark
> Midnight shakes the memory
> As a madman shakes a dead geranium.[4]

Each image in this structure is precise and its connotations clearly fixed. Only the word 'memory' is released with its full connotations, and it is the object of the poem to define the specific

[1] W. Seitz, op. cit., p. 22.
[2] M. L. Rosenthal, op. cit., p. 7.
[3] Quoted by Wylie Sypher, *Loss of Self in Modern Literature and Art* (1964 edition), pp. 60–1.
[4] *Collected Poems*, p. 26.

associations which it has for the observer. From the first fragment, memory is suggested as a storehouse. Genesius Jones gives
us the full connnotations of this image:

Platonic speculation on memory as a sort of broken bridge between the
soul and the divine Ideas was kept alive throughout the Hellenic world
by the neo-Platonists, and realised in a Christian context by St.
Augustine. From his time Christian thinkers saw the memory as an
image in the human soul of the creative *Ars Aeterna* in the Trinity.
. . . But memory has not been regarded merely as a still storehouse.
From the time of Plato onwards, this storehouse has presented a scene
of intense activity as its contents were pressed into service by the
mind of man. Medieval thinkers, especially Hugo of St. Victor and St.
Bonaventure saw it as a medium where the *umbra, vestigia, imagines*
and *similitudines* of the Divinity were to be sought as the soul led the
world of its apprehending back to God.[1]

The floors of this storehouse dissolve and, from the third
fragment, we see the 'objects' which pour out: 'a crowd of
twisted things', 'a twisted branch', 'a broken spring'—rusty,
useless, lifeless objects. The associations of these objects are
juxtaposed with those of the objects from the immediately
perceived world, experienced in the image of the torn, stained
dress of the woman, whose eye is also twisted. The two sets of
images share the connotations which useless, lifeless, 'junkyard'
objects present.

The nausea which the observer senses in the immediate
world is presented in the quick action-image of the cat, lapping
up 'rancid butter'—a useless gesture, contrasted with the automatic grabbing action of a child at a toy, connotatively useless,
since it has been discarded and runs along the quay. 'Memory'
presents a similar picture, now of a crab clutching the end of a
lifeless stick; but a crab will clutch at anything, so this too is a
futile gesture. The common associations of present and past
experience are obvious. Clearly, 'memory' in this poem only
serves to make the present more sordid, more meaningless;
this is the only 'illumination' which it can offer: it can urge the
observer to no meaningful activity since its contents are useless
to him.

The attention of the observer is drawn to the moon, queen of
the night world, whose light *could* illuminate the uselessness

[1] Genesius Jones, op. cit., pp. 169–70.

of the world, and inspire the observer to use his memory in more useful ways. But the moon who sees everything has also lost her faculty for remembering better things. She is identified with a woman 'twisting a paper rose'—another futile gesture. The part she plays in the kingdom of the night is therefore a passive, indifferent one:

> La lune ne garde aucune rancune,

Memory throws up further images, now of dry geraniums—flowers which we associate with city window boxes, which here suggest the neglect they have suffered in the hands of city dwellers—and nauseating 'female smells', 'cigarettes in corridors'. It is obvious that 'memory' has no Platonic associations in this poem.

And so the observer is led 'home'. His only useful memory is the number on his door. The door is opened and a small ring of light is cast on the stairway, illuminating the bed where sleep will prepare the observer for 'life'. But if past memories are of useless things and the present is equally sordid, life ahead has little potential. Hence the irony of the last line:

> The last twist of the knife.

The poem, therefore, as we can see, is not an exercise in completely 'free' association. The connotations of

> Midnight shakes the memory
> As a madman shakes a dead geranium

are painfully clear. The 'memory' is simply a still storehouse for sordid impressions. The faculty of remembering is a useless one.

Graham Hough has perhaps been harsh in attacking Eliot for his lack of 'logical' progression. In his view, 'an order of emotions' such as we have in these poems, is only possible in short lyrics. He points out that 'classical poetic theory'—and it is with this he points out that Eliot would identify himself—'was not deduced from brief lyrics'. He goes on:

One does not insist on Aristotelian rigour of construction; but even in the looser forms the sense of a syntax of events or a syntax of thoughts is preserved; and criticism insisted on it. Emotions are not capable of such a syntax. A pattern can be made of them, by simple juxtaposition, but it will hardly be an integrated pattern, unless there runs through it the thread of narrative or logic.[1]

One could not say that the juxtaposition of the poems I have dealt with so far is simple. Nevertheless, I have attempted to point out that the juxtaposing of fragments is a procedure capable of giving unity to a connotative structure. The emotions juxtaposed in 'Rhapsody' are simple, however, in that they illustrate a consistent disgust at the life of the city. Grover Smith has pointed out that Eliot's poetry goes on to deal with more complex emotions:

> Squalor itself was not his bane; he did not aspire to found a 'junkyard' school of poetry. What perturbed him was the helplessness of sensitivity and idealism against matter-of-factness.[2]

It is true that from 'Rhapsody' onwards, the poetry presents a conflict of emotions, where 'Preludes' and 'Rhapsody' each articulated a 'sick' vision of life. The poet rendered this vision artistically comprehensive, however, by providing, in the case of 'Preludes' for example, two ways for the reader to view the sordid aspects of life which it presented. In 'Rhapsody' the same sick vision is made comprehensive, by being illuminated from the past as well as being contemplated in the present. Whatever way it is viewed, however, the emotions which the individual parts of both these poems represent are simple, in that they indicate no conflict in the emotions of the 'I' of either poem. The poems which follow, however, present a struggle between conflicting emotions and for this reason mark an advance in comprehensiveness and dramatic technique. These emotional conflicts are now given names, which set the poems at a greater distance from the poet than the 'I' of 'Preludes' and 'Rhapsody'. Prufrock, the Lady, Sweeney and Gerontion are the recognizable concrete forms in which emotions, the subject matter of the poems, are embodied. These emotions will therefore be expressed most accurately when the 'persona' is shown as realistically as possible.

I have already mentioned Eliot's belief that even lyric poetry involves a 'praxis' of the Aristotelian theory and quoted

---

[1] Graham Hough, *Image and Experience* (1960), p. 18.
[2] Grover Smith, op. cit., p. 29.

the passage from the *Poetics* which illustrates what Aristotle meant by it:

All human happiness or misery takes the form of action; the end for which we live is a certain kind of activity, not a quality. Character gives us qualities, but it is in our actions—what we do—that we are happy or the reverse.[1]

The same thought is echoed by G. T. Wright who gives an interesting historical interpretation of the 'personae' of modern poetry in general, in *The Poet in the Poem*. In his introductory remarks, Wright sums up what I believe the intention of Eliot is, in his use of dramatic personae to give shape and order to the conflict of emotions which he wishes to present:

. . . the person *is* what he *does*; his actions define him. But as soon as we begin to interpret those actions, we begin to lose our objectivity in observing him.[2]

A dramatic poet, Eliot wrote, must

. . . take genuine and substantial human emotions, such emotions as observations can confirm, typical emotions, and give them artistic form;[3]

This concern for accuracy in the presentation of dramatic characters has its background in twentieth-century philosophy. In Bergson's terms, similar to the notion of personality articulated by Bradley, we cannot 'think' of ourselves, we can only *live*; hence our being can only be found amidst the shifting currents of our most immediate experience. We cannot even conceive of ourselves as having a single clear identity; when we do, we are translating our experiences into logical reconstructions of them, or in other words, transposing the data of experience into concepts that are extraneous to the data themselves. Hence Eliot presents emotions in personae most concretely and accurately, by confining his descriptions of them to perceived, significant acts, illustrating Pound's remarks already quoted in Chapter IV:

I catch the character I happen to be interested in at the moment he interests me, usually a moment of song, self-analysis, or sudden understanding or revelation.[4]

---

[1] See Chapter IV, p. 72.
[2] G. T. Wright, *The Poet in the Poem* (1960), p. 1.
[3] 'Rhetoric and Poetic Drama', *Selected Essays*, p. 41.
[4] See Chapter IV, p. 72.

Eliot similarly catches them amidst the conflicting currents of their experience, since it is only there that they can be seen in their 'reality'.

The technical difficulty for Eliot is, of course, to present in concrete *action*-images conflicting emotions of persons *unable* to act, their 'tragic flaw',[1] as Smith calls it in speaking of Prufrock, being their timidity in the face of action. Eliot surmounts this difficulty in the most concrete poetic language when he shows us the emotions of Prufrock, for example, in images where he *sees himself* acting. Speaking of Shakespeare, Eliot writes:

The really fine rhetoric of Shakespeare occurs in situations where a character of the play *sees himself* in dramatic light.[2]

And he goes on to quote passages from *Othello, Coriolanus, Timon of Athens* and *Antony and Cleopatra*, each passage presenting a visual action-image of the character seeing himself in action.

'Personae' are, then, the means whereby Eliot is able to impose an artistic pattern on the complex, conflicting emotions of experience. At the beginning, as in the early 'personae' poems 'Prufrock' and 'Portrait of a Lady', these emotions are 'worked up' from ordinary flat emotions into a new 'art-emotion'; as the poetry progresses, however, this new art-emotion gains in universal significance as the poet introduces more and more 'appearances' into the texture of his poem, from his knowledge of the literature and culture of the past, and of other countries. Sometimes these conflicts of emotion are presented in two or more personae, as in Eliot's early attempt at an ironical dramatic situation in 'Conversation Galante', or 'La Figlia che Piange', or in the later 'Sweeney' poems. These I call poems *of stage-drama*, in the sense that we can see something of the narrative of stage action in them. Conrad Aiken, in his obituary article on Eliot in *Life* ( 1 January 1965 ), recalls the poet's 'urge for the theatre' and points out that 'Prufrock' is 'full of stage directions'. 'Prufrock' is a dramatic poem, but not in the same sense as, for example, 'La Figlia che Piange', which contains stage directions in overt language, 'So I *would have him* leave', etc. The more significant 'dramatic' poems are those in which a single persona *sees himself* in dramatic light. These poems are less *stage*-drama than *art*-drama. Personae such as Prufrock or

[1] Grover Smith, op. cit., p. 15.          [2] *Selected Essays*, p. 39.

Gerontion are not the 'characters' proper of the stage. They are most complex artistic personae, embodying the most subtle complex emotions, whose 'reality' resides, for the most part, in the structure of the poem.

'Portrait of a Lady'[1] embodies the same theme as the more sentimental Laforguian 'Conversation Galante'. George Williamson sums up its theme best when he sees it as the presentation of a character (that is, the man of the poem) 'suspended between feelings of attraction and repulsion':

Under a sophisticated surface Eliot develops a conflict of feelings which weaves its sensuous imagery into patterns of changing mood and significance.[2]

The structure of the poem is obvious: it is the juxtaposing of the comments of a Lady and the emotions of her visitor, articulated silently to himself. Grover Smith sees the poem as a series of 'scenes'—'episodes of observation and analysis'.[3] This is at once useful and confusing. Analysis suggests interpretation, reasoning, abstraction and judgement, but there is none of this kind of 'thinking' in the poem. The only 'analysis' there is takes the form of the emotions of the man, presented 'dramatically', where he 'sees himself' in visually precise action-images: if there is 'interpretation' of the events, it is merely hinted at.

The first fragment of the poem presents the scene, its artificiality and faked emotion defined by the connotations of 'Juliet's tomb', a dramatic scene which has 'arranged itself' after a concert. The woman's remarks about 'saving' the afternoon for her visitor suggest immediately the 'pose' of a socialite, vividly characterized by the cliché-ridden language of her class; the boredom she arouses in her companion is emphasized by her repetitive remarks:

'You do not know how much they mean to me, my friends,
And how, how rare and strange it is, to find
In a life composed so much, so much of odds and ends,
    • . . .
To find a friend who has these qualities,
Who has, and gives
Those qualities upon which friendship lives.'

[1] *Collected Poems*, pp. 18–21.
[2] George Williamson, *A Reader's Guide to T. S. Eliot* (1962), pp. 70–1.
[3] Grover Smith, op. cit., p. 10.

The 'analysis' of the scene has already begun. This conversation has taken place amid the 'tones of violins' mingled with 'remote cornets', and is taken up again in musical imagery in which the emotional response of the man is embodied. The image of the smooth 'windings of the violins' with its connotations of romance and sweetness is set against the 'capricious monotone' of the tomtom, beating in the imagination of the visitor. The syncopated rhythm of the 'dull tomtom', or the harsh tone of the cornet, is clearly 'out of tune' with the violin and Chopin. The two fragments are thus united and fused into unity by their connotations. It is suggested by this juxtaposing that the pair are also 'out of tune' with each other. Similar connotations form the background against which we place:

> 'So intimate, this Chopin, that I think his soul
> Should be resurrected only among friends
> Some two or three, who will not touch the bloom,
> That is rubbed and questioned in the concert room.'

This is the concrete expression of the delicate, somewhat precarious emotional situation of the woman, who by her later juxtaposing of 'friends' and 'me'—'you do not know how much they mean to me, my friends'—somehow seems to identify herself with Chopin and his need for a few intimate friends. Socially, she is 'the *précieuse ridicule*, to end all preciosity',[1] according to Conrad Aiken, who apparently knew who she was. Bandied around, 'rubbed and questioned' in the concert room, like a fragile bloom, her soul, she feels, could nevertheless be 'resurrected' and preserved among a few friends. Connotatively, the lines suggest hope. 'Resurrection'—the hope of life after death—suggests that she is perhaps old, feels her position of being unable to save herself, hence the passive action of the verb 'should be resurrected'. Her hope is in establishing emotional harmony between her present companion and herself.

Against the self-revealing talk of the woman are set the thoughts of the man. At her struggle to articulate her needs, he feels only repulsion. This is a situation in which he is unable to act. In a series of verbally concrete images his emotions are made clear (my italics):

[1] Quoted by Hugh Kenner, *T. S. Eliot, The Invisible Poet*, p. 22.

—Let us take the air, in a tobacco trance,
*Admire* the monuments,
*Discuss* the late events,
*Correct* our watches by the public clocks.
Then *sit* for half an hour and drink our bocks.

By the choice of concrete verbs Eliot suggest first the anxiety
to escape and then the impossibility of meaningful action. Each
verb, 'admire', 'discuss', 'correct', and finally 'sit', connotatively
suggests no 'action'. No *motion towards* the desires of the woman
is possible.

This pattern is repeated throughout the poem. While a line-
by-line analysis of the poem is not necessary, a look at a few
more examples will emphasize the structural form as it has been
defined above. The emotional anxiety and frustration of the
woman are articulated clearly in a visually concrete image:

'Ah, my friend, you do not know, you do not know
What life is, you who hold it in your hands'
(Slowly twisting the lilac stalks)

The irony is obvious: neither does she. By the action of twisting
the lilac stalks which she holds in her hands she is as surely
destroying her own hope of 'life', as she warns the young man of
his wasted opportunities. Pathetic hope emerges in her diffident
plea:

I am always sure that you understand

The hackneyed phrasing reminds the man once again that he is
'out of tune'. His attraction has brought him to the woman; his
repulsion forces him to leave. This time his incapacity for action
is articulated by a series of the observed actions of other people
who make sensational news headlines:

An English countess goes upon the stage.
A Greek was murdered at a Polish dance,

The connotations are obvious. Here are people capable of
positive action. But the hero is unmoved:

I keep my countenance,
I remain self-possessed

Such actions will not stir him to any desire to do anything, so
that his return to the room with 'the smell of hyacinths' is

ironically proved futile before he even reaches his destination. The
connotations of the lines which articulate his return suggest his
awareness of self-degradation and self-possession:

> I mount the stairs and turn the handle of the door
> And feel as if I had mounted on my hands and knees.

His way of dealing with the situation is to make the easy excuse
of having to go away. The action of this announcement is
deliberately not presented in the poem. It is the woman who
makes it explicit. Eliot's technique is very clear: this man does
not *ever* act. His own awareness of his clumsiness is presented
very vividly in the line:

> My smile falls heavily among the bric-à-brac.

He realizes that he has shattered the fragile hopes of the woman.
The crisis is poignantly expressed in the two parts of the line:

> My self-possession gutters; we are really in the dark.

Again he leaves. 'Analysis' of the scene is again clearly presented:

> And I must borrow every changing shape
> To find expression . . . dance, dance
> Like a dancing bear,
> Cry like a parrot, chatter like an ape.

'Life' for the man is reduced to the automatic habits of the
animals. Activity for him will be like the meaningless antics of a
bear or an ape, his conversation the empty prattle of a parrot.

The conclusion emphasizes for the man his own passivity. If
the woman should die, he will be left sitting, 'pen in hand', not
only having failed to establish any meaningful communication
with her during her life, but also unable to react to or act on the
event of her death and incapable of articulating, even to himself,
the reason for this inertia. Her death would ironically point to
another kind of death: his own emotional 'death'. Her advantage
over him would be that she had made the better 'escape' from a
meaningless life than his. The music returns with a 'dying fall',
'successful' because it brings home to him the futility of his
existence.

It is generally agreed that 'Portrait of a Lady' is, from an
artistic point of view, unequal to 'Prufrock'. Hugh Kenner finds
its defects in the 'tendency to stay closer to the empirical facts

than the poet's essentially portentous and generalizing technique will really permit':

The contours of the situation are so specified, the lady's speech so
clearly reproduced, that decorum requires a comparable definiteness in
depicting the confusions into which she throws her visitor; instead of
which we have an alternation of fanciful symbol and archly impenetrable
behaviour.[1]

The reason why the 'contours of the situation' are so specified,
however, is to give rise to the complex *emotions* of the man which
can only find concrete articulation in the manner shown above.
Yet the emotions of the man lose in complexity, since the basically narrative structure of the poem places greater emphasis on
the particular dramatic situation of the pair than on the dramatic conflict of emotions which he represents. The emotional
conflict suggested from this situation is more that of a young
man anxious to escape from a tight situation than the Bradleyan
emotions of a person who feels

. . . that he needs to preserve the inviolacy of self, and simultaneously
feels that he needs sympathy from others whom he cannot reach and
who cannot decorously reach him.[2]

Smith finds it a less 'incisive' poem than 'Prufrock' because it
'does not communicate tragedy through feeling'.[3] In view of my
previous remarks I should call 'Portrait' a poem *of stage-drama*
but defer comparison of its artistic design with that of 'Prufrock'
until after an examination of its structure. What 'Portrait of a
Lady' achieves is the raising of 'ordinary' emotions of frustration and isolation to a 'new art-emotion' by juxtaposing them
in patterned form.

'The Love Song of J. Alfred Prufrock',[4] Grover Smith writes,
has a better 'architectonic design' than 'Portrait' and draws our
attention to a letter of Eliot's to Harriet Monroe in 1916, in
which he states that it is better than his other poems of the
1910–11 period.[5] The theme of the poem was already contained
in the early poem 'Spleen' in which Eliot had expressed the
emotions of distraction and dejection produced by the self-
satisfied socialities with their Sunday-morning faces. This poem

---

[1] Quoted by Hugh Kenner, *T. S. Eliot, The Invisible Poet*, p. 25.     [2] ibid., p. 27.
[3] Grover Smith, op. cit., p. 9.         [4] *Collected Poems*, pp. 15–17.
[5] Grover Smith, op. cit., p. 15.

had ended with an ironic personification of 'Life'—a Prufrock in
fact, a little bald, a little pale, waiting on the threshold of the
Absolute. It is interesting to note in E. J. H. Greene's article,
'T. S. Eliot et Jules Laforgue', that Eliot rejected this poem
because of its lack of structural unity, the third stanza, he felt, not
being closely enough linked to the first two.[1]

'Prufrock' indicates its own presentative cinematic-type
structure, as we have already pointed out, in the lines:

> It is impossible to say just what I mean!
> But as if a magic lantern threw the nerves in
> patterns on a screen:

As the problem for both the man and woman in 'Portrait of a
Lady' was in part one of communication with each other, so
Prufrock's predicament—and that which appears increasingly
to haunt Eliot's personae—is to say exactly what he means: how
to articulate a complexity of emotions in a society which is so
ridden with smart talk that its members can no longer establish
any meaningful contact with one another, and would register
only shock at the attempt of one who might, like Prufrock, dare
to try. An unpublished poem, 'Death of a Duchess', found with
'The Waste, Land' manuscripts, expresses this problem well, and
is, in my view, an exciting find, not only on its own merit as a
poem, but also for the light which it throws on the emotional
experience central to 'Prufrock' and one of Eliot's preoccupying
themes: the problem of communication. The poem, in fact, reads
like an early attempt at 'Prufrock'. In it, the affluent inhabitants
of Hampstead are described, like the socialites of 'Prufrock', so
bound to the social round, deriving their conventions and
socially acceptable thoughts from the jargon of the newspapers,
that they and their talk become parrot-like. They become in fact,
voiceless beaks. The problem for the speaker in 'Death of a
Duchess' is identical to Prufrock's in a similar situation: '. . .
should I then presume?' Like Prufrock, he can think only of the
possibility of escape. It is easy for him to be part of the society of
bird-like chatter, but terrifying to be faced with the challenge of
striking up a meaningful relationship with one of them. Yet this
is what he longs to do. The same problem faces Prufrock. To
conform to the class to which he inescapably belongs, a crowd

[1] *Revue de littérature comparée* (1948).

who think alike, behave alike and where social contact is restricted to brittle chit-chat over coffee cups and tea cups, is ultimately
to lose identity. At the same time, he cannot presume to alter the
situation. And so the poem becomes a projection of images on a
screen, the poet's (and incidentally Prufrock's) attempt to
resolve in a patterned structure the conflicting emotions which
define and are defined by Prufrock.

The conflicting emotions of Prufrock are shown in the 'data'
which make up the 'you' and 'I' of the poem, the 'conflicting
selves' of personality. Hugh Kenner, in writing of the identity of
Prufrock, reiterates Bergson's theory of personality in Bradley's
terms:

If you ask him [Bradley] what is Mr. Prufrock's essential self, he will
first discard 'essential' as implying that of which Prufrock himself is
self-consciously and therefore distortedly aware; and reply at some
length that the real Prufrockian focus of consciousness (he will not say
the real Prufrock, any more than he will say the real you) is a finite
centre. ('The finite Centre', writes Eliot, 'so far as I can pretend to
understand it, *is* immediate experience').[1]

The 'data', the fragments of 'immediate experience' which make
up the bisected persona of Prufrock, are his repulsion from and
attraction for a meaningful 'life' of communication and activity
which will define 'being' for him.

We have already looked at the emotions of Prufrock in the
previous chapters, and Eliot's concrete ways of presenting them;
the uneasiness of the 'we' of the poem, articulated in the fragments describing the streets and the fog, each a 'finite centre' in
which the Prufrockian emotions are artistically 'empathized'.
Juxtaposed with the fragments articulating Prufrock's uneasiness
is the 'life' offered by the socially assured women who

> . . . come and go
Taking of Michelangelo.

The opportunity to 'prepare a face' to be the 'persona' suited to
those who talk of Michelangelo, and the opportunity to 'murder
and create'—doing something either for good or evil, implied in
transitive verbs—suggest that the 'overwhelming question' to
which his uneasiness leads him is his inability to do anything,
much less be. He *sees himself* dramatically turning and descending

1 Hugh Kenner, op. cit., pp. 52–3.

the stairs, rejecting the conflicting opportunities which 'the
room' offers him. Eliot makes interesting comment on this
ability to see oneself dramatically which is applicable to Prufrock
in this situation:

It is a sense which is almost a sense of humour (for when anyone is
conscious of himself as acting, something like a sense of humour is
present).[1]

The moments in actual life where we see ourselves in dramatic
action are of 'very great usefulness to dramatic verse'.[2] In such a
way Prufrock, not really acting, but seeing himself acting, is able
to visualize himself descending the stair,

> With a bald spot in the middle of my hair—

The question posed at the beginning of the fragment, 'Do I dare?'
is left inarticulated until the end of the section:

> Do I dare
> Disturb the universe?

By the use of the word 'universe' Eliot is able to let us see the
magnitude of Prufrock's problem. For him the little room
assumes worldwide dimensions. To enter it, to disturb it by
acting out of 'character' with the ritual activities which go on in
it, would be as portentous as disturbing the universe. The clipped
rhythm of

> In a minute there is time
> For decisions and revisions which a minute will reverse

connotes the quick movements of Prufrock towards and away
from the door.

Then follows the image of life in the room. Maxwell compares
it with Laforgue's lines:

> Ah! que la vie est quotidienne.
> Tâchons de vivre monotone.[3]

The comparison is interesting in that it points out, not simply a
similarity of tone and atmosphere, but also Eliot's greater
precision of language. Instead of the adjective 'quotidienne',
Eliot presents the same feeling of monotony more concretely by
listing the series of evenings, mornings, afternoons:

[1] *Selected Essays*, p. 41.       [2] ibid.       [3] D. E. S. Maxwell, op. cit., p. 50.

> For I have known them all ready, known them all—
> Have known the evenings, mornings, afternoons,
> I have measured out my life with coffee spoons;

'Known' is here used in the precise sense of being intimately acquainted with and, by the connotations of the coffee-spoon line, in the sense of 'belonging'.

The precise image with which Prufrock articulates his feeling of being 'trapped' in the stifling society of coffee mornings and evenings, is connotatively rich. He sees himself 'pinned and wriggling on the wall', observed and summed up into a neat formula by his fellow 'sufferers'. His identity has been discovered by others, although Prufrock is not sure of himself, so why and how could he presume to throw open his personality for further discussion and a new formulation? How could he begin

> To spit out all the butt-ends of my days and ways?

The precise action of spitting out connotes the decisive and derisive action which would be required of him. 'Spitting out' in such 'genteel' society would indeed disturb it.

Again the question is posed; again Prufrock feels the attraction and repulsion of acting. The fragment which presents the image of 'lonely men in shirt sleeves'—the result of inaction— we have already dealt with. Prufrock dreads this fate as much as he fears what he feels himself condemned to suffer should he surrender to the attraction of the moment. His timidity brings about the crisis of the poem: he desires simply to escape:

> I should have been a pair of ragged claws
> Scuttling across the floors of silent seas.

Here is Eliot's first use of a purely personal symbol. The equivalent image of escape in purely Romantic poetry would be Keats's nightingale or Shelley's skylark. The use of it here is obvious from its context, as we have already seen.[1] Its associations are those of animal existence at the bottom of the sea; the visual action of 'scuttling' denotes the sideways 'progress' associated with crabs, and connotes no progress for Prufrock.

The fog image is taken up again. It was left 'asleep' at the end of the third fragment. 'Asleep' connotatively suggests peace—

[1] See Chapter III, p. 54.

but it is merely pretence at being at peace for it 'malingers'.
Again the connotations are those of escapism.

The first of a series of remembered 'heroes' is introduced.
Prufrock 'sees himself' as John the Baptist—one whose associations are with supreme Christian heroic action and saintliness;
here too a sense of humour is present—hence the bracketed
'(grown slightly bald)'. He sees himself mocked by his fellows,
including the Footman who has assumed 'eternal' dimensions.
Set against this is the short poignant line which fuses together all
the associations of the passage:

> And in short, I was afraid.

The fate, the 'misunderstanding' which would arise if he
possessed the courage of Lazarus, is now vividly articulated.
Lazarus denotes one raised from the dead. By self-identification
with Lazarus, Prufrock recognizes himself—that is his social
self—and his companions, as spiritually 'dead'. He repeats the
same feelings resulting from inactivity—hence the 'death' of the
society to which he belongs—by presenting a list of objects,
with no verb connection, which connotatively suggest their
'lifeless' existence: 'novels', 'teacups', 'skirts that trail along the
floor'.

He cannot assume the dignity of the tragic hero. He is simply
an 'extra' in the drama of life. These lines are good in that they
are denotatively clear and connotatively rich. The associations
with Hamlet, the 'hero' who couldn't act, are obvious. If we also
see association with similar lines in Canto II of Dante's *Inferno*,
as has been shown by Eugene Arden,[1] the image gains in
intensity. The 'hero' of Dante's *Divine Comedy* is also something
of a fool. He cuts a sorry figure, trembling and weeping at what
he is shown in the underworld. He, like Prufrock, would do
anything to escape. He cannot retain his determination to suffer
and fears that his journey through the underworld will appear
foolish. He therefore asserts his position:

> I am not Aeneas, I am not Paul, neither
> I myself nor any other man thinks me fit
> For such an affair. If I am persuaded into going
> I fear the journey will be a mad act.[2]

[1] Eugene Arden, 'T. S. Eliot and Dante', *Notes and Queries*, August 1958, p. 363.
[2] *Inferno* II. 32, quoted ibid.

Allan Gilbert, in a useful study of the *Divine Comedy*, comments
on Dante's 'comic' hero, and throws incidental light on Prufrock:

. . . the sightseer of Dante's imagination is commendably anxious to
see and to learn, but his desires are not the lofty aspirations of a saint
or a philosopher. His eagerness—in itself often amusing—is that of a
character deliberately kept mediocre to fit him for comedy as Horace
describes it. . . . only at the very end of the 'Paradiso' does divine
love possess the weaker's spirit. Otherwise he is still on the comic level,
quite unable to do more than lament weakness preventing expression.[1]

Such understanding of Dante's hero fuses all the associations,
from the epigraph, John, Lazarus and Hamlet, into perspective.
The poem does not *depend* for its communication on the reader's
knowledge of Dante's hero, but if we are acquainted with
Dante's artistic intention, then the whole poem is given added
dimension. The images of 'Prufrock' are raised to a higher
'power', to borrow again from the terminology of mathematics,
so that Prufrock, by being associated with figures from history
and literature, becomes a type of universal figure.

Prufrock's next image bears out the 'ridiculous' comic
associations of the fool. As Eliot writes of Hamlet's buffoonery:

The levity of *Hamlet* . . . [is] . . . a form of emotional relief. In the
character Hamlet it is the buffoonery of an emotion which can find no
outlet in action.[2]

'I shall wear white flannel trousers' and 'I shall wear the bottoms
of my trousers rolled' are the equivalent of the buffoonery of
Hamlet. Since Prufrock has no 'outlet' in significant action, he
will act as befits the fool, like Hamlet. The insignificant and
inadequate action-images are given added dimensions: images
which, as we have seen, connote Prufrock's timidity:

Shall I part my hair behind? Do I dare to eat a peach?

Images of the sea follow, and the choice of 'mermaids' suggests
escape into the world of imagination. Elizabeth Drew sums up
the associations of the mermaids riding the waves and singing as a

. . . glimpse of a life rhythm where living creatures delight spon-
taneously in their natural environment, mastering it and being carried
along by its vital energy.[3]

[1] Allan Gilbert, *Dante and his Comedy* (1964), p. 75.
[2] *The Sacred Wood*, p. 102.
[3] Elizabeth Drew, *T. S. Eliot: The Design of his Poetry* (1950), p. 57.

It is such 'vital energy' that Prufrock yearns for. Death by
drowning of a different sort from that which would take him to
the bottom of the sea—a 'primordial' symbol of destruction
which is also creation[1]—ends the poem. Prufrock 'drowns' in his
social surroundings, not those of his imagination. The 'we' and
'us' of the last line fuse the bisected self into unity.

Bearing in mind that 'persona' as we see it is only the technique whereby conflicting emotions are given 'a name plus a
voice'[2] and become an artistic form, we can see how 'Prufrock' is
an advance on the structure of 'Portrait of a Lady', described as

The quintessence of a James novel, heavily concentrated, epitomised
and sustained in its intensity by the more precise texture and pattern of
verse,[3]

a description which sums up admirably the basically narrative
progression of the poem; 'Prufrock' is more specifically an
assembled Qualitative Progression, heightened by irony. The
images which articulate the emotions of the poem, fragments of
conversation, images in the Imagist manner, dramatic glimpses
and poses, provide a more varied artistic texture than that of
'Portrait'. The 'scenery' of the poem—the streets, the room—
and the connotations aroused by all the fragments provide the
'personality pattern'[4] of Prufrock. Prufrock *is* in all the fragments, which suggest action but are beyond the action of the
stage, for in no part of the poem does Prufrock actually act. For
this reason the comparison with the cinema is most useful.
Leonard Unger pursues 'cinematic' structure by seeing the poem
as

. . . a series of slides. Each slide is an isolated, fragmentary image,
producing its own effect, including suggestions of some larger action or
situation of which it is but an arrested moment.[5]

George Wright describes what I have called Eliot's artistic
personae as personae whose motions are arrested—like a type of
sculpture:

Like the figures on Keats's urn, these personae are caught permanently
in certain attitudes.[6]

[1] Pointed out by Elizabeth Drew, ibid.
[2] Hugh Kenner, op. cit., p. 36.
[3] A. D. Hawkins, *Fiction Chronicle*, April 1936, p. 480.
[4] Elizabeth Drew, op. cit., p. 56.        [5] Leonard Unger, op. cit., p. 22.
[6] George Wright, op. cit., p. 66.

This is only partly applicable to 'Prufrock'; he certainly cannot advance or retreat and so he is an arrested figure, caught, not in the 'ideal' pose of a figure on the Grecian urn, but arrested in art in a moment of unresolved conflict, oscillating between two choices, to act or not to act, and hence to be or not to be. In this sense the poem is more like a Cubist structure, 'cinematic' in that each Cubist painting gives the impression that the objects it presents are moving, when in fact they are arrested in the instances of art which they present. A Cubist portrait attempts to fuse all the facets of character simultaneously in a single complex design. The shape of the person is recognisable here and there in the same way that we can 'see' Prufrock at times among the fragments which form the poem. Nevertheless:

What 'Prufrock' is, is the name of a possible zone of consciousness where these materials (i.e. Hamlet, Lazarus, John the Baptist, mermaids) can maintain a vague congruity; no more than that; certainly not a person . . . Like the thing you look at when you raise your eyes from this page, he is the centre of a field of consciousness, rather yours than his: a focusing of the reader's attention, in a world made up not of cows and stories, but of literary 'effects' and memories prompted by the words.[1]

As Bradley found the Absolute amidst change, reality among the plural aspects of experience and identified being as the concatenation of conflicting selves, so Prufrock finds his being, in the articulation of himself in the poem, which *is* Prufrock.

The opposite emotions of activity and vital energy are articulated in the fragments which make up 'Cousin Nancy' and 'Mr. Apollinax',[2] personae who appear 'mad' in the genteel society to which they refuse to conform. Apollinax presents an energetic liveliness in the world, again like Prufrock's, articulated by its smallness and inactivity—the world of teacups, 'a slice of lemon and a bitten macaroon'. Images, denotatively precise and rich in association, present the effect of the contrasting of the intensely small and fragile with the intensely vital:

His laughter tinkled among the teacups.

I heard the beat of centaur's hoofs over the hard turf
As his dry and passionate talk devoured the afternoon.

[1] Hugh Kenner, op. cit., p. 35.
[2] *Collected Poems*, pp. 32–3.

The effect of the poem is, however, that of the levity of satire rather than the serious irony of dramatic conflict. If Prufrock is the oscillating persona, Mr Apollinax represents one side of the oscillation, Professor and Mrs Channing Cheetah and their society the other. This poem is thus more a poem *of stage-drama* than 'Prufrock', less complex and intense.

The Gautier poems are, generally speaking, experimental and minor poems. The quatrain form, however much Eliot admired Gautier around 1917, seems, from one point of view anyway, to be capable of a negative justification. According to Pound, the two poets imposed the discipline of the quatrain as a 'counter-current'[1] to the diluters of *vers libre*—to show that it was possible for the masters of the *vers libre* form to conform to a more rigid verse structure. If Eliot's chief reason for writing in quatrains was simply to justify his more overtly 'free' forms, then he chose it for no positive reason—certainly not for the reason that the matter of the poems was always suited to the form. One is bound to agree with D. E. S. Maxwell who suggests that while

They have their powers, . . . they impose a restraint which, while not to be dismissed as worthless, cramps almost as much as it disciplines the full operation of the poetic sensibility.[2]

Gautier himself pointed out that his aim in *Emaux et Camées* was 'to treat little subjects within restricted limits of form, as if they were a surface of gold or copper with the bright hues of enamel'.[3] Where Eliot was content with 'little' subjects—as for example the simple juxtaposing of childish daydreams and the 'penny world' of the past, with the stale, unsavoury, cheap present in 'The Cooking Egg', or the acid satire on the Church in 'The Hippopotamus'—the quatrain is successful. 'The Hippopotamus' presents in pictorial, clear action-images, the frustrated reaching out of the clumsy animal, man, and the passive inertia of the Church in the face of its obligations to him. 'Whispers of Immortality' is another instance where a single juxtaposition is sustained throughout the poem. The content of the poem is well known; it presents Eliot's 'apology' for his own

[1] Ezra Pound, *Polite Essays* (1937), p. 14.
[2] D. E. S. Maxwell, op. cit., pp. 95–6.
[3] Quoted by Wylie Sypher, *From Rococo to Cubism*, p. 241.

metaphysical or Imagist manner, and the need of contemporary
poets to avoid 'dissociation of sensibility'. Against the vigor-
ous 'seizing', 'clutching' and 'penetrating' of Donne and Webster
who were able to think 'as if the body thought', and who in the
sexual embrace were able to attain knowledge of an abstract
concept 'Death', Eliot places the vivid picture of the 'promise' of
Grishkin, and the 'crawling' action of contemporary humanity
steeped in tepid metaphysics.

The matter of the 1920 poems however is not always a
simple contrast between past and present; along with contrast is
woven a parallel. Eliot was becoming more and more involved
in his theory of Traditionalism in life and art and the desire to
deal comprehensively with more universal emotions. Time,
therefore, has begun to take on new and lengthened connotations. In 'Preludes' and 'Rhapsody' it was seen simply as the
circling progression from day to day, and man was portrayed in
his epicyclic activities within it. Along with this now is juxtaposed time as the progression of history—running endlessly
from past to future in a new kind of 'durée'. Eliot therefore chose
symbols and images with wide historical connotations. Elizabeth
Drew sums up his intentions by the use of the 'mythical'
method:

The method whereby a definite parallel is manipulated between the
planless panorama of the present and the ordered world of myth . . .[1]

and then again:

He [Eliot] *perceives*, and recreates his perceptions by projecting
patterns which are now much more than nerves upon a screen. The
insights are increasingly moral as well as emotional, they are coloured
by a disgust which is much more bitter and searching, and the power-
ful symbols and rhythms which carry them move in new and complex
poetic pantomime and choreography.[2]

Emotions are therefore gaining in complexity. Eliot is not now
simply concerned with man's spiritual inadequacy, but also with
his spiritual development, which the Sweeney poems show to be
no development at all. A constant comparison with animals is
drawn, in all aspects of their behaviour: Sweeney is apelike in his
laughter and like the orang-outang in his love-making.[3] Modern

[1] Elizabeth Drew, op. cit., p. 58.          [2] ibid., p. 59.
[3] See *Collected Poems*, pp. 44, 59.

man, viewed in this light, is related to no order, he is cut off from a progressive civilization and tradition. Rachel in 'Sweeney among the Nightingales'[1] has not even *any* identity. She was '*née* Rabinovitch', which ironically suggests that she is *now* a nobody. By placing this isolated figure of modern man and his futile activities against the scaffold of myth and history, Eliot is attempting to relate him to a time when he was not so isolated and his activities not so meaningless. He is also attempting to show at the same time, by the parallels that he draws between the events of the past and the present, knowledge like that of the undertaker in 'Aunt Helen' who

> . . . was aware that this sort of thing had occurred before.[2]

It is this emotional complex which Eliot attempts to manipulate into the simple quatrain form.

The structure of these poems, however, is still a connotative structure, the progression, while adhering closely to the narrative of stage drama, broken up here and there by the introduction of a proper name, from history or myth, whose superimposition on the narrative makes of it a complex montage—like Pound's superimposition of excerpts from Eastern and Western history to give the images of the Cantos added dimension. These names are 'cluster-evocations' as G. S. Fraser defined them in speaking of Pound's use of them:

> . . . the use of an historical proper name or more rarely one out of myth or legend to stand not for one abstract idea, but for a cluster of attitudes.[3]

The success of such 'cluster-evocations' depends on the reader's sharing of the poet's mythical or historical knowledge, and the efficacy of the 'convenientia' in which they have been placed. Recalling Genesius Jones's remarks quoted in Chapter III, it is the 'convenientia' which

> . . . determines whether the final pattern is adequate to the state of affairs; and itself can be declared upon only if the symbols have a delimited symbolic connotation. It is the task of the poet so to fix the connotation that there may be no missing the evocation.[4]

Since space forbids an examination of each of the poems in this

[1] See *Collected Poems*, p. 59.                [2] ibid., p. 31.
[3] See Chapter IV, pp. 77–8.                   [4] Genesius Jones, op. cit., p. 39.

section, we shall have to confine our examination of the type of
'convenientia' in which Eliot places them to a few, which
are representative of the method. The epigraph of 'Sweeney
Erect' is from Beaumont and Fletcher's *The Maid's Tragedy*,
where Aspatia, having been deserted by her lover, sees her
position similar to that of Ariadne deserted by Theseus:

> And the trees about me,
> Let them be dry and leafless; let the rocks
> Groan with continual surges; and behind me
> Make all a desolation. Look, look, wenches![1]

Grover Smith informs us that

Seeing the resemblance of her plight to that of Ariadne in a tapestry
that her attendant women are weaving, she bids them use her as their
model.[2]

The words of the epigraph, 'dry and leafless' trees and 'groan-
ing' rocks, suggest desolation and misery, so that we do not have
to know their literary context, although added dimension is
given to the poem if we do. Set against 'the waste shore' of the
first stanza, with its 'snarled and yelping seas', are the breezes
of the second stanza, associated with Aeolus who was given power
to control them, to use them as he pleased either to soothe or
excite. Both activities are suggested here—the winds tangle
Ariadne's hair and swell the 'perjured sails', which recall her
abandonment by Theseus after their arrival on the island of
Naxos.

The present, by contrast, is connotatively stale and lifeless.
No refreshing winds stir the Polypheme, giant-like figure of
Sweeney and his companion, contrasted with the beautiful
Nausicaa. Steam rises from the sheets, and the violent activity
of the two is clearly articulated, resulting in the epileptic fit of the
woman when Sweeney deserts her. Her plight is thus linked
connotatively with that of Ariadne and Aspatia. Unlike Ariadne,
however, there is no 'reconciliation' for her. We may remember
that Ariadne was found by Dionysius who made her his wife and
placed among the stars the crown which he gave her at their
marriage. Reconciliation for the epileptic is in the hands of the
prudish 'ladies of the corridor' and Doris, bringing smelling salts

---

[1] *Collected Poems*, p. 44.        [2] Grover Smith, op. cit., p. 47.

and a glass of brandy. No reconciliation, no spiritual regeneration results from this, hence the ironic comment on Emerson's view of history.

Whether such knowledge of myth can be expected of the reader or not is questionable. The reader will grasp the *contrast* between the past and the present without it, for the evocation of classical names suggests past glory. The parallel, which adds complexity to the poem, is something we may not see without sharing Eliot's knowledge, since he gives us only the names of his mythical characters and we cannot see the actions in which they were involved. From this point of view the structure fails.

Speaking of 'Sweeney among the Nightingales' and the reconciliation pattern which it contains, Miss Drew writes that these mythical stories

. . . create a pattern of reality which gives *meaning* to human hate and horror, and sacrifice and suffering, because they are related to an order and value beyond the temporal and the immediate.[1]

We can see the similarity and contrast implied in the plots against Agamemnon and Sweeney, if we approach the poem with a thorough knowledge of the history of Agamemnon. The characters of the Sweeney plot are incapable even of violent action, however, unlike those who plotted against Agamemnon; hence 'reconciliation' or 'rebirth after death' is impossible for them. The woman who 'tries' to sit on Sweeney's knees succeeds only in overturning a coffee cup and pulling the table-cloth to the floor. Her failure causes no disappointment or disturbance:

Reorganised upon the floor
She yawns and draws a stocking up;

Rachel's 'murderous paws' tear only at grapes, and the remaining personae plot in whispers, and are gaping, yawning, heavy-eyed, tired characters, incapable of any action, either good or evil. Agamemnon, we may recall, after his dishonourable deed of killing the stag sacred to Artemis, which delayed the Greek army from sailing to Troy because they were stricken with pestilence, was willing to sacrifice his daughter in order to appease the angered goddess. Such willingness is impossible for

1 Elizabeth Drew, op. cit., p. 66.

Sweeney and his friends. No one pays any heed to the singing of
the nightingales; their rôle is a passive one.

From the point of view of connotative structure 'Burbank
with a Baedeker: Bleistein with a Cigar'[1] is the most successful
poem. The emotions of Burbank and Bleistein are clearly
articulated and juxtaposed. The language of the present—the
colloquial 'falling' in the first stanza—juxtaposed with 'defunc-
tive'—the refined but dying language of the past prepares us,
Maxwell suggests, for the allusion that follows: the 'direct
juxtapositioning of the ancient and modern "co-supremes and
stars of love"'.[2] Life in modern Venice is expressed in the image
of the Princess Volupine extending her hand to Sir Ferdinand
Klein, whom, according to Smith, we are to take as the 'mean'
between Burbank and Bleistein. But the 'mean' between these
two might be a reasonable fellow since neither Burbank with
his Baedeker, nor Bleistein with his cigar, pompous each in his
own way, offers a satisfactory attitude either to the past or to
the present. Sir Ferdinand, however, is clearly not to be viewed
as a desirable character. The break between the two parts of his
name suggests bathos. He connotes a Fragilian type figure, weak
and passive in the face of the decay of the modern city. We can
grasp this connotation from the fact that he is not seen in any
action-image; he does not *do* anything; he is simply passively
entertained by the voluptuous Princess. The sharp, clear
perspective of a Canaletto is blurred in the 'smoky candle end of
time', or lost in the gaudy brightness of the lights of the modern
city. The pattern of the emotions is very clear in this poem.

In the Quatrain poems Eliot is experimenting with a new
discipline, perhaps because the emotions he is presenting are a
more rigid confrontation of past and present activity than the
emotional indecision of Prufrock. The symbols he gives are
precise and clearly defined in the poems where the particular
emotions of the past to be evoked are capable of being grasped
within the connotative structure. While the principle is sound
enough, the effect is often slight, like 'the levity of Hamlet'—
like the kind of 'buffoonery' on the part of a poet who has not
quite found the means to convey the complex emotions that the
traditional method demands.[3] Taupin, in describing the method

[1] *Collected Poems*, p. 42.          [2] D. E. S. Maxwell, op. cit., p. 88.
[3] *The Sacred Wood*, p. 125.

of Gautier, provides a useful means of summarizing Eliot's identical use of it at his best:

Gautier va de la surface vers la profondeur, complétant à chaque vers la description jusqu'au moment où il juge que l'effet est obtenu, et il s'arrête court, ou bien se permet exceptionnellement un commentaire, une comparaison très rapides pour ne pas ternir l'impression.[1]

Sufficient commentary on the over-erudition of some of these poems has been given to make repetition of it superfluous here. Considerable criticism has been levelled at these poems— especially 'Mr. Eliot's Sunday Morning Service'. An early reviewer in the *Athenaeum* for May and June 1919 asks, 'Is this poetry ?' and answers his own question by replying that it is not —more a kind of 'science'. Elizabeth Drew is bound to admit that

. . . by the time the reader is finished with *Encyclopaedia Britannica* and the Oxford English Dictionary he has not much heart for the intellectual *tour-de-force* of the use of the material in the poem.[2]

Genesius Jones, in speaking generally of Eliot's mythical method, suggests that the reader should

. . . arm himself with the books of Miss Gardner and Professor Smith; he should be thoroughly familiar with the *Divine Comedy*, Shakespeare and the Jacobeans, and French Symbolist theory. Then if he retires to the window seat behind the *Encyclopaedia Britannica* with Mr. Eliot's few thousand lines, the mystery should reveal itself.[3]

Over-erudition, classical names, however 'fixed' they appear in the texture of the poems, often throw open too wide the window on the world of connotation, so that, paradoxically, the symbols are as astronomically distant as the most personal symbol of Mallarmé. One can be as guilty of 'the sin of angelism', as we referred to it in Chapter III,[4] by turning one's back on reality and facing the gilded casements of literature and art, as the purest Symbolists, by retreating inwardly into the world of 'le rêve'.

Eliot, having made it clear that 'the four-sided hollow box'[5] could be used to contain conflicting emotions of growing

[1] René Taupin, op. cit., p. 237.    [2] Elizabeth Drew, op. cit., pp. 59–60.
[3] Genesius Jones, op. cit., pp. 299–300.    [4] See Chapter III, p. 46.
[5] Hugh Kenner, op. cit., p. 73.

intensity, moved on and back to the overtly assembling, fragmentary method again. He returns to it with an extended view of the present, with the addition of precise historical connotation to his symbols and images. Eliot's present is now more that of Baudelaire than of Laforgue. Peter Quennell compares the attitudes of the two French poets to Time:

> One difference between Baudelaire and the later poets, Laforgue, Verlaine, Corbière and Mallarmé, is that Baudelaire not only reveals the troubles of his own age and predicts those of the age to come, but also foreshadows some issue from these troubles. When we get to Laforgue we find a poet who seems to express more clearly than Baudelaire the difficulties of his own age; he spoke to us or spoke to my generation more intimately than Baudelaire seemed to do. Only later we conclude that Laforgue's present is narrower than Baudelaire's and Baudelaire's present extends to more of the past and more of the future.[1]

Eliot's present now takes in more of the past, and the emotional assemblages which result are increasingly 'timeless' because they are experienced by universal mankind.

'Gerontion' is generally acknowledged as Eliot's best poem of the early period. Matthiessen says that it provides the best use of the 'objective correlative', in that it is

> . . . perhaps the best example of the kind of hard precision with which Eliot's reliance upon a 'set of objects' enables him to thread together the range of his associations,

and he quotes as illustration the passage beginning:

> I an old man,
> A dull head among windy spaces

and ending:

> Vacant shuttles
> Weave the wind.[2]

He stresses as most critics do the 'meaning' of the passage in saying that 'there could hardly be a more effective way of stressing the intimate connection between the mysteries of religion and sex than by linking together the Christian story with the upsurging energies of spring'.[3]

[1] Peter Quennell, 'Baudelaire and the Symbolists', *Criterion*, January 1930.
[2] *Collected Poems*, pp. 39–40.          [3] F. O. Matthiessen, op. cit., p. 61.

Hugh Kenner writes more specifically of the poem's poetic
qualities:

One poem like this is enough; it purges the language. *Gerontion*
exploits systematically what a decade later Mr. William Empson was
to denominate as the norm of English poetic effect, describing as 'alien
to the habits of the English language' a Dryden's lack of interest in 'the
echoes and recesses of words'. The author of *Gerontion* is enquiring
into the past of that world made out of words.[1]

Genesius Jones has provided us with an interesting approach to
the historical connotations of some of Eliot's words in *Approach
to the Purpose*—we have already mentioned 'memory' as one,
in dealing with 'Rhapsody on a Windy Night'—which are vital
to a full appreciation of the poems. In 'Gerontion' we have a
series of words released with their full historical connotation—
'history' itself, 'knowledge', 'judas' are a few of them. In
addition to their historical associations, the images of this poem
take on religious association. The word which I should like to
suggest as being particularly relevant to this study is 'thought',
for it is the line

Thoughts of a dry brain in a dry season[2]

which indicates the boundaries within which we may allow our
imaginations to rove among the historical and religious connotations of all the images and symbols of the poem, and thus
gives the poem structural unity.

'Thought' has two chief connotations. The immediate association is with the abstract reasoning, the logic which we impose on
our experiences. The second association is the 'thought' process
referred to throughout this study and summed up in de Gourmont's dictum:

On pense au moyen d'images.

The most accurate way to 'think' was, for Eliot, as it was for
Donne and Webster, to think 'sensuously', as if the body
'thought'. It is this second thinking faculty which Gerontion has
lost in losing his five senses. Hence:

I would meet you upon this honestly.
I that was near your heart was removed therefrom

[1] Hugh Kenner, op. cit., p. 116.         [2] *Collected Poems*, p. 41.

> To lose beauty in terror, terror in inquisition.
> I have lost my passion: why should I need to keep it
> Since what is kept must be adulterated?
> I have lost my sight, smell, hearing, taste and touch:[1]

Although Gerontion has experienced the physically near, which can either be Christian 'physical thought' in Christ the tiger, or a woman, he has lost the beauty of both in 'terror'—the fear associated with the 'devouring tiger', or the Prufrockian fear of realizing a pure physical experience. He then lost his 'terror' in their presence, because of his inquiring mind, the mind which seeks to reduce all experience to the first form of 'thought'—the cold, abstract logic. Being unable to reduce such experiences to abstraction, the result is that his head, which contains such 'thought', is empty and dull. 'History' has two specific connotations: it suggests the time-progression of events, the succession of moments of actual experience which is how Eliot himself would view it. It also suggests the historian's rationalization and interpretation of the events of time, the abstract generalization which he deduces from the events of the past. Both views of 'history' offer ways of 'thinking' about the past. The first is useful, and is that which we associate with Eliot's 'historical sense', the artist's ability to resurrect and re-experience the past:

> . . . a perception, not only of the pastness of the past, but of its presence.[2]

The second way of thinking about the past is, in the context of this study, useless, for the 'reality' of the events is lost in rationalizing and making concepts from them. In the poem 'Gerontion', the 'corridors' of history contain the events of the past, the significance of which is missed because men are never ready for the events when they come, and so are unable to sense their reality. These corridors are also, however, the 'contrived' images of reasoning in which man, here Gerontion, loses himself. The 'truths' which the past has given are either given too soon, or else given in such

> . . . supple confusions
> That the giving famishes the craving.[3]

---

[1] ibid., p. 41.    [2] *Selected Essays*, p. 14.    [3] *Collected Poems*, p. 40.

These are rich lines. Connotatively 'craving' is associated with the flesh. Here it also means craving after more knowledge of historical conjecture. Thus 'famishes' can have two meanings, either 'reducing to hunger' or 'starving'. History, by giving truth, makes Gerontion crave for more truth by way of information, but it can also mean that it *starves* the craving of the flesh. Hence, when 'knowledge' of the physical kind is grasped, it is too late to live by its truth since passion can only be 'remembered'; the senses are therefore unable to function since they are starved, deadened. When Gerontion speaks of 'knowledge', he implies two forms of historical thinking, best summed up by Eliot himself, in 'East Coker':

> There is, it seems to us,
> At best, only a limited value
> In the knowledge derived from experience.
> The knowledge imposes a pattern, and falsifies,
> For the pattern is new in every moment
> And every moment is a new and shocking
> Valuation of all we have been.[1]

When the knowledge of immediate experience is given too soon it is given into weak hands, so that

> . . . what's thought can be dispensed with
> Till the refusal propagates a fear

—the fear we have already dealt with. Neither courage nor fear will save us. 'Heroism', the impudence of man in thinking that his own interpretation of events will save him, brings forth the unnatural vices of 'thoughts'. Virtues, that is, illusions of truth, are forced on us; 'forced on' suggests that man is forced to live by the conceptions of truth which he has fathered. And so the articulation is made:

> Thoughts of a dry brain in a dry season.

The poem can be viewed as the presentation of 'thoughts', with historical, religious and poetic connotations.

The first fragment presents in the passive verb 'being read to', the passive inactive attitude of the little old man. 'Reading'— the action of searching after the kind of knowledge to be found in books—is lost to him, because he has lost his faculty to read.

[1] 'East Coker', *Collected Poems*, p. 199.

A boy reads to him. Ironically, the young boy, in reading, may become like Gerontion. History repeats itself in becoming tradition. The old man waits for rain, which, ironically, he will be unable to feel, since he has lost his touch. The fact that he is speaking at the same time as the boy reads, suggests that he cannot hear the boy. His only faculty is articulation of his position in the decayed house, given by the series of objects:

> Rocks, moss, stonecrop, iron, merds.[1]

The second fragment presents the 'sign', the physical manifestation of 'meaning' which man has always sought for. But man also seeks for 'meaning' in the abstract sense, so that the mere physical presence of the silent babe in swaddling clothes is insufficient. The Blakean 'tiger' Christ is then given in May, at Easter, but it is 'depraved May', because man in the meantime is so distracted by his own ways of giving meaning to his world, in commercialism, etc. that the Easter-tiger is a fearful object. One wonders at Eliot's use of *'flowering* judas'. 'Sprouting', or a word with more sordid connotations, would surely be more suitable for the figure of betrayal; the connotations of 'flowering' are of beautiful blossoms. The irony of Judas was, of course, that by his betrayal of Christ he brought about the second major physical reality of religion, that of life after death, like blossoms after winter—the beauty of the physical knowledge of the whole of Christian teaching. The judas-flowers thus bring forth fruit. Fruit, in its first historical instance, blossomed on the tree of the Knowledge of Good and Evil. The fruition of Christianity in the death of Christ is also the fruit of knowledge: the two stem from the same source. This fragment suggests the perverted eating of the fruit, 'among whispers', by characters preoccupied with their own illusions of perverted knowledge and the meaning of life. Hence the next fragment:

> After such knowledge, what forgiveness?[2]

Knowledge, the physically real and the knowledge of perversion, is also the knowledge of history:

> These with a thousand small deliberations
> Protract the profit of their chilled delirium,
> Excite the membrane, when the sense has cooled,

[1] *Collected Poems*, p. 39.          [2] ibid., p. 40.

With pungent sauces, multiply variety
In a wilderness of mirrors.[1]

Gerontion suffers; the membranes of the mind and the body are
moved as the earlier observer was

. . . moved by fancies that are curled
Around these images.[2]

But he is, unfortunately, only 'moved' when both the 'senses'
and the reasoning 'sense' have cooled. As Brotman has pointed
out in speaking of 'East Coker':

. . . as in the constellated wars in which heat and cold oppose until
both are extinguished, as 'Leonids fly' wildly and blindly 'whirled in
the Vortex', so man is in darkness, knowing not where he is going.[3]

So the profit of the 'chilled delirium'—suggesting both heat and
cold—is that Gerontion is shattered into fragments, driven by
the Trades, the activating, vital sea winds, to 'knowledge' of
nothing. He has become and is a

Gull against the wind, in the windy straits
Of Belle Isle, or running on the Horn.
White feathers in the snow, the Gulf claims,
And an old man driven by the Trades
To a sleepy corner.[4]

Gerontion is tired as he 'waits', connotatively now, not for rain
but for death. Unlike Simeon to come, he will not 'depart in
peace'. He has not 'seen' salvation, never having been at the
'hot gates', never having participated in any meaningful action
of either religious or sexual significance.

If Gerontion is incapable of the physical sensation of 'thought',
this is not true of the artist's persona which articulates the
poem. Each fragment is presented in sensuously real, emotion-
ally and vividly precise images, and the creator, the poet, has
arranged them so that the conflict moves from one form of
'thought' to another, the physical and the abstract. The 'abstract'
thought passages, for example, the fragment on history, are seen
and felt. It is at once a house with contrived corridors and a

---

[1] *Collected Poems*, p. 41.        [2] 'Preludes', ibid., p. 24.
[3] D. Brosley Brotman, 'T. S. Eliot, the Music of Ideas', *University of Toronto
Quarterly*, October 1948, p. 25.
[4] *Collected Poems*, p. 41.

woman who gives but fails to give fulfilment. Perverted knowledge is seen in personae acting: Mr Silvero, in Limoges, whose
name connotes money and commercialism, has 'caressing hands',
which suggests that he is capable of sensing, but does not use
them, for he 'walked all night in the next room'; Hakagawa,
preoccupied with the Titians, 'bowing' among them so that she
is deprived of 'seeing'; Madame de Tornquist, preoccupied with
'shifting the candles' in the dark room; Fräulein von Kulp,
'who turned in the hall one hand on the door', but turned *away*.
All these images present the activity of twisting, gyrating,
turning humanity. This is summed up in a weaving motion—
the final perfect articulation of doing nothing:

> Vacant shuttles
Weave the wind.

'Gerontion' stands at the apex of all the previous artistic
methods and devices of communication used by Eliot. It is the
culmination of the 'persona' poem, in that Gerontion does no
more than give artistic shape and name to the poem, whose
subject was emotion. Since 'personae' have to be believed in, so
in previous poems they were given 'human' attributes. We can
see Sweeney, we can hear the Lady—all the personae borrow
their literal qualities from the world which they inhabit. George
Wright expresses the 'being' which they articulate:

We are accustomed to thinking of people as individuals, or at least as
types familiar to our culture, but, for the purposes of his poetry at least,
Eliot gives us people whose archetypal roles characterize them more
fully than do their cultural and individual peculiarities.[1]

In the sense that they borrow their personal attributes from the
world and act their ritual roles in their poems, the personae like
the Lady, Sweeney and his companions, the personae of 'Lune
de Miel' and the French poems, belong to the drama of the stage,
whereas Prufrock and Gerontion, whose only reality exists in
the poem, are more specifically dramatic characters of art. The
'drama' which they present is not the narrative which belongs
to the stage, since it has no counterpart in the exterior world of
action. Gerontion is in this respect an advance on Prufrock, more
personalized than Gerontion—(one can argue that we see Pru-

[1] George Wright, op. cit., p. 61.

frock ascending and descending the stair, going through the
streets, etc.)—who is the most depersonalized of all Eliot's
personae, except perhaps for Tiresias in 'The Waste Land'.
Rosenthal sees Gerontion as a persona who is not susceptible to
literal psychological analysis:

. . . nor does he symbolise a particular social class. He is an allegorical figure who represents the shrunken state of Western religious
tradition and the morbid preoccupation of modern man with his own
degradation.[1]

When Hugh Kenner describes Prufrock as 'the centre of a field
of consciousness, rather yours than his',[2] he gives us at the same
time a valuable way of looking at 'Gerontion'. Perhaps F. R.
Leavis sums up this artistic, dramatic 'persona' poem best when
he writes:

It has neither narrative nor logical continuity, and the only theatre in
which the characters mentioned come together or could, is the mind of
the old man. The Jew who squats on the window-sill could not hear
the old man even if he spoke his thoughts aloud, and the field overhead
in which the goat coughs has no geographical relation to the house. All
the persons, incidents, and images are there to evoke the immediate
consciousness of the old man as he broods over a life lived through and
asks what is the outcome, what the meaning, what the residue.[3]

This suggests to us 'Gerontion's' crowning achievement as an
instance of art. He is like a pure Cubist assemblage, for which
Wylie Sypher provides an interesting definition:

At its extreme purity . . . cubism is a study of the very techniques of
representation-painting about the methods of painting, a report on the
reality of art.[4]

'Gerontion' is this for the method of Eliot's poetry, showing
how thought can become poetry without showing how poetry is
thought. Genesius Jones speaks of the artist's gift

. . . so to have seen and heard and touched, so to have tasted and
smelt; and then, in the intuitive sense, so to have *seen* the pure forms of
his sensuous experience, that in his hands they can symbolize every
aspect of human experience.[5]

[1] M. L. Rosenthal, op. cit., p. 84.        [2] Hugh Kenner, op. cit., p. 35.
[3] F. R. Leavis, *New Bearings in English Poetry* (1932), p. 84.
[4] Wylie Sypher, op. cit., p. 269.        [5] Genesius Jones, op. cit., p. 251.

The 'new art-emotion' of 'Gerontion' is universal in this sense;
it has the 'immanent universality' of pure art in Jones's words
because it is given only in 'sense-experience', and 'timeless'
because

> [art] 'distances' the whole of human experience without neutralising it,
> contemplates it in time and space with a vision out of time and space,
> formalises it without generalising it.[1]

It is in this sense that Gerontion is a persona but transcends the
personae of the stage, is in history, in religion, in art and out
of all three—in time and out of time, so that 'meaning' need not
be constant. The poem will bear a religious or a sexual reading
according to the 'values' the reader gives each image and symbol.
At its extreme, I have tried to show that it provides a commentary on all that Eliot meant by Traditionalism in art, and the
'new art-emotion' of poetry. 'Gerontion' thus stands at

> The point of intersection of the timeless
> With time . . .[2]

For Eliot this is still a poetic and artistic occupation.

[1] ibid., p. 252.
[2] 'The Dry Salvages', *Collected Poems*, p. 212.

# VI   'The Waste Land'

'Eliot's "Waste Land" is, I think, the justification of the "movement" of our modern experiment since 1900', wrote Ezra
Pound to Felix Schelling in 1922.[1] Whether or not all readers
and critics would agree that the poem is the 'justification' of the
movement of modern poetry, it would be true to say that no
other poem between 1910 and 1922, apart from the few *Cantos*
already written, pushes so far the poetic theories and beliefs of
the period. Certainly no other poem has made such demands on
the type of structure defined in this study. 'The Waste Land'[2]
provides us with a mathematical-type progression of emotions
raised to epic dimension. The emotions which Eliot explores in
the poem are little different from those of 'Gerontion', but, as if
the single presiding poetic consciousness of the little old man,
Gerontion, restricted the connotations of the images used to
articulate them too much, Eliot throws his structure open to
embrace in its 'convenientia' the whole of society for all time.
Man, the social unit, Gerontion, becomes all men, and it is this
timeless Everyman, this Tiresias, who becomes the assembled
'persona' of the poem: a completely depersonalized Gerontion,
without even the semblance of humanity about him, except when
he is fragmented into his many temporal manifestations in the
poem:

Tiresias, although a mere spectator and not indeed a 'character', is yet
the most important personage in the poem, uniting all the rest. Just as
the one-eyed merchant, seller of currants, melts into the Phoenician
Sailor, and the latter is not wholly distinct from Ferdinand, Prince of
Naples, so all the women are one woman, and the two sexes meet in
Tiresias.[3]

As if the 'decayed house' of Gerontion confined the geographical
connotations of the poem to too small an area, the persona of
'The Waste Land' inhabits the assembled city of

---

[1] Quoted by Noel Stock, *Poet in Exile* (1964), p. 82.
[2] *Collected Poems*, (1963 edition), pp. 61–80. All quotations are taken from these
pages.
[3] Notes on 'The Waste Land', *Collected Poems*, p. 82.

Jerusalem Athens Alexandria
Vienna London.

M. L. Rosenthal described 'Gerontion' in these words:

He is an allegorical figure who represents the shrunken state of Western religious tradition and the morbid preoccupation of modern man with his own degradation. Art, love and religion seem to him debilitated and perverted simultaneously by a selfish secularism.[1]

The poetic sensibility which presides over the timeless, space-less world of 'The Waste Land' explores emotions which make up a similar 'theme'. The aim of the poet is to construct something like a modern epic, not in the form of a traditional narrative or sequence of events, but by assembling a complex montage of images, symbols and series of events which 'intensify the world'[2] to these emotions.

The method of the poem owes much to Pound, and many of the comments which Hugh Kenner and other critics have made on *The Cantos* can be applied, as we shall see, with equal efficacy to 'The Waste Land'. The composite persona, which we have already noted, is one which he attributed Eliot has to Pound. This sudden transition from one persona to another is a new technique for Eliot, and, in describing Pound's use of it as early as 1919, he makes indirect comment on his own:

Such a method involves immense capacities of learning and of dominating one's learning, and the peculiarity of expressing oneself through historical masks. Mr. Pound has a unique gift of expression through some phase of past life. This is not archaeology or pedantry, but one method and a very high method of poetry. It is a method which allows of no arrest, for the poet imposes upon himself, necessarily, the condition of constantly changing his mask; *hic et ubique*, then we'll shift our ground.[3]

It is the assembling of historical masks to make up the conscious-ness of Ulysses which Hugh Kenner describes as the unifying factor of *The Cantos* and, in fact, compares his function in Pound's poem to that of Tiresias in Eliot's:

In one sense, the substance of 'The Cantos' is what Odysseus sees, as that of 'The Waste Land' is what Tiresias sees.[4]

[1] M. L. Rosenthal, *The Modern Poets* (1960), p. 84.
[2] *The Sacred Wood*, p. 102. See also Chapter V., p. 91.
[3] T. S. Eliot, 'The Method of Mr. Pound', *Athenaeum*, 24 October 1919. p. 1065
[4] Hugh Kenner, *The Poetry of Ezra Pound* (1951), p. 317.

The only difference between the two is that Pound's composite persona, Odysseus, 'many minded, fertile in strategems, is engaged in active amelioration of conditions for himself and his men, involved as factive protagonist in what he sees', whereas Tiresias 'is capable only of psychic action, motions of fascination, revulsion, purgation'.[1] The reason why such a technique is possible in 'The Waste Land', as for *The Cantos*, is that each persona which makes up the assembled personae articulates very much the same basic emotion. We are made aware early in *The Cantos* that

. . . we are going to hear all through, in a sense, the 'same' story, but in 'different' shapes. Adams, Jefferson, Confucius, Sigismundo de Malatesta, a variety of Chinese Emperors, Pound himself in the 'Pisan Cantos', Mussolini, will all in a sense *be* Odysseus.[2]

The same is true of 'The Waste Land'. Each individual persona feels the same emotion and defines it as he experiences it. As the personae merge to become Tiresias, so he feels the emotion in its ensemble, the total of its multiple appearances. Tiresias thus becomes a 'universal' consciousness:

And I Tiresias have foresuffered all.

For many readers and critics 'The Waste Land' represents a complete breakaway from the technique of the earlier poems, and, while they accept 'Prufrock' or 'Gerontion', they find the apparent lack of structural coherence of the later poem generally unacceptable. Nevertheless, both the emotions from which the poetic structure is made, and the method by which the images which articulate them are brought together, represent a natural development of the methods of the earlier poems. It is difficult, therefore, to approach the poem without understanding and appreciating the methods of poems like 'Preludes', 'Rhapsody on a Windy Night', 'Prufrock' and the Quatrain poems. Once these poems are grasped, the method of 'The Waste Land' is clear. The poem represents for Eliot the same stage in his poetic development as *The Cantos* for Pound. Eliot's comment on Pound's poem and his advice to its readers, provide direction for the understanding of his own poem:

[1] Hugh Kenner, *The Poetry of Ezra Pound* (1951), p. 317.
[2] G. S. Fraser, *Ezra Pound* (1960), pp. 74–5.

. . . when anyone has studied Mr. Pound's poems in chronological order and has mastered *Lustra* and *Cathay*, he is prepared for the *Cantos*—but not till then. If the reader then fails to like them, he has probably omitted some step in his progress, and had better go back and retrace his journey.[1]

In attempting an elucidation of the method of 'The Waste Land', we shall do so best by considering it in relation to the methods of the earlier poems which we have examined.

The emotions at the basis of the structure are a development of the emotions of the earlier poems. We noted in the previous chapter Eliot's growing 'historical sense' as his poetry pro-gressed, and particularly the lengthening connotations of 'time' and 'tradition'. We noted his progress from the intensely immediate sense of present time in the images of 'Preludes' and 'Rhapsody', to a confrontation of the present with equally vivid images of the past in the Quatrain poems and 'Gerontion'. His sense of the present was thus linked with the past to form a 'durée'.[2] We remarked that after his experiment with the quatrain form, he returned to his initial and more valuable frag-mentary method with a view of the present which we described as more Baudelairean than Laforguian. The quotation is useful for present purposes:

When we get to Laforgue we find a poet who seems to express more clearly than Baudelaire the difficulties of his own age; he spoke to us or spoke to my generation more intimately than Baudelaire seemed to do. Only later do we conclude that Laforgue's present is narrower than Baudelaire's and that Baudelaire's present extends to more of the past and to more of the future.[3]

Allied to this sense of time was Eliot's progress from concern with man's spiritual inadequacy to his spiritual development. Up to 'The Waste Land', the future was hardly mentioned. We can now say that by 1922, Eliot's 'present' is completely Baudelairean. Ian Alexander has made an interesting study of Baudelaire's consciousness of time in a way that describes more accurately than any specific comment on Eliot has done the emotions which underlie 'The Waste Land':

[1] T. S. Eliot, *To Criticize the Critic* (1965), p. 182.
[2] See Chapter V, p. 98ff.
[3] Peter Quennell, 'Baudelaire and the Symbolists', *Criterion*, January 1930, quoted Chapter V, p. 125.

Time is not so much the passage as the substitution of identical and isolated moments, precluding both continuity and progress: behind, a load of sin, before, an endless recurrence of sin, and in the present, vain gnawing remorse, with at the end death as the final term.

This experience of time is very much the 'temps clos' of Bergson. It is the sense of time as a slow, monotonous recurrence. The feeling can reach a point where time seems to become motionless. At that point it is linked with the sensation of stifling, for, instead of its being an instrument at the service of man's will, time takes on a life of its own and becomes a vast cloud or blanket weighing upon the self and suffocating it. The self is then divorced from the temporal flow of life and becomes a stranger to the world of living creatures; the flux of effort dried up, it is petrified into an object, lost in a desert among unfamiliar, silent things. . . . In this state all hope is lost, the will paralysed.[1]

Time, from 'Preludes' onwards, was seen as a cyclic repetition. Particularly we remember images like:

> The worlds revolve like ancient women
> Gathering fuel in vacant lots

and

> . . . sleep, prepare for life.
> The last twist of the knife.[2]

It is the suffering personae of these early poems, locked in their squalid rooms, who now inhabit an equally squalid waste land, but who have reached the point of consciousness where time is motionless; people whose sensations are stifled, where all hope is lost, and where the springs of effort and desire are dried up. Their position is described by Eliot himself in *The Cocktail Party*, in terms like Alexander's description of Baudelaire:

> The final desolation
> Of solitude in the phantasmal world
> Of imagination, shuffling memories and desires.[3]

Baudelaire has explored the emotions arising from such a view of time in 'Spleen' (LXXVI), from which Alexander quotes, where the past weighs heavily, stopping up the vital activity of the mind, being no more than:

[1] Ian W. Alexander, 'The Consciousness of Time in Baudelaire', from *Studies in Modern French Literature* presented to P. Mansell Jones (1961), p. 4.
[2] *Collected Poems*, pp. 25, 28.
[3] *The Cocktail Party* (1930), p. 141.

> . . . un vieux boudoir plein de roses fanées
> Où gît tout un fouillis de modes surannés.[1]

So the Lady's bedroom in 'A Game of Chess' offers the same
view of 'temps clos', where the past weighs like the nauseating,
synthetic perfume which chokes the atmosphere, where the
bric-à-brac she has collected are simply 'withered stumps of
time':

> . . . staring forms
> Leaned out, leaning, hushing the room enclosed.

The future is mentioned more specifically than it was in the
earlier poems, but it is contemplated with the same feeling of
panic-stricken recurrence which characterized them:

> 'What shall I do now? What shall I do?'
> 'I shall rush out as I am, and walk the street
> 'With my hair down, so. What shall we do tomorrow?
> 'What shall we ever do?'
> The hot water at ten.
> And if it rains, a closed car at four.

This is the emotion which is at the basis of each fragment of the
poem. The same feeling of suffocation is given historical and
religious dimension in the fragment which suggests another
shut-up room, where the disciples sat waiting for 'a knock upon
the door' after the Crucifixion:

> After the torchlight red on sweaty faces
> After the frosty silence in the gardens
> After the agony in stony places
> The shouting and the crying
> . . .
> He who was living is now dead
> We who were living are now dying
> With a little patience

It is a similar awareness of time which has come to a standstill,
which the Fisher King and Ferdinand share in the stifling
environs of the gasworks, beside the stagnant waters of the
canal:

> While I was fishing in the dull canal
> On a winter evening round behind the gashouse

[1] Ian Alexander, op. cit., p. 5.

Musing upon the king my brother's wreck
And on the king my father's death before him.

This 'consciousness of time' has reached the point where each
man is 'locked within himself'[1] and 'becomes a stranger to the
world of living creatures', one who can neither act in the present,
nor hope to go forward with any assurance into the future:

We think of the key, each in his prison
Thinking of the key, each confirms a prison

The sense of isolation which accompanies such a consciousness of
time leads him to an 'ignorance of locality' as Pound calls it, his
inability to 'place' himself in relation to the culture in which he
lives.[2] In 'Canto LXXXII' he writes:

let the herbs rise in April abundant
. . .

but I will come out of this knowing no one
neither they me.[3]

The woman of 'Burial of the Dead' struggles in the same way
towards self-identification:

Bin gar keine Russin, stamm' aus Litauen, echt deutsch.

This, then, is the view of time and tradition which Eliot explores
in 'The Waste Land', and the images which articulate its various
manifestations throughout the history of religious belief and art,
he seeks to assemble into a new and complex instance of art. It is
the efficacy of this assemblage which we wish to examine in this
chapter.

That 'The Waste Land' is an assemblage of shorter poems
need not be restated, and the 'cutting' operation performed by
Pound on the original collection, which for so long has intrigued
students of Eliot's poetry, is no longer a matter for speculation.
The long-lost manuscripts of the poem were finally released in
October 1968, and now form part of the Berg Collection of the
New York Public Library. From my own examination of these
manuscripts, it would appear that Pound's 'Caesarian' role was

[1] Leonard Unger, T. S. Eliot (1960), p. 12.
[2] See Roy Harvey Pearce, 'Towards an American Epic', Hudson Review, Autumn
1959.
[3] Ezra Pound, The Cantos (1964 edition), p. 561.

justified and that Eliot was right to dedicate his poem to one
whom he acknowledged in his epigraph as 'il miglior fabbro'.[1]
Pound himself justified his suggestions to Eliot on the grounds
that everything should be cut which was not 'of the first
intensity',[2] and I hope in the space of this chapter to show how
this process worked. The final poem thus appeared, reduced to
half its original length. What remained, however, were, in
Pound's view, sufficient 'gists and piths'[3] to make the inclusion
of any further items unnecessary to an understanding of the
complete scheme from which they were excerpted.

Critics, since the poem was first published, have faulted it for
the final separateness of the assembled fragments and have not
been able to identify even the 'thousandth part of a quality'[4]
which they have in common with one another. For these critics,
the interference of Pound simply destroyed any possible unity
which the poem in its original form might have had. What they
appear to assume, without knowledge of the manuscripts, is that
Pound rendered the poem more difficult by demanding that
Eliot cut the connecting links between the disparate parts, which
now, without them, somehow do not hang together. The manuscripts in fact reveal that Eliot never attempted a continuous
poem in even a rough narrative sequence, and that the original is
no 'easier' than the published version. The changes Pound
advised simply reduced the number of fragments. Eliot's intention from the beginning was obviously that which he frequently
asserted during his lifetime—that is, to explore the possibility of
bringing together into a single poem a number of shorter pieces
which he had composed separately. From the marked differences
in handwriting, paper and typescript, the manuscripts reveal that
'The Waste Land' is not only made up of such pieces, but that
they were also written over a considerable period of time. Some
critics have, however, denied the right of the fragments to be
included in the single context of the poem. An early reviewer in
*New Statesman and Nation* for November 1922, speaks of
'several separate poems entitled "The Waste Land"'. Another
reviewer writes:

[1] See *Letters of Ezra Pound 1907–1941* (1951) (ed. D. Paige).
[2] Hugh Kenner, *T. S. Eliot: The Invisible Poet* (1965), pp. 125ff.
[3] Hugh Kenner, *The Poetry of Ezra Pound*, p. 204.
[4] See Chapter IV, p. 84.

'The Waste Land', for all the suggestion made by calling it a poem, is but a set of shorter poems . . . tacked together.[1]

Other critics have determined to defend its seemingly chaotic structure, by attempting to prove that somehow, when a poet is dealing with chaos, he can only render it by chaos. Leonard Unger appears to take this stand by reading lines like 'I could not speak' and 'I can connect nothing with nothing' as overt statements of the poet's 'own despair of ever succeeding in fully articulating his meaning'. He therefore justifies the poem in these terms:

> If the poet's own voice fails him, he can at least intimate that much, confirm his prison, by withdrawing almost altogether, while his poem dies away with the echo of other voices, and thus reaches a termination which is, appropriately, not a conclusion. It is impossible for the poet to say *just* what he means and yet he manages to say that much. And to say that much, to make the claim persuasively is after all a kind of consummation . . . If he could have entirely articulated his meaning, then it would no longer have been the meaning with which he was concerned.[2]

At the other extreme, critics like Cleanth Brooks and Grover Smith have felt the need to 'make sense' of the poem, and, by supplying the bricks in the scaffold of the myths which support the poem, have denied the fragmentariness of its structure in threading the pieces together to make a rough narrative progression of it.[3] Somewhere between these extremes there is a need to view the poem and to justify its structure on its own terms. We must guard against over-emphasizing the fragmentary nature of Eliot's presentation by underestimating the assembled wholeness. Too much attention to the *analytic* process which the emotional complex has undergone and the resultant apparent shattering of subject matter into fragments undervalues the more important *creative* process of reassembling and re-integrating them; the danger here is to pay too much attention to the detail and ignore the type of synthesis which the poem makes. Nevertheless, the separateness of the fragments

---

[1] Alex Brown, 'The Lyric Impulse in T. S. Eliot', *Scrutinies II* quoted by D. E. S. Maxwell, *The Poetry of T. S. Eliot* (1952), p. 98.
[2] Leonard Unger, op. cit., p. 25.
[3] See Grover Smith, *T. S. Eliot's Poetry and Plays* (1956), pp. 72ff.; Cleanth Brooks, *Modern Poetry and the Tradition* (1965 ed.), pp. 136ff.

should not be ignored in demanding from the poem a kind of unity which it is not its intention to provide.

Conrad Aiken perhaps sums up the structural form best for us in a short essay entitled 'The Anatomy of Melancholy', included in a recent collection of articles on Eliot which originally appeared separately in various issues of *The Sewanee Review*.[1] He begins by defining its seemingly chaotic appearance:

I think, therefore, that the poem must be taken—most invitingly offers itself—as a brilliant and kaleidoscopic confusion; as a series of sharp, discrete, slightly related perceptions and feelings, dramatically and lyrically presented, and violently juxtaposed (for effect of dissonance), so as to give us an impression of an intensely modern, intensely literary consciousness which perceives itself to be not a unit but a chance correlation or conglomerate of mutually discolorative fragments.[2]

He goes on to point out that, while the cutting of any individual part of the poem would not seriously affect or destroy the 'plan', since it has no overt plan, it would 'seriously detract from the value of the portrait':

These things are not important parts of an important or careful intellectual pattern; but they are important parts of an important emotional ensemble.[3]

Aiken does not pursue the point, but it is an important one. His way of viewing the structure of the poem implies the same analogy between poetry and painting that has been made throughout this study. In Chapter I, the characteristic, modern art-structure was defined as an assemblage of particular appearances or aspects of an object which rendered it, in the art-form, in something approaching its 'total existence'[4] To omit a single view in the Cubist portrait would not destroy the 'plan' of the portrait, but would detract from its 'value', which is the comprehensiveness of its presentation. The significance of 'The Waste Land' is a similar comprehensiveness. The 'loss' of a Lady Fresca passage from 'The Fire Sermon' or the initial 'Death by Water' sequence deleted by Eliot at Pound's suggestion from the original manuscripts, did not interfere with the poem's sequence or 'plan'. *Technically* speaking, neither, in

---

[1] *T. S. Eliot: The Man and his Work*, (1967) (ed. Allen Tate).
[2] ibid., p. 201     [3] ibid.,     [4] See Chapter I, p. 4.

fact, should the elimination of the 'April is the cruellest month' or 'The chair she sat in' passages. Though each passage in the published version of the poem has its place, it is not like a vital part in a 'plot' sequence; its significance is of a different kind.

The method of testing the right of each fragment to be included in the final context is implied, I think, in Pound's suggested revision. He obviously thought that nothing would be lost by cutting, for example, the Lady Fresca passage because the frustration felt by the lady in question had been parallelled and expressed by another lady in 'A Game of Chess'. Both women experience frustration with their social activities. Each attempts to communicate with another and fails. The lady in 'A Game of Chess' says:

> 'My nerves are bad to-night. Yes, bad. Stay with me.
> 'Speak to me. Why do you never speak. Speak.
> 'What are you thinking of? What thinking? What?
> 'I never know what you are thinking. Think.'

Lady Fresca's letter to a friend atttempting, but failing, to describe her boredom at a dull party is a diluted form of the same sort of breakdown in communication. She indicates that she has a lot to say if only she could say it. For all their similarities, the Lady Fresca passage has none of the intensity of the passage quoted from 'A Game of Chess'. The impression that it gives is simply that Fresca is as much bored by her letter-writing as her party-going. On these grounds, I think, the cut is justified. To cut the passage from 'A Game of Chess' would, on the other hand, take away from the comprehensive emotional ensemble which the poem presents. Consequently, in examining the structural unity of the poem, we should aim solely to see the interrelationship of the parts to this end: the presentation of an emotional complex whose 'total existence' is made up of aspects of it taken from the past—historical and religious views of it— which render the present appearances of it comprehensive.

'The Waste Land' is Eliot's most ambitious experiment in the 'unification of sensibility'; he sees the theme of his poem reflected in many widely scattered instances, and constructs his poem from these units, drawing them together to give a more complete sense of his emotional complex than he could by limiting himself to the poetic potentialities of any single one of them.

The method, as the above comments indicate, has a good deal in common with that of the analytic Cubists who, in an attempt to see their subjects in their entirety, and in order to transcend the limitations of conventional perception, as Eliot is trying to do, dissected their subjects to reintegrate them in a way that would provide a new autonomous artistic construction. Few poems illustrate better this method, Eliot's description of the poet's mind as

. . . a receptacle for seizing and storing up numberless feelings, phrases, images, which remain there until all the particles which can unite to form a new compound are present together.[1]

or Baudelaire's description of creative activity leading to new art-emotion:

It decomposes all of creation, and, with the materials gathered, set forth according to rules whose origin cannot be found except in the deepest part of the soul, it creates a new world, and produces the experience of the new.[2]

The 'numberless feelings and images' which are the allotropic components of the poet's structure are those which he picks and chooses from the immediate world of his observation, fragments of myth, fragments of literature, the Upanishads, the Bible, all 'worked up' into a new and complex instance of art.

We have shown how the emotions of 'The Waste Land' develop out of the emotions of the earlier poems, and indicated the necessity of examining the method as a similar development. The techniques of all the earlier poems are used but advanced in the later poem. Like 'Rhapsody on a Windy Night' in intention, 'The Waste Land' is an attempt to show us 'memory', the floors of which have been 'dissolved'. In place of the 'crowd of twisted things'—the broken spring, a twisted branch, the 'objets trouvés' of the quayside and the beach—the memory of Tiresias throws up instances of dramatic conflict. They are presented to us, however, with the same connotative intention as the objects in 'Rhapsody': they are 'objets trouvés' from literature, art and

[1] 'Tradition and the Individual Talent', *Selected Essays* (1951 edition), p. 19.
[2] Translated from 'La Reine des facultés', Salon de 1859, quoted by Jacob Korg, 'Modern Art Techniques in the Waste Land', *Journal of Aesthetics and Art Criticism*, No. XVIII, (1960), pp. 456–63.

myth which 'retain marks of their previous form and history'[1]
like the found objects in the earlier poem. Let us look at one
example:

> I remember
> Those are pearls that were his eyes.

The connotations of such a fragment as this are no longer the
simple associations of uselessness—the basic connotations of the
broken spring, etc. At one level the image does arouse these
emotions, in that the 'objet trouvé', a fragment from tradition,
has not been integrated into any useful functioning of the mind
of the persona—time weighs with a dead weight: traditional
thinking is lifeless and useless. At another, deeper level, the
associations are the emotions of Ferdinand in *The Tempest*. Like
the woman in 'A Game of Chess', Ferdinand has reached a
motionless moment in time, in which he can no longer act or go
forward, overcome by emotions aroused by his father's death.
At the same time, the allusion to *The Tempest* also suggests
metamorphosis, by indicating a 'sea-change'; the 'death' of the
king and his sea-burial bring about reconciliation and regeneration. No happy issue is forecast for the woman or for any of the
inhabitants of the modern waste land. Similarity and difference
are thus pointed out simultaneously, and we can see how the
fragment supports, in a complex way, the emotions of isolation
and 'temps clos' which caused it to be 'thrown up'. It identifies
the emotions in their present manifestation with the same
emotions felt in the past. At the same time, it shows the present
in a new perspective by directing the imagination of the reader
to *new* emotions which make a contrast between past and present.
Such quotations as this from *The Tempest*, along with the frequent allusions to past literature and the fragments of nursery
rhymes included in the poetic structure of 'The Waste Land',
function in the same way as the 'objects' thrown up by memory
in 'Rhapsody on a Windy Night', and provide for the poem the
same collage-like texture which we examined in the earlier
poem. Jacob Korg writes of artistic collage:

. . . when actual bits of our own world take their place in a picture side
by side with forms created by a painter, the real object seems to
demarcate the limit of the painting, forming what Guillaume Apollin-

---
[1] William Seitz, *The Art of Assemblage* (1961), p. 17.

aire called an 'inner frame', and impressing the observer with the sharp contrast between the realms of art and actuality, thereby freeing him from the assumptions underlying imitative art.[1]

The found objects from other literatures in 'The Waste Land' function like 'real objects' in the picture, and provide an 'inner frame' for the connotations of the fragments surrounding them, which in their turn provide an ironic comment on them:

> The real and the imagined are made to support each other, the real bringing in to the work a powerful and unexpected authenticity and the imagined serving to control the significance of the real elements.[2]

These 'objets trouvés', the material which the poet borrows from other literatures, are like the 'marked' materials that Seitz mentioned in the passage quoted in the previous chapter:

> When paper is soiled or lacerated, when cloth is worn, stained or torn, when wood is split, weathered or patterned with peeling coats of paint, when metal is bent or rusted, they gain connotations which unmarked materials lack.[3]

The associations of the objects excerpted from past literature and art are more comprehensive in association than those of 'Rhapsody' and indicate a gain in dramatic intensity for 'The Waste Land'.

It is easy to see how the fragments, 'Da, Dayadhvam, Damyata', incorporated into the section 'What the Thunder said', function as objects in a similar way. It is this section which has caused more than one critic to view the poem as 'a Christian sermon in disguise',[4] and to 'interpret' these words as the 'message' of the poem. The artistic intention of 'Da, Dayadhvam, Damyata', affixed to the structure of the poem, yet apart from it, since they have no syntactical function where they occur, seems to me to be similar to the technique of 'papier collé' in collage art, or the Cubist method of introducing a letter or a word within the framework of the picture. Picasso was experimenting with the technique as early as 1911–12 when he painted 'Still Life with Chair Caning', in which the letters JOU, representing a realistic symbol of 'Journal', 'float ambiguously from their position in space towards the surface of

[1] Jacob Korg, op. cit., p. 460.        [2] ibid.
[3] W. Seitz, op. cit., p. 17, quoted Chapter V, p. 98.
[4] M. L. Rosenthal, op. cit., p. 88.

the picture'.[1] Mallarmé had attempted the same kind of thing
in 1897 with 'Un Coup de dés jamais n'abolira le hasard', where
the title is fragmented and distributed as four topical headings
throughout the context of the poem. Roger Fry notes of such a
method that the theme is

. . . frequently as it were broken to pieces in the process of poetical
analysis and is reconstructed not according to the relations of experience, but of pure poetical necessity.[2]

Both Picasso's method and that of Mallarmé make interesting
contrast with the technique of 'The Waste Land'. The words of
the Thunder seem to be intended to communicate rather by their
associations than by their denotative abstract values. They
*embody* meaning. Korg writes:

They are realistic exhibits which illustrate directly instead of discussing. They have the irreducible opaque solidity of *tranches de vie*,
communicating on a different level from that of Eliot's own words and
illuminating his meaning from a different direction.[3]

These words act as a kind of trajectory, a 'broken theme' moving
through the various sections of the poem, defining the boundaries of the associations of each fragment, floating ambiguously
throughout the context of the poem to the surface at the end.
Like the mathematical progression where the 'answer' is given,
each section can be seen to betray through its own kind of fear a
lack of giving, sympathy and control.

The technique of the poem can therefore be defined from one
standpoint as a highly sophisticated advance on 'Rhapsody on a
Windy Night'. It presents the same perspectiveless structure,
past and present coexisting in a new dramatic amalgam.

We can now go on to examine in greater detail the type of
dramatic structure which 'The Waste Land' represents. The
drama of the poem, like that of 'The Love Song of J. Alfred
Prufrock' or 'Gerontion', is not that *of stage-drama* which
we associated with a poem like 'Portrait of a Lady'. A poem
*of stage-drama* was defined in the last chapter as one which
presented a narrative sequence of events similar to that which

[1] W. Seitz, op. cit., p. 9.
[2] Roger Fry, *The Poems of Mallarmé* (1951), p. 290, quoted by Seitz, op. cit.,
p. 13.
[3] Jacob Korg, op. cit., p. 459.

the audience sees enacted on the stage. Opposed to it was the purely artistic drama of poems like 'Prufrock' or 'Gerontion', where there was no narrative progression, the 'drama' simply an emotional conflict which took place in the imagination of the persona, who, alone, 'saw himself' acting. The drama of 'The Waste Land' appears to have more stage drama than either 'Prufrock' or 'Gerontion', yet it is obviously not a narrative poem like 'Portrait', in that each scene gives rise to no subsequent development, and there is no beginning, middle and end to any sequence of events. Like those of 'Portrait', however, the scenes of 'The Waste Land' are there primarily to *define* an emotion. No event in the poem is intended to advance a plot. When we realize this, we can appreciate the invalidity of comment like that of Graham Hough who criticizes the poem for the ways in which it shows 'the use of language in different and unrelated fashions in different parts of the poem'.[1] Hough dislikes Eliot's mixing connotative language in, for example, the passage dealing with the Hyacinth girl, and the purely denotative language of narrative progression in the typist passage. That the intention of this passage is not literal or narrative, but emotive, in the same way as that of the Hyacinth girl passage, has been adequately commented on by Hugh Kenner:

> The typist passage is the great *tour de force* of the poem; its gentle lyric melancholy, its repeatedly disrupted rhythms, the automatism of its cadences, in alternate lines aspiring and falling nervelessly . . . constitute Eliot's most perfect liaison between the self-sustaining gesture of the verse and the presented fact . . . the texture is lyric rather than dramatic because there is neither doing nor suffering here but rather the mutual compliance of a ritual scene.[2]

In other words, the intention is to focus our attention on the connotations of the passage—automatic gestures, futile activity—rather than to present a theatrical 'scene' which we are to watch. Perhaps a look at the syntax of part of a passage of the same type will make this point clearer:

> I Tiresias, though blind, throbbing between two lives,
> Old man with wrinkled female breasts, can see
> At the violet hour, the evening hour that strives

---

[1] Graham Hough, *Image and Experience* (1960), p. 22.
[2] Hugh Kenner, *T. S. Eliot: The Invisible Poet*, pp. 142–3.

Homeward, and brings the sailor home from sea,
The typist home at teatime, clears her breakfast, lights
Her stove, and lays out food in tins.

First of all let us look at the verbs of the last four lines. The
'evening hour' 'strives homewards' and 'brings the sailor home
from sea'. By implication it also brings the typist home. This
much is clear. The subject of the verbs 'clears' and 'lights'
is not so clearly denoted, however. It is obviously the typist
who does these things, but the syntactical arrangement of the
lines suggests that it is also the evening hour which does them.
The connotative intention is clear. The actions of the typist are
so automatic, geared so rigidly to her regular homecoming, that
the evening hour is also implicated in them. If we now turn to
the verb 'can see' in the second line we find a similar ambiguity
in syntax. The subject of 'can see' is 'I, Tiresias'. What can he
see? Either there is no direct object and the lines mean 'I,
Tiresias, though blind *can* see, however, at the evening hour',
or else the verb 'can see' is used transitively and means that he
can see 'the evening hour' and all the activities which it brings.
Clearly, both are intended. Tiresias, by his ability to see at the
violet hour, is aware of all the events of the evening and acts as
a presiding consciousness over them. The ambiguity of syntax
of the passage indicates that the function of the language is not
literal but connotative.

The 'scenes' of the poem are there for the same purpose as the
lyric passages in Pound's *Cantos*:

. . . not for indulgence but for definition: they are surveyor's pegs or
records of emotional absolutes. When they are over, they stop.[1]

The reader is less 'involved' in them than he is in scenes of stage
drama. In 'Portrait' we were invited to share the emotions of the
man:

I take my hat: how can I make a cowardly amends
For what she has said to me?[2]

The effect of the typist passage in 'The Waste Land' is somewhat different. Here we are offered a passage for inspection not
submersion. It corresponds exactly to the Imagist technique

[1] Hugh Kenner, *The Poetry of Ezra Pound*, p. 229.
[2] *Collected Poems*, p. 20.

which Hugh Kenner examines in Pound. In comparing a soporific passage in Tennyson's 'Lotos Eaters' with a corresponding passage in Pound's poem, he writes:

The excitement with which the Pound passage infects us is on the contrary that of inspecting, as it were from behind glass, a new and exotic mode of being. The presentation is not 'cold', the Lotos-eater feelings are 'there', but the passion is attached to cognition, not submersion.[1]

Thus we can see that each passage in its own way functions as an item of exact definition, not pushing forward any action in the narrative sense. Remembering that we defined exact language in Chapter IV as implying an action, we can see how each passage has the same function as Pound's ideograms. Kenner describes Pound's method as the articulation in ideograms of 'gists and piths':

The Chinese ideogram imitates an action: it is a picture of a metaphor. On p. 35 of his *Unwobbling Pivot* pamphlet, Pound reproduces an ideogram showing, literally, 'a man standing by his word'. That this lies in the province of 'gists and piths' may be seen by contrasting the vaguer ambience of an abstract noun like 'fidelity' or 'honesty'. The ideogram is not a makeshift. It is more specific, not less. It defines by imitation a particular mode of honesty, adherence to the word previously given . . . Ideogram and metaphor, then, are sharply focused as to action, relatively indifferent as to material. The essential action of 'maintaining one's defined intention' is the same whether the 'given word' relate to marriage vows, rates of taxation, or acceptance of responsibility for a bundle of laundry. Hence the suitability of the ideogrammic method for the use to which it is put in the *Cantos*, that of establishing 'a hierarchy of values' by isolating either volitional dynamics or persistent emotional currents from hundreds of different material contexts.[2]

The action-images resulting from actual observation and excerpted from Eliot's knowledge of tradition have a similar function in 'The Waste Land'.

The technique of the poem is a clear advance on the methods of 'Prufrock' and 'Gerontion'. Each persona in the poem is, like Prufrock or Gerontion, only 'a name plus a voice'.[3] In 'The Waste Land', however, this technique is pushed to its farthest

[1] ibid., p. 69.      [2] ibid., p. 204.
[3] Hugh Kenner, *T. S. Eliot: The Invisible Poet*, p. 35.

extreme. We can say that the personae of this poem are only
voices, for only rarely are they given names and they are never
personalized. We cannot 'see' the personae here as we can
sometimes catch a glimpse of Prufrock 'grown slightly bald', or
the little old man, Gerontion. The personae of 'The Waste
Land' can only be called assembled voices, ranging from the
voice of Isaiah to Ferdinand, Lil's friend to the Buddha, each
articulating his own 'fear in a handful of dust'. Eliot himself
appears consciously to have adopted the technique of merging
voices in calling his first two sections in the original version
'He do the Police in different Voices'. He abandoned the title, of
course, but in his poem he does, in fact, do 'humanity in many
voices'. Eliot has presented in the poem 'a harmony of all the
voices that had ever struck his ear', as Auerbach wrote of Dante.[1]
Like Dante, Eliot has remembered:

> . . . and remembering turned to his purpose—all that he had heard and
> read, from the market place exchanges of his fellow-citizens to the
> liturgical Latin of the church.[2]

As the speaker changes, so the poetic tone changes with him,
but all are united, however, in the single dominant tone—the
tone of conversation. Allen Tate describes the method of 'The
Waste Land' well, in attempting a definition of the form of *The
Cantos*:

> The secret of his form is this: conversation. *The Cantos* are *talk, talk,
> talk* . . . the length of a breath, the span of conversational energy, is
> the length of a Canto. The conversationalist pauses; there is just
> enough unfinished business left hanging in the air to give him a new
> start; so that the transitions between the Cantos are natural and easy.[3]

The talk of 'The Waste Land' reflects in turn, through the
voice of the speaker, aspiration, desire, despair, capacity for
ecstasy, capacity for humour, all the voices by natural and easy
transition becoming the voice of Tiresias, the voice of all time,
who has experienced all these forms of emotion:

> And I Tiresias have foresuffered all

---

[1] Auerbach, *Dante*, p. 127, quoted by T. G. Bergin, *Approach to Dante* (1965), p.
278.
[2] T. G. Bergin, op. cit., p. 278.
[3] Quoted A. Alvarez, *The Shaping Spirit* (1958), p. 62.

Seen in the way Tate suggests we look at *The Cantos*, 'The Waste Land' thus forms a complex assemblage of moments of the motionless time of Baudelaire, moments of fear in which the voice of the persona articulates his isolation in his surroundings : an assemblage of the voices in the wildernesses of all time in which all hope of establishing meaningful communication is lost. The length of each fragment is 'the span of conversational energy of each speaker'. The voice of the woman at the beginning of 'Burial of the Dead' soon loses its articulating energy as the fragment progresses :

> And when we were children, staying at the arch-duke's,
> My cousin's, he took me out on a sled,
> And I was frightened. He said, Marie,
> Marie, hold on tight. And down we went.
> In the mountains, there you feel free.
> I read, much of the night, and go south in the winter.

As Hugh Kenner notes :

We have only to delete 'there' to observe the collapse of more than a rhythm : to observe how the line's exact mimicry of a fatigue, which supposes it has reached some ultimate perception, can telescope spiritual bankruptcy, deracinated ardour, and an illusion of liberty, which is no more than impatience with human society and relief at a temporary change.[1]

There is a similar dying away of conversational energy at the end of the passage on the Hyacinth girl :

> I could not
> Speak, and my eyes failed, I was neither
> Living nor dead, and I knew nothing,
> Looking into the heart of light, the silence.

'A Game of Chess' has the same feeling of the short 'length of a breath' as the voice of the woman fades :

> 'You know nothing? Do you see nothing? Do you remember
> 'Nothing?'

The omission of the inverted commas at the end of the line ' "Do you remember" . . .' indicates that the final question is left unfinished.

[1] Hugh Kenner, *T. S. Eliot: The Invisible Poet*, p. 136.

A detailed analysis would labour the point. We can see clearly how each fragment is similar in representing the same brief span of articulating energy. The voice of Lil's friend weakens in the sudden burst of the barman's voice:

> And they asked me in to dinner, to get the beauty of it hot—
> HURRY UP PLEASE ITS TIME

The end of the final section of the poem indicates the dying fall of all the voices of the poem.

'Prufrock' and 'Gerontion' are made up of fragments showing the personae in moments of peculiar intensity. As Pound described the method of his own dramatic lyric:

> I catch the character I happen to be interested in at the moment he interests me, usually a moment of song, self-analysis, or sudden understanding.[1]

Eliot's personae are caught in similar moments, moments not unlike the Joycean epiphany. His structural unit, like that of Joyce and Pound, is 'a highly concentrated manifestation of a moral, cultural, or political quiddity'.[2] The woman of 'Burial of the Dead' points to a sudden moment of abandonment to terror, which is in some ways invigorating and free, but the moment dies. The lover of the Hyacinth girl articulates the sudden moment of ecstasy in love which is also a kind of fear. The moment is that which Helen Gardner describes as the point

> . . . when love passes beyond its object, and seems for a moment held in a kind of silence that seems outside time.[3]

The voice of Stetson addressing the crowd flowing over London Bridge expresses a momentary fear of the Dog, the 'cluster-evocation'[4] which suggests the inexplicable attraction for and repulsion from the 'cruel' spring of the beginning of the poem. Voices articulating more and more moments of sudden revelation are added together until the voices of the disciples merge with all the voices of the poem to become the composite universal voice of Tiresias in an almost ritual chant in the final section of the poem:

---

[1] See Chapter IV, p. 72.
[2] Hugh Kenner, *The Poetry of Ezra Pound*, p. 186.
[3] Helen Gardner, *The Art of T. S. Eliot* (1961), p. 91.
[4] G. S. Fraser, op. cit., p. 56, See also Chapter IV, p. 77.

> Here is no water but only rock
> Rock and no water and the sandy road
> The road winding above among the mountains
> Which are mountains of rock without water
> If there were water we should stop and drink
> Amongst the rock one cannot stop or think

The moment here is a frantic moment of terror in the dry, arid mountains where there is only the sterile voice of the thunder. In his 'London Letter', published in the *Dial* in 1921, Eliot wrote of *Le Sacre du Printemps* that the music of the ballet metamorphosed the 'rhythm of the steppes' into

> . . . the screams of the motor horn, the rattle of machinery, the grind of wheels, the beating of iron and steel, the roar of the underground railway and the barbaric cries of modern life.

In 'The Waste Land', he is making his own attempt at such a metamorphosis—only here it is voices that are metamorphosed. The cries of the prophets of all time, the Sibyl, Tiresias, Isaiah, St. Augustine, the disciples, Ferdinand, the Fisher King and Ophelia, are metamorphosed into the despairing voices of the croaking Madame Sosostris, the Lady, the Thames Daughters and Lil's friend. The music of *The Tempest*, the songs of Philomel and Spenser become the songs of the Thames Daughters, the sounds of the motor horn and the rhythms of modern jazz:

> O O O O that Shakespeherian Rag—
> It's so elegant
> So intelligent

At the same time Eliot adds, by connotation, the assembled voices of the poets of all time, metamorphosed into the voice of the modern poet, struggling to articulate the timeless condition of man in the world. Herbert Howarth writes of the ballet of Stravinsky with its similar technique:

> It brought home the continuity of the human predicament: primitive man on the dolorous steppes, modern man in the city with its 'despairing noises'; the mind of the one a continuation of the mind of the other, the essential problem unchanging.[1]

The technique of assembled voices is possible for the reason we have already given at the beginning of the chapter—mainly

[1] Herbert Howarth, *Notes on Some Figures Behind T. S. Eliot* (1965) p. 235.

that the persona is given no individual qualities. G. T. Wright
makes the same point:

> Since Eliot's characters do not usually receive substantial individuality,
> and since even their cultural characteristics give way to their human
> ritual roles, they are often unstable. Different persons who play the
> same archetypal role tend to 'melt' into one another and even the
> different roles merge into abstract humanity.[1]

Thus the transition from the voices of the Thames Daughters,
for instance, to the voice of St Augustine, is a natural and easy
one, the emotion expressed by the prostitutes, easily intensified
by an ironic twist to include the emotion of the saint:

> 'My people humble people who expect
> Nothing.'
>             la la
>
> To Carthage then I came
>
> Burning burning burning burning

The poetic intention of Eliot, however, in this poem, as in
all the early poems, is to guard the separateness of each voice.
Not only the lineation of the passage quoted above, but also the
change both in poetic tone and often language, testify to this.
The texture of the poem is thus like Stravinsky's, as Jacques
Rivière describes it:

> L'oeuvre est entière et brute, les morceaux en restent tout crus; ils
> nous sont livrés sans rien qui ne prépare la digestion; tout ici est franc,
> intact, limpide et grossier.[2]

Like the film director, he deliberately 'cuts' after each fragment.
Like Pound in *The Cantos*, his concern is to express his emotion
as exactly as possible and, when his articulation is complete, he
stops. Apollinaire, one of the chief spokesmen for the art of
poetic and artistic assemblage, writes:

> *Psychologically* it is of no importance that this visible image be com-
> posed of fragments of spoken language, for the bond between these
> fragments is no longer the logic of grammar but an ideographic logic
> culminating in an order of spatial disposition totally opposed to dis-

[1] G. T. Wright, *The Poet in the Poem* (1962), p. 62.
[2] Quoted by Herbert Howarth, op. cit., p. 236.

cursive juxtaposition . . . It is the opposite of narration. Narration is
of all literary forms the one which most requires discursive logic.[1]

Eliot's method, like that described by Apollinaire, is an attempt
to dispose of nineteenth-century story and theatrical plot and to
replace it by a cinematographic technique, which makes of his
sophisticated assemblage of voices an extremely complex
montage.

This cinematic technique we have already noted in Pound and
Eliot, where Aristotelian 'praxis' is built up from a series of
shots, perceived immediately and set down simultaneously into
a collage which aims deliberately to resist unification into a
schematized plot by an 'easy lateral sliding'.[2] The aim of both
poets in this seems to coincide with that of Eisenstein in the film
—to 'dismember' events into a montage of various shots and

> . . . by combining these monstrous incongruities, we newly collect the
> disintegrated event into one whole, . . .[3]

The object is to create a new art-emotion by the superimposing
of incongruous elements on one another. The method is similar
to the Japanese 'hokku' which deals in Aristotelian *'peripeteia'*.
Hugh Kenner describes Pound's use of it and quotes as an
example:

> Fu I loved the high cloud and the hill
> Alas he died of alcohol.[4]

Here Pound, like the film director, 'cuts' from one image to the
next, in a cinematic 'peripeteia'. Kenner justifies it in these terms:

> In judging epigrammatic verse the reader must distinguish between
> the rhetorical gesture that chucks in one component to negate another
> and the *peripeteia* that juxtaposes two worlds of perception to strike
> light from their interaction . . . Fu I's sozzled exit doesn't debunk his
> love of the high cloud and the hill, but inflects it with a wry pathos of
> inadequacy.[5]

It was a similar cinematic device which Eliot had used at the end
of 'Preludes':

---

[1] Guillaume Apollinaire, *Soirées de Paris*, quoted by Seitz, op. cit., p. 15.
[2] See Donald Davie, *Ezra Pound: Poet as Sculptor* (1965), p. 121.
[3] Eisenstein, *Film Form*, quoted by Wylie Sypher, *From Rococo to Cubism in Art and Literature* (1960), p. 283.
[4] Ezra Pound, 'Epitaphs', *Selected Poems* (1928), p. 120.
[5] Hugh Kenner, *The Poetry of Ezra Pound*, p. 63.

I am moved by fancies that are curled
Around these images, and cling:
The notion of some infinitely gentle
Infinitely suffering thing.

Wipe your hand across your mouth, and laugh;
The worlds revolve like ancient women
Gathering fuel in vacant lots.[1]

Here the second image inflected the first with the same 'wry pathos of inadequacy' which Kenner noted in Pound. The same cinematic progression occurs throughout 'The Waste Land':

O the moon shone bright on Mrs. Porter
And on her daughter
They wash their feet in soda water
*Et O ces voix d'enfants, chantant dans la coupole!*

The last line, introducing the singing of children into the lines which suggest a very different kind of singing—that of Mrs. Porter and her daughter—intensifies it with an ironical pathos. Each remains separate and distinct however. Another passage, this time from 'The Fire Sermon', achieves the same effect:

The river's tent is broken; the last fingers of leaf
Clutch and sink into the wet bank. The wind
Crosses the brown land, unheard. The nymphs are departed.
Sweet Thames, run softly, till I end my song.

The last line here is as unexpected as the second line in the fragment of Pound which we quoted. With the addition of an image in a completely different tone, the movement of the verse shifts direction. The purpose of the image, like the 'Fu I' line, is not to 'debunk' what has gone before but to point up the pathetic contrast that the modern Thames scene makes with the splendid scenes of Spenser's river. It corresponds exactly to Pound's 'one-image' poem where, in true Imagist fashion,

. . . one is trying to record the precise instant when a thing outward and objective transforms itself, or darts into a thing inward and subjective.[2]

Like the Imagist, Eliot is concerned to render his emotions as

[1] *Collected Poems*, pp. 24–5.
[2] Ezra Pound, *Gaudier-Brzeska* (1916), p. 103.

directly as possible, and he will do so best, not by translating them and interpreting them for the reader, but by setting them down with the immediacy in which they occurred to him, like 'planes in relation' in a Cubist painting. It is

. . . harmony in the sentience, harmony of *the sentient* where the thought has its demarcation, the substance its *virtu,* where stupid men have not reduced all 'energy' to unbounded undistinguished abstraction,[1]

which Eliot, along with Pound, is looking for—the 'radiant world'

. . . where one thought cuts through another with a clean edge, a world of moving energies, *mezzo oscuro rade, risplende in so perpetuale effecta,* magnetisms that take form, that are seen, or that border the visible, the matter of Dante's *paradiso* . . .[2]

Having found the data by which to articulate and present his emotional complex, he does not proceed to deduce a general statement from them. He does not instruct the reader what to feel by drawing conclusions about them himself, but rather directs him in the way in which he may come to his own conclusions. Allan Gilbert makes much the same point about Dante's *Divine Comedy.* In Dante's search for spiritual liberty, Gilbert says, he does not interpret the events which present the chief character's change from fear and the 'wearied vigour'. The passage continues:

The poet assumes that to present the evidence is enough; a man of sense cannot but draw the right conclusions. So in his journey the traveller is to see . . . such opportunity for seeing is all that is required to establish in the observer's mind confidence in divine justice and love.[3]

Eliot's structure is far from being observations within the strict Christian scaffold which is Dante's *Comedy.* Nevertheless, Gilbert's analysis of Dante's structure offers analogous comment on Eliot's. Tiresias, like Dante's observer in the *Purgatorio,* 'sees' enacted before him scenes, in which he takes no part himself:

[1] Ezra Pound, 'Mediaevalism', quoted by Hugh Kenner, op. cit., p. 236.
[2] ibid., p. 237.
[3] Allan Gilbert, *Dante and his Comedy* (1964), pp. 21-2.

. . . we do not say 'Dante the visitor did something' so much as 'Dante saw something'.[1]

The observation reads very much like the Tiresias note to 'The Waste Land' which we quoted at the beginning of the chapter. The 'scenes' experienced by Dante's observer are presented in a similar manner to those of 'The Waste Land'. Gilbert points out that the

. . . sequence from one group of saints or sinners to another is slight. One interview does not lead to another. Thus the construction of the poem is that of beads on a string, each bead distinct.[2]

A narrative or discursive progression is not necessary in such a structure as this, if the connotations of the data are clear enough. As Kenner writes again, quoting from Eisenstein:

The plot is no more than a device without which one isn't yet capable of telling something to the spectator![3]

The progression of 'The Waste Land' is thus comparable to the series production of the modern cinema. We noted this in 'Preludes' and pointed out how scene was added to scene in the first three sections, as the camera moved along the street and into the room, until the poetic 'statement' was completed in the final Prelude. 'The Waste Land' similarly strives after a cinematic statement by a continuous assembling of fragments or 'urges', to borrow the term used for it in the film form, until at the end, the emotional complex which the poem presents is generated. One feels the 'sameness' of each urge. At the beginning of each section the poet appears to begin again, to offer a new articulation of the same emotion, so that each fragment seems a restatement, and the whole a continuous succession of them. Examined in detail, however, we realize that, although each section is a fresh definition of the same emotion, something new is added in each, as Eliot probes more and more deeply into the emotional complex, seeking to define it in more and more accurate images, and presenting it in its connotative fullness. Gertrude Stein defines this cinematic technique when she describes the method of her early stories, which were

[1] Allan Gilbert, *Dante and his Comedy* (1964), pp. 21–2.
[2] ibid.        [3] Hugh Kenner, op. cit., p. 262.

. . . made up of succession and each moment having its own emphasis that is its own difference and so there was the moving and the existence . . .[1]

A detailed analysis of the structure is not necessary here, but a brief look at the general cinematic 'movement' of the poem will indicate something of the 'sameness' and 'emphasis' of each section.

We defined the general emotional complex of the poem as being the aggregate of emotions felt by individuals in isolation, resulting from their particular consciousness of 'temps clos'. The past bears down like a burden, the present a suffocating fear, the future impossible to contemplate. The result is a kind of panic-stricken 'madness' from which articulation begins. Each persona, locked within himself, indicates, by his articulation of this consciousness of time or the 'action' in which we find him, a lack of sympathy, love, control or sacrifice. In 'Burial of the Dead' the camera introduces all aspects of this emotional complex. The scene is presented, a dried-up modern waste land which assumes the dimension of the wilderness of all the prophets. All forms of fear are articulated, fear in consciousness of the past in the Stetson passage, fear of the future in Madame Sosostris and that fear in the present moment which leads to the separateness of the assembled individuals in the crowd, so stifled by the fog that

Sighs, short and infrequent, were exhaled,
And each man fixed his eyes before his feet.

Historical dimension is given to the same emotion in the fragment of Tristan, who is by implication in the same circumstance, looking out over a waste sea, aware that Isolde will never come, and yet powerless to do anything about it. All humanity shares the condition, even the reader is implicated:

'You! hypocrite lecteur!—mon semblable,—mon frère!'

The next three sections provide, in fragments articulating the same emotion, their own special 'emphasis'. Lack of sympathy and love for the lady and Albert's wife are presented in 'A Game of Chess', which moves on towards the isolation of

1 Gertrude Stein, *The Making of Americans*, quoted by Wylie Sypher, op. cit., p. 267.

Ophelia whose tortured madness led finally to her 'selfish' act of self-destruction, which connotes no sacrifice. 'The Fire Sermon' provides a rhapsodic-type structure of the same emotions, but emphasizes recurrent action of a mechanical, ritual nature, which indicates humanity out of control. Eugenides, the typist and the Thames daughters all provide images which suggest stagnation in this ritual recurrence of meaningless activity. While Elizabeth and Leicester mark refreshing contrast, at the same time their activities on the Thames connote an ironic similarity. In this fragment we are shown briefly an image of invigorating, fresh wind which contrasts with the sluggish movement of the modern river:

> The brisk swell
> Rippled both shores
> Southwest wind

These lines, along with the clean, clear lines suggesting the white splendour of Magnus Martyr, the singing of children and the final image—

> The boat responded
> Gaily, to the hand expert with sail and oar
> The sea was calm, your heart would have responded
> Gaily, when invited, beating obedient
> To controlling hands

—only serve to intensify the images of stagnation which characterize the rest of the poem, defining the inactivity and claustrophobic conditions in which the personae find themselves. They correspond to the image of the mermaids in 'Prufrock'— moments of 'vital energy' which are lacking in the lives of the articulating personae. In 'Death by Water', cyclic or ritual activity is connoted in the image of the wheel. Isolation and fear which result in a similar act of self-destruction to that of Ophelia, are given emphasis. Over-indulgence in selfish commercialism brings about a feeling of suffocation which once again takes on associations of drowning. The drowning of Phlebas, like that of Ophelia, connotes no sacrifice, only waste and death as the final terms.

In 'What the Thunder Said', the images of the previous sections are assembled in a patterned, surrealist collage. Emotions are 'worked up' into a final design which completes the poem. Emotions which result in the self becoming a 'stranger to the world of living creatures', 'lost in a desert among unfamiliar silent things', generate surrealist-type images of the woman drawing out her long black hair, bats with baby faces, voices suffocating in 'empty cisterns' and 'exhausted wells'. The implications of the last lines with their complex references to Kyd, Dante, the myth of Philomel and Nerval, indicate, however, that it is only from this final point, this extreme conscious-ness of motionless time, that a vision of peace will emerge. Selfish isolation may lead to the selfish act from which more meaningful community life will emerge:

> Shall I at least set my lands in order?

Madness, like that of Hieronimo, may bring its own useful prophecy. For the moment all is silent, however. Tiresias only observes. He 'sees', but seeing connotes no active participation in the events of the poem. No hope of prophecy is expressed. Part V, therefore, does not indicate a climax in any dramatic or narrative sense—unless it be that of clearer definition in the assembled poetic statement or the completion of a 'vortex of perception'.

The cinematic technique of the poem is an obvious advance on that of 'Preludes', however. There the images that added up to the concatenation were images taken from the present. The camera did not move out of the present context. In 'The Waste Land', the camera moves out of time and brings into contempor-ary focus images from the past, to illuminate, from another angle, the poet's images from the present. It is the multi-dimensional vision arising from such complex juxtaposition of past and present that Eliot calls the 'mythical method'. The passage in which he describes Joyce's use of it in *Ulysses* is well known:

. . . In using myth, in manipulating a continuous parallel between contemporaneity and antiquity, Mr. Joyce is pursuing a method which others must pursue after him . . . It is simply a way of controlling, of ordering, of giving a shape and a significance to the immense panorama of futility and anarchy which is contemporary history . . .[1]

[1] T. S. Eliot, Review of *Ulysses, Dial*, November 1923.

Joyce, like Eliot, is making a continuous, simultaneous confrontation of past and present, by drawing images from the past into the present with the immediacy of film presentation, to give us an impression of the various facets of time-consciousness. The mythical method has an important technical function; it points out a 'constant' value in all Eliot's images.

Much has been written about Eliot's use of myth, but we must turn our attention to it in making concluding comment on the poem. The mythical method is, for Eliot, something distinct from narrative, as we see from the review of *Ulysses* from which we have just quoted:

> Psychology (such as it is and whether our reaction to it be comic or serious), ethnology, and 'The Golden Bough' have concurred to make possible what was impossible even a few years ago. Instead of narrative method we may now use mythical method.[1]

His use of myth is not the use of a controlling story form, but a system of symbol, and a way of bringing his fragments together into an ordered structure. George Dekker, in discussing Pound's use of myth and metamorphosis, uses a definition of myth by Denis de Rougemont on which to base his comments:

> Speaking generally, a myth is a story—a symbolic fable as simple as it is striking—which sums up an infinite number of more or less analogous situations. A myth makes it possible to become aware at a glance of certain types of *constant* relations and to disengage these from the welter of everyday appearances.[2]

This 'constant' or recurring value is what Pound calls 'rhythmic accord'.[3] It is the common connotations which the fragments share with one another, and which are linked with analagous images in myth, that form the 'convenientia' of 'The Waste Land'. Genesius Jones's definition of the connotative structure is a useful one:

> . . . the symbols come together because each one is needed to build up the particular pattern of evocation required. The *convenientia* determines whether the final pattern is adequate to the state of affairs; and

---

[1] T. S. Eliot, Review of *Ulysses*, *Dial*, November 1923.
[2] Denis de Rougemont, *Passion and Society* (1956), p. 18, quoted by George Dekker, *Sailing After Knowledge* (1963), p. 63.
[3] Ezra Pound, *Cavalcanti* preface, p. 12, quoted by Hugh Kenner, op. cit., p. 279.

itself can be declared upon only if the symbols have a delimited symbolic connotation. It is the task of the poet so to fix the connotation that there may be no missing the evocation.[1]

Where the fragments are linked together so that one can see the constant value in each, the 'convenientia' is adequate to the structure. When fragments are not intensified by connotation, are not linked together in the world of association, then they remain isolated and the result is simply an amalgam of fragments. *The Cantos* of Pound which are least successful are those in which his concern for exact language and his guarding of the separateness of each fragment are carried to the extreme that one cannot see the interrelatedness of the various parts. We remember Warren Ramsey's comment that the Cantos which fail will be those

. . . in which Pound fails to rise from the particular to the general, those in which he follows most faithfully his so-called 'ideographic' or Chinese picture-writing method of heaping disconnected particulars together.[2]

Warren Ramsey considers the best Cantos are those early poems which relate to a mythical 'convenientia', where the language does not 'stay on the page',[3] as Alvarez describes it, but directs us to some general, but defined, field of association. In praising the early Cantos, the mythical Cantos, Warren Ramsey writes:

In a kind of poetry wherein literary reference is of the process, as he would say, in which knowledge on the reader's part is essential to the understanding, Pound has passed from the particular to the ordering universal.[4]

That is, in the early Cantos, the images have some archetypal pattern.

Elizabeth Drew has made fairly extensive study of Eliot's use of myth, and has described its origin in terms of modern Jungian psychology. The myths which primitive man created were a

---

[1] Genesius Jones, *Approach to the Purpose* (1964), p. 39, also quoted Chapter III, p. 45.
[2] Warren Ramsey, 'Pound, Laforgue and the Dramatic Structure', *Comparative Literature* (1951), III.
[3] A. Alvarez, op. cit., p. 60.
[4] Warren Ramsey, op. cit.

functioning of his psyche. Archetypal patterns of images in-
habited a psychic territory which Jung called the 'collective
unconscious', which was for him '*un*conscious inherited wisdom
of the race' in the same way that tradition is the *expressed* wisdom
of the race. This, Elizabeth Drew says, accounts not only for
striking analogies between the themes and patterns of myths in
many different countries, but also for 'the presence of recurring
mythological and archaic symbols in dreams, even in the dreams
of those who have no knowledge of the traditional and literary
sources which perpetuate them.[1] It is easy to see how a system
of belief evolves from a common stock of archetypal images,
articulating the constant mythical and religious idea that through
death comes life. Eliot, by relating his images to this common
store—and not confining them to any single manifestation of
belief in Christian or fertility rite—is giving 'meaning' and
import to his images, without necessitating his interpreting and
developing them for the reader in his poetic context. The images
which he uses in 'The Waste Land' are thus given a general
dimension which those of the earlier poetry did not possess. The
image of Prufrock drowning connoted his submersion in the
world of his immediate social surroundings. The image of the
drowning Phlebas in 'The Waste Land' connotes his death by
the commercialism by which he has sought to control his life, but
is also related to the death of a god which brings about life for
men. Against this pattern, Phlebas' death shows no sacrifice, no
regeneration. It is the contribution of each image to basic
mythical symbolism which raises it from the particular to the
general, and which gives the total assembled structure of the
poem shape and significance. For Eliot it represents an important step in his personal as well as his poetic development.
Susanne Langer shares with Elizabeth Drew and indeed all
modern psychologists the belief that myth is the first 'primitive
phase of metaphysical thought, the first embodiment of *general
ideas*'.[2] It represents the same stage in Eliot's poetic development.
From 'The Waste Land' onwards, Eliot incorporates general
ideas in his poetic context. The concrete image can bear no more
universal significance than that given to it in 'The Waste Land'.

[1] Elizabeth Drew, *T. S. Eliot: The Design of his Poetry* (1950), p. 27.
[2] Susanne Langer, *Philosophy in a New Key* (1942), p. 9, quoted by Wimsatt
and Brooks, *A Short History of Literary Criticism* (1957), p. 705.

In his use of the concrete language of myth, by observing around him images which share the archetypal connotations of the images of historical and literary myths, Eliot is creating a new type of modern myth. Kenner, again writing on Pound, points up Eliot's achievement in 'The Waste Land':

'One of the rights of masterwork is the right of rebirth and recurrence.' Here we have the link between 'Make it New', Pound's translating activities, and the sense of historical recurrence that informs the *Cantos*, not a bulldozed 'All this happened before', but a lively sense of forms asserting their immortality in successive material opportunities.[1]

Eliot, in describing Dante's achievement in *The Divine Comedy*, adequately sums up his own in 'The Waste Land'. In 'What Dante means to me', he writes of the poem which he perhaps admired above all others:

*The Divine Comedy* expresses everything in the way of human emotion, between depravity's despair and the beatific vision, that man is capable of experiencing. It is therefore a constant reminder to the poet, of the obligation to explore, to find words for the inarticulate, to capture those feelings which people can hardly even feel because they have no words for them, and at the same time, a reminder that the explorer beyond the frontiers of ordinary consciousness will only be able to return and report to his fellow-citizens, if he has all the time a firm grasp on the realities with which they are acquainted.[2]

In an earlier essay he writes that the *Purgatorio* and *Paradiso*

. . . are to be read as extensions of the ordinarily very limited human range.[3]

'The Waste Land' is Eliot's *Divine Comedy*. In it he attempts to explore everything in the way of emotion 'between depravity's despair and the beatific vision', and to find the language by which to formulate a new, timeless emotion beyond the frontiers of limited human consciousness. The emotions with which he deals in the poem are those 'real' emotions with which we are all acquainted, and those inspired in him from the fragments of literature and myth which he excerpts and includes in his structure. By the assemblage Eliot makes of the fragments which articulate these realities, he creates a new art-emotion

---

[1] Hugh Kenner, op. cit., p. 234.     [2] *To Criticize the Critic*, p. 134.
[3] *Selected Essays*, p. 268.

which has no referent in any single human experience, however, a new art-emotion which arises from the multidimensional, timeless vision of myth, arrested in a single instance of art. 'The Waste Land' has a completeness and a penetration of vision which has no precedent in Eliot's poetry—and no successor.

# VII The final pattern

To conclude a study of the method of T. S. Eliot's poetry at this particular point in his development—to make an arbitrary division between the earlier and later poetry as if there was somehow a sudden difference between the way the poet's mind worked in the earlier years and the later—is to create the wrong impression of the poetry: we are in danger of destroying the *wholeness* of his work. In his criticism of other writers, Eliot has frequently emphasized this wholeness, saying that the entire output of Shakespeare, for example, constitutes a single poem; that there is meaningful connection between one work and another, and that any single work is endowed with added meaning by being considered in relation to the completed context:

. . . what is 'the whole man' is not simply his greatest or maturest achievement, but the whole pattern formed by the sequence of plays; . . . we must know all of Shakespeare's work in order to know any of it.[1]

It is the same emphasis which we should place on Eliot's poetry, and what I have attempted to show in this study is the continuity and development of the themes and method as the poet progressed from one group of poems to another: the pattern as well as the parts. We have examined the 'fragmentary method' of Eliot's composition, the piecemeal mode of 'doing things separately' and then of seeing the possibility of 'making a kind of whole of them'.[2] Just as the assembling of fragments articulating 'ordinary' emotions added up to the complex structure of significant art-emotion, 'minor' poems added together to form major poems so the complete assemblage of the poetry forms another unity. As Kenneth Muir expresses it:

The whole body of Eliot's poetry is greater than the sum of its parts.[3]

[1] 'John Ford' (1932), *Selected Essays* (1951 edition), p. 193.
[2] See Chapter V, p. 94.
[3] Kenneth Muir, 'A Brief Introduction to the Method of Mr. T. S. Eliot', *Durham University Journal*, June 1944, p. 84.

While I do not wish to examine the later poetry in any detail, we cannot ignore the 'wholeness' of the final pattern, and must therefore conclude by attempting a brief examination of how the later poetry develops out of the earlier. We shall see that, although the emotions of the later poetry indicate an advance on those of the earlier, the method of assembling parts to form a whole remains unchanged.[1]

The purpose of this study has been to examine the poetic method of the earlier poetry: how the poet set out to assemble a comprehensive, universal articulation of experience from individual and very particular aspects of it. His first aim as a poet was to improve his medium, to make language more exact for the projection of individual images, and then to raise the 'meaning' of these images to a higher and higher degree by the connotations which they would have within the complex structure which he made of them, as a result of his 'studied selection and artificial arrangement'.[2] Images were charged with associations within the 'formula' which the poet offered as the 'objective correlative' of emotions which he felt, or those of others which could be added to his own to make them more comprehensive. The particularity of the parts was thus transcended in becoming a general or universal instance of art. I examined the ways in which Eliot participated in the experiments which the Imagists and Pound carried out with language for the projection of the concrete Image, and how he saw the possibilities of the Symbolist structure in making a comprehensive poem. The poetry developed from the relatively simple and undramatic vision of 'Preludes' to the dramatic poems presented in personae like 'Prufrock' and 'Gerontion', and then to the final assemblage of concrete images raised to the mythical dimension of 'The Waste Land'. Eliot's purpose throughout was to make words express more and more, to free the 'meaning' of verse from the single statement, and to make the poem inclusive of the greatest possible number of meanings. Ezra Pound defined 'great literature' as

[1] The method of publication testifies to this continuation; various fragmentary poems which appeared in the journals *Chapbook* and *Criterion* over the period 1924–5 were assembled to form 'The Hollow Men', and 'Ash Wednesday' is a similar collage of poems which were composed between 1929 and 1930. See Grover Smith, *T. S. Eliot's Poetry and Plays* (1956), pp. 100, 135.
[2] Coleridge, quoted by D. E. S. Maxwell, *The Poetry of T. S. Eliot* (1960), p. 33.

. . . simply language charged with meaning to the utmost possible degree,[1]

and according to this criterion, 'The Waste Land' and 'Gerontion', by virtue of the number of readings possible for them within the connotative structure, are 'great'. No poem could be more exact in its parts and more general or universal in its meaning than 'Gerontion' or 'The Waste Land'. Having discovered, however, how to perfect the connotative structure, Eliot decided that he was no longer disposed to the 'comprehensive' poem of this sort. In a sense, the experiment of 'The Waste Land' could not be repeated. The only development from the mythical method of ordering experience is towards acceptance of general 'belief'. Cleanth Brooks and William Wimsatt in *A Short History of Literary Criticism* quote Susanne Langer's definition of myth as the first

. . . primitive phase of metaphysical thought, the first embodiment of *general ideas*[2]

and go on:

In due course mythic conception gives way when discursive language has been developed.[3]

In the poetry which follows 'The Waste Land', we find passages which surrender the concreteness of the earlier images and take on the conceptual phrasing of discursive theology. For example, in 'The Hollow Men', we read:

Between the conception
And the creation
Between the emotion
And the response
Falls the Shadow[4]

and in 'Ash Wednesday':

Because I know that time is always time
And place is always and only place
And what is actual is actual only for one time

[1] Ezra Pound, *A.B.C. of Reading* (1961 edition), p. 28.
[2] Susanne Langer, *Philosophy in a New Key*, quoted by Wimsatt and Brooks, *A Short History of Literary Criticism* (1957). p. 705.
[3] ibid.
[4] *Collected Poems* (1963 edition) p. 92.

And only for one place
I rejoice that things are as they are . . .[1]

as well as purely abstract passages in 'The Four Quartets':

What might have been is an abstraction
Remaining a perpetual possibility
Only in a world of speculation.[2]

Nevertheless, we cannot say that these are 'statement' poems
any more than the earlier poems. The abstract language of discourse is not suitable on its own for the articulation of the emotions of the later poetry, even if it is by this time acknowledged
as possible 'argument' in the new equation which the poet is
making of them. The problem for the developing poet is still

. . . the intolerable wrestle
With words and meanings.[3]

In an interview with the poet which Leonard Unger quotes,
Eliot said of his earlier poetry:

I think that in the early poems it was a question of not being able to—
of having more to say than one knew how to say, and having something
one wanted to put into words and rhythm which one didn't have the
command of words and rhythm to put in a way immediately apprehen-
sible.

   That type of obscurity comes when the poet is still at the stage of
learning how to use language. You have to say the thing the difficult
way. The only alternative is not saying it at all, at that stage. By the
time of 'Four Quartets' I couldn't have written in the style of 'The
Waste Land'.[4]

The progress from the earlier poetry to the later marks a desire to
do something different from what the poet was doing in poems
like 'The Waste Land'. If the earlier poetry can be considered, in
the light of this statement, to be the poet's discovery of language,
then the later poetry marks a further period of experimentation
which the poet carries out with the language he has discovered.
Having found 'a proper modern colloquial idiom', 'a period of
musical elaboration'[5] can follow in which the poet is concerned

[1] *Collected Poems* (1963 edition) p. 95.
[2] 'Burnt Norton', ibid., p. 189.
[3] 'East Coker', ibid., p. 198.
[4] Leonard Unger, *T. S. Eliot* (1960), p. 41.
[5] T. S. Eliot, 'The Music of Poetry', *On Poetry and Poets*, (1957), p. 38.

with the uses to which he can put the actual form which he has perfected. This is the natural development of any craftsman. In Eliot the period of 'musical elaboration' indicates the desire to articulate emotions different from those of the earlier poems, for, of course, historically speaking, the period following 'The Waste Land' is characterized by his acceptance of the Christian faith. The problems of the young poet may be solely form and technique, or as Yeats expressed it, to 'sing in a marrowbone'. As the poet grows older, the 'prose part' of life takes on added significance and his artistic talent often dies. With Eliot the 'prose part' is an increasing interest in morality, but as this basically religious apprehension of life grows, his poetry does not die but develops with it. In his comment on Yeats, Eliot expresses well this development of the poet:

> It is my experience that towards middle age a man has three choices: to stop writing altogether, to repeat himself with perhaps an increasing skill of virtuosity, or by taking thought to adapt himself to middle age and find a different way of working. . . . Maturing as a poet means maturing as the whole man, experiencing new emotions appropriate to one's age and with the same intensity as the emotions of youth.[1]

In 'East Coker' he describes the direction which this maturity takes:     .

> Love is most nearly itself
> When here and now cease to matter.
> Old men ought to be explorers
> Here and there does not matter
> We must be still and still moving
> Into another intensity
> For a further union, a deeper communion
> Through the dark cold and the empty desolation,[2]

The new 'intensity' would no longer be that sought for in life itself, but discovered in the meaning of life. Poetic style should not be solely directed towards the articulation of experience, but must seek ways of finding the significance of that experience; a style which would represent 'further union', not of language with the 'objects' of the real world, but a 'deeper communion' with the 'still point',[3] the centre in which all experience is resolved into

[1] Quoted by Elizabeth Drew, *T. S. Eliot, The Design of his Poetry*, (1950), pp. 240–1.
[2] *Collected Poems*, pp. 203–4.     [3] 'Burnt Norton', ibid., p. 191.

meaning. This shift in emphasis to the newly-directed focus of attention on the 'still point' is the mark of maturity in any individual, which, as Elizabeth Drew indicates, is called by Jung 'the process of individuation' or 'the integration of personality'. Elizabeth Drew, who concentrates on these pyschological aspects of the poet's development, writes of Jung's definition:

It is the experience of detachment from the world of objective reality as the centre of existence and the finding of 'a new dimension' in which it can and must be contemplated and lived.[1]

This higher form of reality is not the world itself but the new dimensions of Heaven and damnation, the 'still point' around which the 'turning world' revolves. While the earlier poetry was mainly concerned with finding the language to express the 'turning world', the later poetry seeks means for expressing the 'still point'. Images of the 'turning world' are still present, many apprehended in the same form as we found them in the earlier poems. Modern life is still seen as

> Tumid apathy with no concentration
> Men and bits of paper, whirled by the cold wind[2]

Image after image suggest the same apathetic condition expressed in all the poems from 'Preludes' to 'The Waste Land'. In the later poetry, however, as D. E. S. Maxwell points out:

Urban imagery ceases to be a predominant factor, and its place is taken by a revised symbolism.[3]

This is the poetry of Eliot's 'high dream'[4] as he called the poetry of Dante. In it the 'object' appears to be abandoned and the poet approaches a new form of expressionism, in that he attempts less and less to depend on the recording of actual experience for his poetic articulation. In the previous chapters, I have made frequent comparison between Eliot's early method and the methods of modern painting; the later method more nearly approaches musical form, the most essentially non-figurative art. In 1933, Eliot said in an unpublished lecture on D. H. Lawrence that he sought

1 Elizabeth Drew, op. cit., p. 31.
2 'Burnt Norton', *Collected Poems*, p. 193.
3 D. E. S. Maxwell, op. cit., p. 119.
4 'Dante', (1929), *Selected Essays*, p. 262.

. . . to write poetry which should be essentially poetry, with nothing poetic about it, poetry standing naked in its bare bones, or poetry so transparent that we should not see the poetry, but that which we are meant to see through the poetry, poetry so transparent that in reading it we are intent on what the poem *points at*, and not on the poetry . . .[1]

It is interesting to note in passing, however, the same tendency in art, a movement away from the concrete forms of Cubism and collage towards the abstract art of Mondrian,who wrote of his aim to unburden painting

. . . from the tragic content of material and individual things; thus it becomes the purest expression of the universal.[2]

We emphasized in Chapter III that Eliot's early interest in the French Symbolist movement was concentrated on its technical aspects. As his poetry develops, he seems to draw closer and closer to its aesthetic aim to express the ineffable. Kristian Smidt has made much the same point:

His view of life as unreal and of a transcendent existence as real owes a a great deal to the symbolists as well as to more purely philosophical sources. For Symbolism, though to a large extent a matter of form and technique, was essentially a search for mystic reality behind physical manifestations.[3]

He goes on to quote Arthur Symons's comment in *The Symbolist Movement*, that

. . . the literature of which I write in this volume [is] a literature in which the visible world is no longer a reality, and the unseen world no longer a dream.[4]

In a sense the wheel has come full circle. We find Eliot now stating, in terms reminiscent of poets like Mallarmé and Rimbaud, that 'consciousness' is awareness of another reality. As he puts it in 'Burnt Norton':

To be conscious is not to be in time[5]

[1] Unpublished lecture on 'English Letter Writers', New Haven, Connecticut, (1933), quoted by F. O. Matthiessen, *The Achievement of T. S. Eliot* (1959 edition), p. 90.
[2] Quoted by Wylie Sypher, *From Rococo to Cubism in Art and Literature* (1960), p. 317.
[3] Kristian Smidt, *Poetry and Belief in the Work of T. S. Eliot* (1961), p. 153.
[4] ibid.    [5] *Collected Poems*, p. 192.

At the same time, however, he goes on to say that

Only through time is time conquered.

In other words, Eliot realizes that it is only by analogy with the objects of time that poetry can attempt expression of a higher reality. Language must not come too close to the particular, however, for to come too close is to realize the ultimate unsuitability of the things of time and space to express the 'high dream'. As he puts it in another context, in the image of the dancing men and women round the bonfire in 'East Coker':

If you do not come too close, if you do not come too close,
On a summer midnight, you can hear the music[1]

To 'come too close' is to discover the impermanence of moments of sudden illumination—here expressed in the meaningful rhythmical movement of dancing and music. The dancing feet are only:

Feet rising and falling.
Eating and drinking. Dung and death.[2]

As pure Symbolist poetry had to rely on personal symbols from the world of imagination for the articulation of the Absolute, so now we find in Eliot a predominance of personal symbols in his revised symbolism. The efficacy of such symbols in the Symbolist structure depended, however, as we discovered, on their 'convenientia',[3] the way in which the poet 'fixed' their connotations within the scaffold of the poem. If they did not have any 'constant' value, then they would fail to evoke anything; if they were not placed in some 'external framework', the poem became 'a constellation of images astronomically distant, nearly invisible to the naked eye'.[4] Apart from the symbols of 'Ash Wednesday' whose connotations are fixed by their Biblical reference, the personal symbols of the later poetry avoid this obscurity as a result of their having been carefully 'worked up' from concrete images of the earlier poems, so that their 'constants' are the accumulated meanings which they have gathered throughout the poetry. Since Eliot is aware that consciousness of a 'higher reality' can only be apprehended through time, but at the same time must be at some remove from it, he attempts to resolve the

1 *Collected Poems*, p. 196.          2 ibid., p. 197.
3 See Chapter III, p. 45.               4 ibid., p. 47.

impossible struggle between words and meanings by 'trans-
forming' the images of the earlier poetry to become the new
symbolic centre of the later. As he wrote in 'The Dry Salvages':

> We had the experience but missed the meaning,
> And approach to the meaning restores the experience
> In a different form, . . .[1]

The later poetry attempts to 'restore the experience' of the
earlier in a different form.

Much has been written about the recurring themes and images
of Eliot's poetry, enough to illustrate the point which I am
making here to require no detailed re-examination of them. A
few examples will suffice. Let us look at a well-known passage
from 'East Coker';

> Whisper of running streams, and winter lightning.
> The wild thyme unseen and the wild strawberry,
> The laughter in the garden, echoed ecstasy
> Not lost, but requiring, pointing to the agony
> Of death and birth.[2]

The aim of the passage is to evoke a higher reality in images
which suggest release from the world of temporal things. The
effect depends on five personal symbols: running water, light,
garden and laughter, along with the cycle of the seasons. The
effect will be missed if we do not see how the connotations of
these symbols have been worked up from their use in the earlier
poems. The fresh-flowing stream of this passage was originally
the water of the gutter of 'Preludes' and 'Rhapsody on a Windy
Night', and the 'peevish gutter' of 'Gerontion'. It became the
'burning canal' of 'Burbank with a Baedeker' and the rat-
infested water of the River Thames in 'The Waste Land'. The
connotations of this unmoving water were uniformly sordid; by
its filth and stagnation, it suggested the inert and sluggish lives
of those who lived around it. From there it became 'the strong
brown god' of 'The Dry Salvages' whose 'sullen, untamed and
intractable' movement suggested the stubborn will of man himself. The associations of the image in the 'East Coker' passage
are obviously similar to the 'running stream' in 'Journey of the
Magi', which indicated the arrival of the Magi at the temperate

[1] *Collected Poems*, p. 208.     [2] ibid., p. 201.

valley where the Birth took place. In 'East Coker', however, it is
emptied of its specifically Christian connotation, and its value as
a symbol of spiritual release depends on our being aware of the
sordid connotations which its counterparts had in the earlier
poetry. 'Laughter' has been similarly worked up from the
cynical laugh at the end of 'Preludes' and the indifferent smile of
the visitor in 'Portrait of a Lady':

> I feel like one who smiles, and turning shall remark
> Suddenly, his expression in a glass.[1]

It becomes the irresponsible laughter of Mr Apollinax, the
debauched laughter of Apeneck Sweeney, and then the innocent
laughter of children in 'Burnt Norton':

> There rises the hidden laughter
> Of children in the foliage
> Quick now, here, now, always—[2]

The fresh, unseen scent of wild thyme in the garden has for its
connotative background the 'smells of steaks in passage ways' of
'Preludes',[3] the 'female smells in shuttered rooms',[4] the 'perfume
from a dress',[5] and then the 'strange synthetic perfumes' of 'The
Waste Land'.[6] The garden itself is a symbol which has developed
out of the smoky window boxes connoted by the dead geraniums
and the rich associations of the 'hyacinth garden'. 'Winter
lightning' is a combination of the cyclical symbolism of the
seasons along with the symbol of light. The light of the earlier
poetry was of a winter dawn, yellow, smoky and grey, and the
moonlight of 'Rhapsody on a Windy Night'. It becomes the
'twilight' of 'The Hollow Men' and then the sudden illumination
of 'the shaft of sunlight' in 'Burnt Norton'.[7] In the passage from
'East Coker', it is associated with winter, the season of death and
burial, the season necessary for the spring of new life. Only
when we are aware of the unpleasant associations which each
symbol had in the earlier poetry, can we realize its force in the
new context of 'birth and death' in which Eliot places them.

Only when we are aware of the complete 'convenientia' can
we appreciate the connotations of each symbol when it is finally
abstracted from the concrete to articulate the 'still point'. At the

[1] *Collected Poems*, p. 21.   [2] ibid., p. 195.
[3] ibid., p. 23.   [4] 'Rhapsody' ibid., p. 28.
[5] 'Prufrock', ibid., p. 15.   [6] ibid., p. 66.   [7] ibid., p. 195.

source of the motionless water of the early poems and the running streams which connote more meaningful movement, is the
perfect stillness of the pool in 'Burnt Norton', where all the
infernal rivers of man's life are transformed and given meaning:

> And the pool was filled with water out of sunlight,
> And the lotos rose, quietly, quietly,
> The surface glittered out of heart of light,[1]

Light itself has become motionless and still:

> . . . After the kingfisher's wing
> Has answered light to light, and is silent, the light is still
> At the still point of the turning world.[2]

The smells become abstracted in the vision of 'Little Gidding':

> . . . There is no earth smell
> Or smell of living thing. This is the spring time
> But not in time's covenant. Now the hedgerow
> Is blanched for an hour with transitory blossom
> Of snow, a bloom more sudden
> Than that of summer, neither budding nor fading,
> Not in the scheme of generation.[3]

The 'action' images which connoted no action in the earlier
poems, and therefore meaningless existence, become images of
movement towards something, images of travelling and the
sudden rhythmical movement of the 'daunsinge'[4] in 'East Coker'.
They are finally transformed into the dance which is 'neither
arrest nor movement'[5] in 'Burnt Norton'. This passage from
'Burnt Norton' lets us see the revised symbolism in its final,
abstract form:

> The release from action and suffering, release from the inner
> And the outer compulsion, yet surrounded
> By a grace of sense, a white light still and moving,
> *Erhebung* without motion, concentration
> Without elimination, both a new world
> And the old made explicit, understood
> In the completion of its partial ecstasy,
> The resolution of its partial horror.[6]

The earlier poetry thus forms the 'convenientia' for the personal

[1] ibid., p. 190.   [2] ibid., p. 194.   [3] ibid., p. 214.   [4] ibid., p. 197.
[5] ibid., p. 191.   [6] ibid., pp. 191–2.

symbolism of the later. Because of the concreteness of the earlier images and the exact 'convenientia' which they form, the poet is able to render the abstract forms which they take in the later poetry meaningful for the apprehension of the Absolute. As I have attempted to show in the few examples which I examined, the images and symbols of the later poetry have been carefully and systematically transformed from the world of experience which was their 'subject' in the earlier poetry. They are removed from it, however, since they have no particular referent in the world as we know it. Elizabeth Drew sums up the nature of Eliot's revised symbolism in these words:

> The still point can be approached only through paradox and negation. It is nothing that can be measured in terms of time, or of movement and fixity, of body or spirit, of ascent and descent. And yet it cannot be detached from these things because though it is the point where there is no movement, it controls all the movement, and it is only through the measured movements that its presence can be known. It exists, but cannot be captured in a *Where* or *When*.[1]

The later poetry can therefore be seen in technical terms as the attempt in poetic form to

>                    Redeem
>      The time. Redeem
>      The unread vision in the higher dream[2]

The objects of memory are no longer 'useless', like the memories which result from the madman's shaking of a dead geranium in 'Rhapsody on a Windy Night'. The purpose of

>      Disturbing the dust on a bowl of rose-leaves[3]

is no longer simply to illuminate the actual moment of experience of life, but to point to that moment which is

>      The point of interesection of the timeless
>      With time,[4]

the religious apprehension of man's timeless existence, which is in time and yet beyond it.

The method of putting these newly-apprehended symbols

---

[1] Elizabeth Drew, op. cit., pp. 190–1.
[2] 'Ash Wednesday', *Collected Poems*, p. 100.
[3] 'Burnt Norton', ibid., p. 189.
[4] 'The Dry Salvages', ibid., p. 212.

together is basically unchanged, however. We cannot say that the apprehension of the 'still point', the 'higher reality', or the 'high dream' is rationalized into any dogmatic statement of Christian belief, although it is true, none the less, that the poetry becomes more specifically Christian in connotation as it progresses. Apart from 'Marina' and 'Burnt Norton,' all the poems from 'The Waste Land' onwards can be referred to some part of Christian teaching. 'East Coker' has its references to the 'wounded surgeon', 'The Dry Salvages' refers to the Annunciation, and 'Little Gidding' to the Baptism and the feast of Pentecost. All may be specifically Christian in connotation, yet there is no attempt on the part of the poet to provide a statement 'answer' to the progression of images which he provides in the later poems. The passages of analytical exploration are simply a newly-admitted way of 'approaching the meaning'. They in no way *substitute* the method of direct sensuous apprehension. As Elizabeth Drew writes:

The approach by way of analytical exploration, and the direct intuitive revelation through symbol alternate throughout, merge into one another by subtle transitions and become one in the total rhythmical structure.[1]

What we therefore have in the later poetry are the concrete images of the early poetry restored in the effort to 'redeem the time', having as their origin the actual experiences of life, but 'transformed' as in a dream to something 'higher' in the form in which they are now apprehended. Along with them we have passages of philosophical speculation. like the opening of 'Burnt Norton', which do not form the statement of the poem for which the passages of concrete image and symbol are illustrative, but rather function along with 'objects, situations, chains of events' in the final 'objective correlative' by which the 'still point', the Absolute, is pointed out. Eliot himself, writing of Dante, illustrates his own intention in the later poems very well:

The insistence throughout is upon states of feeling; the reasoning takes only its proper place as a means of reaching these states.[2]

The poetry does not say 'This is the Truth as I see it', or 'This

1 Elizabeth Drew, op. cit., p. 179.
2 'Dante' (1929), *Selected Essays*, p. 266.

is what I believe'. It is not an attempt to make us believe something, but marks the poet's preoccupation

. . . with establishing from among the illusions, evanescences and unrealities of life in time an apprehension of an assured reality—a reality that, though necessarily apprehended in time, is not of it.[1]

The reality with which the later poetry deals is the actuality of believing; it is the poet's aim to find through the medium of his verse a way of expressing what it feels like to believe.

Since the aim is not to make a statement of belief, there is no need to alter the early method of assembling the parts to form the whole. The same fragmentary-type progression forms a meditation on the 'still point'. The method of meditation, according to the great religious teachers like St John of the Cross or Loyala, is not the method of discursive logic, but rather a means whereby the mind ponders the associations of words like 'Father', 'Heaven', 'Love'—words which are the common currency of Christian teaching. Roger Shattuck, in *The Banquet Years*, defines this kind of meditation as it is described by Loyola in *Spiritual Exercises*:[2]

Loyola's means of raising one's mind to God relies not at all on logic but on a methodical alternation of attention between the degradation of man and the holiness of the Almighty. It is designed to release the mind into a state of spiritual suggestion, a free association of ideas and symbols leading to divine knowledge.

In 'Burnt Norton', Eliot himself refers to the method of St John of the Cross, whose religious contemplation was represented in 'the figure of the ten stairs', which, as Elizabeth Drew points out, 'the soul is ascending and descending continually in ecstasy and humiliation until it has acquired perfect habits.'[3] This new 'circling of the object' has been summarized for us by Helen Gardner, writing of 'Ash Wednesday', as

. . . less a progress of thought than a circling round, and the centre around which this meditative poetry revolves is not an idea or an experience so much as a certain state of mind which is aspired to . . . The subject is an aspiration to a state which can only be suggested, by

---

[1] F. R. Leavis, 'T. S. Eliot's Later Poetry', *Twentieth Century Views*, (1962), p. 111.
[2] Roger Shattuck, *The Banquet Years* (1959), p. 31.
[3] Elizabeth Drew, op. cit., p. 197.

experiences drawn from dreams, or by the figures of the Lady and the veiled sister, types of the blessed soul.[1]

Just as the artist in the world of objects was limited by the bounds of his physical perception to a single view of them, and attempted to transcend this limitation in his art form by assembling fragmentary views of his object to give a fuller, more comprehensive view of it, so Eliot attempts a similar 'collage' of a 'higher reality', which human kind is prevented from experiencing in full. Such 'reality', he states in 'Burnt Norton', can only be experienced in moments; for man, by his very nature, is 'protected' from a complete realization of it:

> Yet the enchainment of past and future
> Woven in the weakness of the changing body,
> Protects mankind from heaven and damnation
> Which flesh cannot endure.[2]

The later poetry marks Eliot's attempt to perfect a poetical means by which we can apprehend this reality; it indicates a new comprehensive vision. In his essay on Andrew Marvell, Eliot praises the comprehensive art of the Elizabethan and Jacobean poets, which resulted from their 'firm grasp of human experience'.[3] He goes on:

This wisdom, cynical perhaps, but untired . . . leads toward, and is only completed by, the religious comprehension.

No comment can better sum up Eliot's own development from one form of artistic comprehension to another.

I have attempted to show how the later poetical technique develops and continues the earlier method, without denying it. It is only by stressing the 'completion' of the earlier method in the later that we see the irrelevance of comparing the earlier and the later poetry with the aim of evaluating the 'better'. D. S. Savage seems to miss this point by claiming that the poet's mind works less 'poetically' by working less concretely in the later poems:

But where the world of the early poems carries real and intense conviction, the atmosphere of the later verse, because of its intellectual

---

1 Helen Gardner, *The Art of T. S. Eliot,* (1961), p. 114.
2 *Collected Poems,* p. 192.
3 *Selected Essays,* p. 297.

rather than sensuous nature, fails to impose its reality sharply and
definitely upon the reader's perceptions.[1]

When one appreciates how concrete presentation of the actual
experience of life is worked up into a pattern whose function is of
a different intensity from the earlier, one sees, not the poetical
failure of the later poetry as compared with the earlier, but a
realization of a completion in it. A higher reality as subject
matter for poetry does not necessarily make for a higher form of
art, and the critics, like Helen Gardner, who prefer the later
poetry, are generally prejudiced by its religious connotations
rather than impressed by its poetic form, which, as we see it, is
essentially the same as that of the earlier poems.

The value of any experiment in art, as F. O. Matthiessen
wrote,

. . . lies in the length to which it is carried, whether it is merely the
by-product of erratic or undisciplined fancy, or whether it has built up
into a completed masterwork.[2]

The 'masterwork' in Eliot is not a single poem or even a single
group of poems—it is the complete pattern of poetic achievement
in the total assemblage of the parts which make it up: each poem
is made possible by the experiment of the others. In this vast
design, the 'masterwork' is the 'complete consort dancing
together'.[3] The complete poems form an exploration of experience, from the minute-by-minute experiences of human life as it is
actually felt and lived, to the final experience of apprehending
God. The later poetry throws the earlier into another perspective, which is why a critic like Genesius Jones can give a
specifically religious reading to all of the poems and point out
the way they develop in a Christian context. All that I wish to
emphasize in conclusion is the continued efficacy of the earlier
method for the later poetry—which seems to indicate the value
of Eliot's early artistic experiment and thereby justifies it.

The total experience of life is material for the man, who is,
before he is anything else, a poet. Throughout his career as an
artist, Eliot has been consistently concerned, above all else, with
the art of writing. His constant aim has been to find 'the perfect

[1] D. S. Savage, *The Personal Principle: Studies in Modern Poetry* (1944), pp. 96–7.
[2] F. O. Matthiessen, *The Achievement of T. S. Eliot*, p. 135.
[3] 'Little Gidding', *Collected Poems*, p. 221.

order of speech'[1] by which human experience can be recreated into
the new life, the new form of art. This urge to create is best
described by him in Choruses from 'The Rock':

> Out of the meaningless practical shapes of all that is living or life-
> less
> Joined with the artist's eye, new life, new form, new colour.
> Out of the sea of sound the life of music,
> Out of the slimy mud of words, out of the sleet and hail of verbal
> imprecisions,
> Approximate thoughts and feelings, words that have taken the
> place of thoughts and feelings,
> There spring the perfect order of speech, and the beauty of incanta-
> tion.

If his poetry marks, as Donald Davie points out, 'the end of an
era',[2] it is simply because the language which the poet has
perfected has been temporarily purged by the use which he
himself had made of it and therefore defies further use or
imitation.

In the complete consort of poems he has given us, we are
invited to share, not the opinions of the artist, but the art-form,
the poem, which is a process of exploration, an effort to circle the
object which is its focus, and return to the starting point with a
fuller comprehension of it. Art of this kind draws no conclusions
on its subject. Arrival at the fuller comprehension can only be
experienced in the poetic method of apprehending it and cannot
be separated from it. If it is the achievement of the earlier
poetry to have made the modern world possible for art, then the
final pattern, by its exploration into the meaning of experience
in that world, brings us back to it, 'the point of departure', and
makes us see it anew, as if for the first time:

> We shall not cease from exploration
> And the end of all our exploring
> Will be to arrive where we started
> And know the place for the first time.[3]

[1] Choruses from 'The Rock', No. IX, *Collected Poems*, pp. 181–2.
[2] Donald Davie, 'T. S. Eliot: The End of an Era', *The Twentieth Century* CLIX,
No. 950, April 1956, pp. 350–62.
[3] 'Little Gidding', *Collected Poems*, p. 222.

# Bibliography

PRIMARY SOURCES

*Works of T. S. Eliot*

(a) *Poetry and plays:*
*Collected Poems*, 1909–1962, Faber, 1963.
*Collected Plays*, Faber, 1962.

(b) *Prose works:*
*The Sacred Wood* (first published 1920), Methuen, 1950.
*Selected Essays* (first published 1932), Faber, 1951.
*The Use of Poetry and the Use of Criticism*, Faber, 1933.
*On Poetry and Poets*, Faber, 1957.
*Knowledge and Experience in the Work of F. H. Bradley*, Faber, 1964.
*To Criticize the Critic*, Faber, 1965.

(c) *Articles contributed to periodicals:*
'A Sceptical Patrician' *The Athenaeum*, 23 May, 1914.
'The Method of Mr. Pound', *The Athenaeum*, 24 October, 1919.
'London Letter', *Dial*, November 1923.
'Note sur Mallarmé et Poe', *Nouvelle Revue Française*, November,1926.
'The Poetry of Jules Laforgue', *Scrutiny*, September 1936.
Commentary (on Imagism), *Criterion*, July 1937.
'That Poetry is made with words', *New English Weekly* XV, No. 2, 27 April, 1939.
Ezra Pound, *Poetry* LXVII, September 1946.

*Critical and interpretative studies*

(a) *Collections of essays:*
*T. S. Eliot: A Collection of Critical Essays by Several Hands*, (ed. B. Rajan), Dennis Dobson, 1947.
*T. S. Eliot: A Collection of Critical Essays* (ed. H. Kenner), Spectrum, Prentice-Hall, Englewood Cliffs, N. J., 1962.
*T. S. Eliot: The Man and His Work* (ed. Allen Tate), Chatto & Windus, 1967.

(b) *Books:*
R. Aldington, *Ezra Pound and T. S. Eliot*, The Peacock Press, 1954.
Elizabeth Drew, *T. S. Eliot: The Design of his Poetry*, Eyre & Spottiswoode, 1950.
Helen Gardner, *The Art of T. S. Eliot* (first published 1949), fifth impression, Crescent Press, London, 1961.

E. J. H. Greene, *T. S. Eliot et la France*, Paris, Boivin, 1951.
Philip R. Headings, *T. S. Eliot*, Grosset & Dunlap, New York, 1964.
Herbert Howarth, *Notes on some Figures behind T. S. Eliot*, Chatto & Windus, 1965.
Genesius Jones, *Approach to the Purpose*, Hodder & Stoughton, 1964.
Hugh Kenner, *T. S. Eliot: The Invisible Poet*, (first published U.S.A. 1959), W. H. Allen (London), 1960.
Robert E. Knoll, *Storm over the Waste Land*, Scott, Foresman & Company, Chicago, 1964.
F. O. Matthiessen, *The Achievement of T. S. Eliot* (first published 1935), O.U.P., London, 1959 edition.
D. E. S. Maxwell, *The Poetry of T. S. Eliot*, Routledge & Kegan Paul, 1952.
Kristian Smidt, *Poetry and Belief in the Work of T. S. Eliot*, Routledge & Kegan Paul, 1961.
Grover Smith, *T. S. Eliot's Poetry and Plays*, University of Chicago Press, 1956.
Leonard Unger, *T. S. Eliot*, University of Minnesota Pamphlets, No. 8, 1961.
George Williamson, *A Reader's Guide to T. S. Eliot*, (first published G. B. 1955), Thames & Hudson, 1962.

(c) *Articles in periodicals:*
Eugene Arden, 'T. S. Eliot and Dante', *Notes and Queries*, August 1958.
D. Brosley Brotman, 'T. S. Eliot, the Music of Ideas', *University of Toronto Quarterly*, October 1948.
Donald Davie, 'T. S. Eliot: The End of an Era', *The Twentieth Century* CLIX, No. 950, April 1956.
E. J. H. Greene, 'T. S. Eliot et Jules Laforgue', *Revue de littérature Comparée*, 1948.
A. D. Hawkins, 'Fiction Chronicle', *The Criterion*, April 1936.
M. J. J. Labouille, 'T. S. Eliot and some French Poets', *Revue de littérature comparée*, 1936.
Bruce A. Morissette, 'T. S. Eliot and Guillaume Apollinaire', *Comparative Literature*, Summer 1953.
Kenneth Muir, 'A Brief Introduction to the Method of Mr. T. S. Eliot', *Durham University Journal*, V, June 1944.
George Williamson, 'The Structure of "The Waste Land"', *Modern Philology* XLVII, February 1950.

(d) *Reviews:*
'Prufrock' and other Poems, *The Athenaeum*, 2 May 1919; 20 June 1919.
'The Waste Land', *New Statesman and Nation*, November 1922: November 1923. *The Times Literary Supplement*, 20 September, 1923.

Secondary sources

*Works of Ezra Pound*
(a) *Poetry:*
*Selected Poems*, Faber & Gwyer, 1928.
*The Cantos* (first published 1954), New Collected edition, Faber, 1964.
(b) *Prose works:*
*Spirit of Romance* (first published 1910), Peter Owen, 1952.
*Gaudier-Brzeska, A Memoir*, Bodley Head, London, 1916.
*Instigations* (including an essay on the Chinese Written Character, by Ernest Fenollosa), Boni & Liveright, New York, 1920.
*A.B.C. of Reading*, Routledge, 1934.
*Polite Essays*, Faber, 1937.
*Literary Essays* (ed. T. S. Eliot), Faber, 1954.
*Letters of Ezra Pound 1907–1941* (ed. D. Paige), Harcourt Brace, New York, 1950.
(c) *Articles contributed to periodicals:*
'How I began', *T.P.'s Weekly*, 10 June 1913.
'Imagisme and England', *T. P.'s Weekly*, 20 February 1915.

*Critical and interpretative Studies*
Donald Davie, *Ezra Pound: Poet as Sculptor*, Routledge & Kegan Paul, 1965.
George Dekker, *Sailing after Knowledge*, Routledge & Kegan Paul, 1963.
G. S. Fraser, *Ezra Pound*, Writers and Critics, 1960.
Hugh Kenner, *The Poetry of Ezra Pound*, Faber, 1951.
Noel Stock, *Poet in Exile, Ezra Pound*, Manchester University Press, 1964.

*Collection of essays:*
Ezra Pound: *A Collection of Critical Essays* (ed. Walter Sutton), Twentieth Century Views, Prentice-Hall, New York, 1963.

*Articles in periodicals:*
Roy Harvey Pearce, 'Towards an American Epic', *Hudson Review*, Autumn, 1959.
Warren Ramsey, 'Pound, Laforgue and the Dramatic Structure', *Comparative Literature* III, 1951.

Imagists and the French Symbolists

*Imagists*

*Books:*
Graham Hough, *Image and Experience*, Duckworth, 1960.

Glenn Hughes, *Imagism and the Imagists* (first published 1931), Bowes & Bowes, 1960.
T. E. Hulme, *Speculations*, Kegan Paul, Trench, Trubner & Co., 1924.
Frank Kermode, *Romantic Image*, Routledge & Kegan Paul, 1957.

*Articles in periodicals:*
Conrad Aiken, 'The Place of Imagism', *New Republic*, 22 May, 1915.
F. S. Flint, 'The History of Imagism', *The Egoist*, 1 May, 1915.
O. W. Firkins, 'The New Movement in Poetry', *Nation*, 14 October, 1915.
Lewis Worthington Smith, 'The New Naïveté', *Atlantic Monthly*, April 1916.

*The French Symbolists:*

*Books:*
Roger Fry, *The Poems of Mallarmé* (first published 1936), Chatto & Windus, New York, 1951.
Ian W. Alexander, *Studies in Modern French Literature*, presented to P. Mansell Jones, Manchester University Press, 1961.
M. Raymond, *De Baudelaire au surréalisme* (Paris, 1933)—From Baudelaire to Surrealism (translated by 'G.M.'). Documents of Modern Art, George Wittenborn Inc., 1949.
Warren Ramsey, *Jules Laforgue and the Ironic Inheritance*, O.U.P., New York, 1953.
Roger Shattuck, *The Banquet Years—the Arts in France, 1885–1918*, Faber, 1959.
Arthur Symons, *The Symbolist Movement in Literature*, Heinemann, 1899.
R. Taupin, *L'Influence du Symbolisme Français sur la Poésie Américaine de 1910 à 1920*, Paris, Librairie Ancienne Honoré Champion, 1929.
Edmund Wilson, *Axel's Castle*, Charles Scribner's Sons, New York, London, 1931.

*Article in periodical:*
Peter Quennel, 'Baudelaire and the Symbolists', *The Criterion*, January 1930.

MODERN ART

*Books:*
Paul Klee, *On Modern Art*, Faber, 1959.
Herbert Read, *Art Now*, (first published 1933), Faber, 1960.
Herbert Read, *The Philosophy of Modern Art*, Faber, 1952.
William Seitz, *The Art of Assemblage*, The Museum of Modern Art, New York, 1961.

Wylie Sypher, *Loss of the Self in Modern Literature and Art* (first published 1962), Vintage Books, Alfred A. Knopf, Random House, New York, 1964 edition.

Wylie Sypher, *From Rococo to Cubism*, Vintage Books, Alfred A. Knopf, Random House, New York, 1960 edition.

F. Worringer, *Abstraction and Empathy* (translated by Michael Bullock from the German: 'Abstraktion und Einfühlung', first pub. 1908), Routledge & Kegan Paul, 1953.

*Article in periodical:*
Jacob Korg, 'Modern Art Techniques in "The Waste Land"', *The Journal of Aesthetics & Art Criticism* XVIII, 1960.

GENERAL

*Books:*
A. Alvarez, *The Shaping Spirit: Studies in Modern English and American Poets*, Chatto & Windus, 1958.

T. G. Bergin, *Approach to Dante*, Bodley Head, London, 1965.

R. P. Blackmur, *Language as Gesture*, Allen & Unwin, 1954.

Cleanth Brooks, *Modern Poetry and the Tradition* (first published 1939) Galaxy, O.U.P., New York, 1965.

E. Cassirer, *The Philosophy of Symbolic Forms* (first published 1955), Yale University Press, 1965.

Donald Davie, *Articulate Energy: An Enquiry into the Syntax of English Poetry*, Routledge & Kegan Paul, 1955.

Allan Gilbert, *Dante and his Comedy*, Peter Owen, 1964.

Murray Krieger, *The New Apologists for Poetry*, University of Minnesota Press, 1956.

Suzanne Langer, *Philosophy in a New Key*, Harvard University Press, 1951.

F. R. Leavis, *New Bearings in English Poetry*, Chatto & Windus, 1932.

Edgar Allan Poe, *The Poetic Principle, Works* XIV (ed. R. Brimley Johnson), Frowde, 1909.

Herbert Read, *The True Voice of Feeling*, Faber, 1953.

I. A. Richards, *Principles of Literary Criticism* (first published 1925), Routledge & Kegan Paul, 1926 edition.

M. L. Rosenthal. *The Modern Poets*, O.U.P., New York, 1960.

D. S. Savage, *The Personal Principle: Studies in Modern Poetry*, Routledge & Kegan Paul, 1944.

Stephen Spender, *The Creative Element*, Hamish Hamilton, 1953.

Stephen Spender, *The Struggle of the Modern*, Hamish Hamilton, 1963.

C. K. Stead, *The New Poetic*, Hutchinson University Library, 1964.

William K. Wimsatt and Cleanth Brooks, *Literary Criticism: A Short History*, Alfred A. Knopf, Random House, New York, 1957.

Yvor Winters, *In Defense of Reason*, Allan Swallow, New York, 1947.
Yvor Winters, *On Modern Poets* (first published 1943), Meridian
Books Inc., New York, 1959 edition.
G. T. Wright, *The Poet in the Poem*, University of California Press,
Berkeley and Los Angeles, 1960.

# Index

Aiken, Conrad, 32, 104, 106, 143
Aldington, Richard, 27
Alexander, Ian W., 137, 138, 139n.
Alvarez, A., 57, 62, 152n., 165
'Angelism', 46, 124
Apollinaire, Guillaume, 16, 146, 156–7
Arden, Eugene, 114
Aristotle, 7, 29, 101; 'praxis', 72, 73, 75, 102–3, 157; 'peripeteia', 157
Art (modern), 3, 11–12, 15, 16, 17, 90, 175, (See also Assemblage, Collage, Cubism, Impressionism, 'Simultanéisme', Papier collé, Primitivism)
Assemblage (art of), 15, 90, 143, 156–7
Auerbach, Erich, 152

Baudelaire, Charles, 11, 41, 42, 46, 55, 56, 125, 137, 138, 145, 153; consciousness of time in, 138; 'Spleen', 138
Beaumont & Fletcher, 121
Berg Collection (The), 140
Bergin, T. G., 152n.
Bergson, Henri, 4, 33, 95, 96n., 97, 98, 103, 111; 'durée', 98, 119, 137; theory of personality, 103, 111; 'temps clos', 138, 139, 146, 161
Blackmur, R. P., 70
Blake, William, 3, 9, 10n., 129 (See also Eliot's Prose Works)
Bradley, F. H., 4, 5, 11, 33, 95, 103, 109, 111, 117; Appearance and Reality, 4, 5; Essays on Truth and Reality, 4; definition of 'reality', 5, 11; identification of objects, 5; 'appearances', 5; 'finite centre', 95, 111; theory of personality, 103, 111
Braque, Georges, 98
Brooks, Cleanth, 142 (See also Wimsatt and Brooks)
Brotman, D. Brosley, 130
Brown, Alex, 142n.
Browning, Robert, 29

Canaletto, Antonio, 123
Cézanne, Paul, 12, 93
Chapman, George, 29, 64
Cinema, technique of, 4, 72, 157; cinematic 'cut', 72, 157; Pound and, 73–5, 120, 157; 'series production' of, 96, 160–1; and 'Preludes', 74,

94, 95, 157–8; and 'Prufrock', 94n., 110–11, 116–17; and Quatrain poems, 120; and 'The Waste Land', 135, 156, 157, 160–4 (See also Eisenstein and Montage)
Claudel, Paul, 48
Cocteau, Jean, 73
Coleridge, S. T., 3, 170n.
Collage, method of, 84, 97–8, 146, 157, 162, 175, 183
Collins, Churton, 6
Connotation (See also Language) of history and myth, in 'Gerontion', 126–9, 137; in Quatrain poems, 119–23, 137; in 'Rhapsody', 99–100, 126, 180; in 'The Waste Land', 139, 144, 161
of religion, in 'Burnt Norton', 181; in 'Gerontion', 126–9, 130, 133; in 'Little Gidding', 181, 185; in 'The Dry Salvages', 181; in 'The Waste Land', 51, 139, 144
over-connotation, in Eliot, 124; in Pound, 85; in Symbolist poetry, 46
Connotative Structure, 43–6, 47, 50–1, 81, 164; Eliot and, 51, 54, 87–8, 97, 102, 120, 123, 149–50, 164–5, 170 (See also 'Convenientia', Qualitative Progression, Structure, Symbolism)
'Convenientia', 45, 85, 98, 120, 121, 134, 164, 165, 176, 178, 179, 180
Confucius, 60, 136; Ta Hio, 83
Conrad, Joseph, 99
Corbière, Tristan, 42, 46, 48, 56, 75, 125
Cubism, 5, 11, 12, 84, 99, 132, 175; theory of composition, 5; Eliot and Cubism, 11–12, 117, 143, 145, 147, 159

Daniel, Arnaut, 67
Dante, Alighieri, 12, 28, 30, 32, 39, 40, 50, 56, 60, 67, 85, 93, 114, 115, 124, 152, 159–60, 163, 167, 174, 181; form and structure of Divine Comedy, 40, 85; 'hero' of Divine Comedy, 114–15; language of, 56; De Vulgari Eloquio, 60
Davie, Donald, 63, 64n., 65, 66n., 72, 73, 74, 75, 76, 78, 79, 80, 81, 84, 87, 157n., 185

Dekker, George, 83n., 164
Delacroix, Eugène, 12
Delaunay, 15
Donne, John, 29, 89, 90, 119, 126
Drama, dramatic (conflicting) emotion
    in poetry, 90–1, 102, 103, 104;
    dramatic function of irony, 53–4,
    81–2; drama and lyric poetry, 72
    (*See also* Aristotle 'Praxis');
    drama and psychology, 9; poem *of
    art-drama*, 104–5, 149; poem *of
    stage-drama*, 104, 148; 'seeing one-
    self' dramatically, 104, 105, 111,
    112 (*See also* 'Persona')
Drew, Elizabeth, 115, 116n., 119, 122,
    124, 165–6, 173n., 174, 180, 181,
    182
Dryden, John, 52, 55, 126
Dujardin, Edouard, 49
'Durée', 98, 119, 137 (*See also* Bergson,
    'temps clos', Time
Duret, 4n.

Ecole Romane, 41
Eisenstein, Sergei, 72, 94, 157, 160
Eliot, T. S., and assemblage (poetic),
    91, 92, 169–70 (*See also* Assem-
    blage); and cinematic technique,
    74–5 (*See* cinema); and 'compre-
    hensiveness' in poetry, 5–7, 9,
    10–11, 12, 18, 88, 96–7, 102, 119,
    143, 144, 170, 171, 183 (*See*
    Language and Connotation); and
    Cubism (*See* Cubism); and Ima-
    gism (*See* Imagism and the
    Image); and the action-image,
    67–70, 80, 82, 88, 100, 104, 105,
    107, 115, 118, 123, 162, 179;
    Impersonality of Art, 3, 7–8, 89–
    90; and the 'meaning' of poetry, 2,
    11, 18, 170–1; and musical form,
    155, 174; and 'mythical method',
    119–23, 163–8, 171; on the nature
    of poetry (literature), 28, 29, 88;
    and new art-emotion, 88–90, 96,
    104, 109, 133, 145, 157, 167, 169;
    and the 'objective correlative', 30,
    43, 55, 74, 78, 79, 87, 88, 125, 170
    (*See* Imagism); and personality, 8,
    10, 88–9 (*See* Persona); and
    Quatrain form, 118, 123, 124–5;
    recurring imagery in, 177–80; and
    structure (*See* Structure); and
    Symbolism (*See* Symbolism); use
    of personal symbols, 51, 54, 176–
    80; Traditionalism of, 12, 119,
    127, 133, 137 (*See* Time)
    *Poetry and Plays*
    'Ash Wednesday', 26, 93, 170n., 171,
    176, 180n., 182–3

'Aunt Helen', 120
'Burbank with a Baedeker: Bleistein
    with a Cigar', 123, 177
'Burnt Norton', 15, 16n., 46n., 172n.,
    174, 178, 179, 180, 181, 182,
    183 (*See* Connotation, of religion)
'Choruses from *The Rock*', 185
*The Cocktail Party*, 138
'Conversation Galante', 104
'The Cooking Egg', 118
'Cousin Nancy', 117
'Death of a Duchess' (unpublished),
    110–11
'The Dry Salvages', 133, 177, 180,
    181 (*See* Connotation, of religion)
'East Coker', 128, 130, 172, 173,
    176, 177, 178, 179
'Gerontion', 7, 23, 51, 68, 91, *125–33*,
    134, 135, 136, 148, 149, 170, 171,
    177 (*See* Persona, Connotation, of
    history and religion)
'The Hippopotamus', 118
'The Hollow Men', 93, 170n., 171,
    178
'Journey of the Magi', 177
'La Figlia che Piange', 37, 104
'Little Gidding', 179, 181, 184, 185n.
    (*See* Connotation, of religion)
'The Love Song of J. Alfred Prufrock',
    7, 22, 35–6, 53–4, 67–8, 80n., 82,
    94n., 104, *109–18*, 127, 136, 148,
    170 (*See* Cinema, Persona)
'Lune de Miel', 131
'Marina', 181
'Morning at the Window', 68
'Mr. Apollinax', 117–18, 178
'Mr. Eliot's Sunday Morning Ser-
    vice', 124
'Portrait of a Lady', 80–1, 82, 104,
    *105–9*, 131, 148, 149, 150, 178
    (*See* Persona)
'Preludes', 15, 22, 36, 74, 91, *93–7*,
    102, 119, 136, 137, 138, 160, 163,
    174, 178 (*See* Cinema, Persona)
'Rhapsody on a Windy Night', 23,
    *97–102*, 119, 126, 136, 137, 145–8,
    177, 178, 180 (*See* Connotation, of
    history, Persona)
'Spleen', 109
'Sweeney among the Nightingales',
    120, 122–3
'Sweeney Erect', 121–2
'The Waste Land', 1, 8, 15, 23, 26,
    69, 71, 73, 84, 91, 132, 134–68,
    170, 171, 173, 174, 177, 178 (*See*
    Cinema, Connotation, of history
    and religion, Persona, Pound,
    'cutting' of 'The Waste Land')
'The Waste Land' manuscripts, 110,
    140–1, 143–4

'Whispers of Immortality', 118
*Prose Works*
'Blake', 9–10
*Criterion* 'Commentary', 26–7 (on
    Imagism)
*To Criticize the Critic*, 12n., 28n., 30n.,
    39n., 56n., 78n.
'Dante', 30, 85, 93, 174, 181
'What Dante means to me', 12, 28,
    56, 167
'Dialogue on Dramatic Poetry', 53
'Dryden', 55
'Essay on Dramatic Poetry', 72
'John Ford', 169
'The Function of Criticism', 89
'Hamlet', 30, 43, 79, 90, 115, 123
*Knowledge and Experience in the
    Philosophy of F. H. Bradley*, 4, 5n.
'London Letter', *Dial*, 155
'Andrew Marvell', 6, 7n., 55, 183
'The Metaphysical Poets', 29, 30
'The Music of Poetry', 2n., 3, 11,
    172n.
'Note sur Mallarmé et Poe', *Nouvelle
    Revue Française*, 89–90
*On Poetry and Poets*, 2n., 6n., 7n.,
    11n., 16n., 172n.
'The Perfect Critic', 7n., 17–18
'The Possibility of a Poetic Drama',
    29
'Ezra Pound', *Poetry* LXVII, 57, 59
'Ezra Pound : His Metric and Poetry',
    57, 78
'The Method of Mr. Pound',
    *Athenaeum*, 67n., 135n.
'Reflections on *Vers Libre*', 39
*The Sacred Wood*, 7n., 9n., 10n., 18n.,
    27–8, 29, 85n., 88n., 92n., 115n.,
    123n., 135n.
'A Sceptical Patrician', *Athenaeum*,
    29
*Selected Essays*, 6n., 7n., 8n., 13n.,
    14n., 19n., 29n., 30n., 43n., 55n.,
    72n., 88n., 89n., 103n., 169n.,
    174n., 181n., 183n.
'Shakespeare and the Stoicism of
    Seneca', 88
'Swinburne as Poet', 13, 19
'That Poetry is made with Words',
    *New English Weekly*, 9, 10, 13
'Cyril Tourneur', 6
'Tradition and the Individual Talent',
    8, 88
'Review of *Ulysses*', *Dial* 163
'What is a Classic ?', 6
Emerson, R. W., 122
Empson, William, 61, 126


Fenollosa, Ernest, 62, 63, 64, 65, 66,
    67, 70, 75, 76

Firkins, O. W., 32
Flint, F. S., 21, 27, 48, 60
Ford, Ford Madox, 30, 58
Fowlie, Wallace, 42
Fraser, G. S., 61, 77, 78n., 120, 136n.,
    154n.
Fry, Roger, 148

Gardner, Helen, 124, 154, 182, 183n.,
    184
Gaudier-Brzeska, 25, 62, 75, 76, 79n.
    (*See also* Pound, Prose Works)
Gautier, Théophile, 118, 124
Gilbert, Allan, 115, 159, 160
Gladstone, 77
Goldsmith, Oliver, 69
de Gourmont, Rémy, 24 (*Problème du
    Style*) ; 26, 29, 48, 49, 75, 76, 126
Gray, Thomas, 6
Greene, E. J. H., 110

Hawkins, A. D., 116n.
H. D. (Hilda Doolittle), 25, 27, 49, 55
'hokku', 157
Hough, Graham, 2, 42n., 44, 79, 88,
    101, 102n., 149
Howarth, Herbert, 73, 155, 156n.
Hueffer, Ford Madox, (*See* Ford
    Madox Ford)
Hughes, Glenn, 19n., 20n., 21n., 27n.,
    32n., 35, 42n.
Hugo, Victor, 20
Hulme, T. E., 22, 27, 28, 29, 30, 31, 46,
    60, 66; on Classicism and Romanti-
    cism, 19–20; on 'exquisite
    moments' of reality, 20–1; on the
    Image, 21, 24; on inspiration, 24;
    on 'intensive' and 'extensive'
    manifolds, 52, 87; on poetic craft,
    26; 'Autumn', 'Conversion', 33;
    *Notes on Language and Style*, 20n.,
    24n.; *Speculations*, 19, 20, 21, 22,
    26n., 27n., 33n.

Ideogram, the Chinese (Ideogrammic
    method), 62, 64, 66, 85, 151, 165
    (*See also* Imagism)
Imagism and the Image, 2, 19–37, 54,
    95; autonomy of Imagist poem,
    25; Eliot amd Imagism, 26–32, 68,
    116, 118–19, 150–1, 158–9, 170;
    'The History of Imagism', 21;
    Imagism and French Symbolism,
    24, 38, 48, 49, 55–6; Imagist Mani-
    festo, 22, 60; Imagist-Symbolists,
    52, 76, 77, 79, 81, 88; Imagism
    and *vers libre*, 39; limitations of
    Imagist poetry, 32–5, 38–9, 71;
    Pound and Imagism, 22, 27, 60–3,

71, 75, 77; Traditionalism of, 24–5, 58
the Image, 21, 23, 92; the archetypal image, 166; the Image and the Chinese Ideogram (the action-image), 64, 66–70; the 'moving' image, 74; the Image and the 'objective correlative', 30–1, 55, 87 (See also T. E. Hulme, individual Imagist poets and Symbolism)
Impressionism, French, 4

James, Henry, 116
Jammes, Francis, 75
Jarry, 34
John, St, of the Cross, 182
Johnson, Lionel, 58
Jones, Genesius, 43, 44, 45, 46, 51n., 76, 77n., 85n., 87, 100, 120, 124, 126, 132, 133, 164, 165n., 184 (See also 'Convenientia')
Joyce, James, 154, 163–4; mythical method in Ulysses, 163
Jung, Carl, 165, 166, 174; 'the integration of personality', 174; 'the process of individuation', 174

Kahn, Gustav, 34
Keats, John, 57, 113, 116
Kenner, Hugh, 18, 31n., 63, 64, 72, 79n., 83n., 85n., 92, 106n., 108, 109n., 111, 116n., 117n., 124n., 126, 132, 135, 136n., 141n., 149, 150n., 151, 153, 154n., 157, 158, 159n., 160, 164n., 167
Kermode, Frank, 2–3
Klee, Paul, 86
Korg, Jacob, 145n., 146, 147n., 148
Kyd, Thomas, 163

Laforgue, Jules, 11, 41, 42, 52, 54, 56, 73, 85, 105, 110, 112, 125, 137
Langer, Susanne, 77, 166, 171
Language, development of discursive language from myth, 171; language of myth, 167; Eliot on importance of connotation in poetry, 55; importance of language in Eliot's poetry, 12–15, 18, 56, 170, 172–4, 176, 184–5; Ford on contemporary language, 58; generalizing tendency of language, 87; gesture of language, 70–1; Hulme on language of poetry, 21; Pound and language 59–60; Pound and the Chinese language (ideogram), 62–7; Pound, the importance of connotative language in, 77–9; Symbolist theory of connotation, 42–3, 55 (See also Symbolism, principles of; Connotation)

Lawrence, D. H., 174–5
Leavis, F. R., 83, 132, 182n.
Leonard, William Ellery, 32
de l'Isle-Adam, Villiers, 41
Lowell, Amy, 27
Loyola, Ignatius, 182

Mallarmé, Stéphane, 41, 42, 46, 47, 50, 78, 89, 90, 124, 125, 148, 175; 'Apparition', 50
Malraux, André, 26
Manet, Edouard, 4n.
Manning, Fred, 58
Maritain, Jacques, 13
Marsden, Dora, 27
Marvell, Andrew, 6, 7n., 183; 'The Nymph and the Faun', 55
Matisse, Henri, 12
Matthiessen, F. O., 53, 55n., 84, 93, 125, 175n., 184
Maxwell, D. E. S., 97, 112, 118, 123, 142n., 170n., 174
Metaphysical Poets, 29, 30, 32
Mondrian, Piet, 175
Monroe, Harriet, 57, 109
Montage, 72, 75, 94, 120, 135, 157 (See also Cinema)
Morris, William, 55
Muir, Kenneth, 69n., 169

Newbolt, Henry John, Sir, 58

'Objets-trouvés' (found objects), 36, 37, 97, 98, 100, 145, 147

Palmer, Samuel, 3
Papier collé, 147
Parnassianism, 20, 41
Pearce, Roy Harvey, 140n.
'Peripeteia', (See Aristotle)
Persona(e), Eliot's poetic use of, 72, 88, 102–4, 138; Pound's poetic use of, 72, 103
Persona(e), artistic, 104–5, 116–17, 131
Persona(e), assembled (composite), in 'The Waste Land', 134–5; in Pound's Cantos, 135–6; assembled voices, in 'The Waste Land', 151–6; in Pound's Cantos, 152
Persona(e), of the stage, 104–5, 131–2
Persona(e) in 'Cousin Nancy', 117; in 'Gerontion', 130–3, 135, 152, 154; in 'Lune de Miel', 131; in 'Mr. Apollinax', 117–18; in 'Portrait of a Lady', 116, 131; in 'Preludes', 102; in 'Prufrock', 111, 116–17, 118, 131–2, 151–2, 154; in 'Rhapsody on a Windy Night', 102 (See also Bergson, Bradley, Theory of personality)
Philippe, Charles-Louis, 95, 97

Picasso, Pablo, 12, 98, 147–8
Plato, 100, 101
Poe, Edgar Allan, 11, 40–1, 89, 90
Poets' Club (The), 19, 21
Pope, Alexander, 52
Pound, Ezra, 13, 18, 25, 26, 27, 31, 57–86, 92, 118, 120, 134, 135–7, 150, 151, 154, 156, 157, 158, 159, 164, 165, 167, 170, 171n.; and the Chinese Ideogram, 62–7, 151; and cinematic montage, 72–5; and the 'cutting' of 'The Waste Land', 73, 140–1, 143; and dramatic lyric, 72, 103, 154; and French Symbolism, 75–9; use of historical names, 77; and Imagism, 22, 27, 60–3, 71, 75; the one-Image poem, 33, 61–2, 157; persona of, 72, 135–6; *See also* Persona, assembled; personal symbols, use of, 78; structural forms of, 79–86; and Symbolist-Imagists, 77, 79; and Vorticism, 62, 75 (*See also* Connotation, Language)
*Poems*
    *Cantos, The,* 83–6, 134, 135, 136, 150, 151, 152, 153, 165, 167; *Cathay,* 61, 79, 137; 'South Folk in Cold Country', 79; 'The River Merchant's Wife', 80; *Hugh Selwyn Mauberley,* 82, 83; 'Yeux Glauques', 77; *Lustra,* 61, 75, 82, 137; 'Epitaphs', 157; 'In a Station of the *Métro*', 61; 'Provincia Deserta', 73–4; 'The Garden', 82–3
*Prose Works*
    *A.B.C. of Reading,* 64n., 71n., 171n.; *Cavalcanti* preface, 164n; *Gaudier-Brzeska: A Memoir,* 25, 62n., 75, 76n., 79n., 158n.; 'How I began', *T. P's Weekly,* 59n.; 'Imagisme and England', *T. P's Weekly,* 62; 'Immediate Need of Confucius', 60; *Instigations,* 66n.; *Literary Essays,* 76n.; *Polite Essays,* 61n., 118n.; *The Spirit of Romance,* 60, 67, 79n.
'Praxis' (*See* Aristotle)
Primitivism, 34

Qualitative Progression, 44, 45, 49, 51, 52, 54, 72, 81, 116; progression by Double Mood, 52, 81, 116 (*See also* Connotative structure and Yvor Winters)
Quennell, Peter, 125, 137n.

Ramsey, Warren, 85, 165
Raymond, Marcel, 46

Read, Herbert, 11, 17, 24n., 31, 38–9, 49, 61, 66n., 86, 94n., 95n.
Reality, appearance and, 5, 11, 12, 18 (*See also* Bradley)
    Cubist theory of, 5
    Eliot and, 8, 14
    'higher reality' of Eliot's later poetry, 174, 176, 177, 181, 182, 183
    Hulme's definition of, 20
    'réalisme symbolique', 49
    'total existence' of objects, 4, 143
de Régnier, Henri, 56, 75
Richards, I. A., 6, 52n., 91–2
Rilke, Rainer Maria, 47
Rimbaud, Arthur, 11, 34, 41, 42, 48, 175
Rivière, Jacques, 156
Romanticism, The Romantic tradition, Eliot and, 2–3; Hulme on Romanticism and Classicism, 19–20, 46; Romantic image, 2–3; visionary sense of Romantic poet, 3, 20, 46 (*See also* 'Angelism')
Rosenthal, M. L., 71, 91n., 97n., 99, 132, 135, 147n.
Rossetti, D. G., 77
de Rougemont, Denis, 164
Rousseau (Douanier), 34
Ruskin, John, 77

St Jacques, Louis, 48
Salmon, André, 4n.
Samain, Albert, 56
Sandburg, Carl, 57
Satie, 34
Savage, D. S., 183
Schelling, Felix, 134
Seitz, William, 15n., 96n., 97n., 98, 99n., 146n., 147, 148n., 157n.
Shakespeare, 88, 124, 169; *Antony and Cleopatra,* 104; *Coriolanus,* 104; *Hamlet* (*See* Eliot's Prose Works); *Othello,* 70, 104; *The Tempest,* 146, 155; *Timon of Athens,* 104
Shattuck, Roger, 16, 182
Shelley, Percy Bysshe, 64, 113
Sidney, Philip, Sir, 63
Simultanéisme, 15
Smidt, Kristian, 36–7, 98, 175
Smith, Grover, 1, 93n., 95n., 96, 97, 102, 104, 105, 109, 121, 123, 124, 142, 170n.
Smith, Lewis Worthington, 33, 61
Spender, Stephen, 19, 23, 39, 47
Spenser, Edmund, 155, 158
Spinoza, 30
Stead, C. K., 2, 7, 25, 26
Stein, Gertrude, 16, 96, 160–1
Stock, Noel, 57, 58, 60, 62n., 63, 72n., 134n.

Strachey, Lytton, 77
Stravinsky, 155–6
Structure, 15–16; Eliot on importance
  of, 39–40 (*See also* Connotative
  structure, Eliot and; 'Convenien-
  tia'; Qualitative Progression; Sim-
  ultanéisme)
Surrealism, 44, 46, 162, 163
Swinburne, Algernon Charles, 13, 14,
  55, 77
Symbolism, The French Symbolist
  Movement, 38–56, 124, 175
  Eliot and French Symbolists, 38, 40,
    42, 45–51, 54–6, 78, 170, 175;
    historical significance of, 41;
    mystical element in, 41, 175;
    Pound and French Symbolists,
    75–9, 86
  Principles of, 40–3 (*See also* Conno-
    tation, Language)
  Structural forms of, 40–1, 43–6, 49,
    50–3, 54, 170 (*See also* Connotative
    structure, 'Convenientia', Qualita-
    tive Progression)
  Symbol and Image, 48, 56; Sym-
    bolism and Imagism, 24, 48–9, 55
    (*See also* Imagist-Symbolists);
    Symbolism and Music, 47; Sym-
    bolism and Romanticism, 46 (*See
    also* 'Angelism'); Symbol and
    Sign, 76–7; use of personal sym-
    bols (system of 'correspondances'),
    46, 176
Symons, Arthur, 9, 41, 42, 52, 175
Sypher, Wylie, 4n., 5n., 11n., 47n.,
    94n., 96n., 99n., 118n., 132,
    157n., 161n., 175n.

Tailhade, Laurent, 75

Tate, Allen, 12n., 46, 143n., 152, 153
  (*See also* 'Angelism')
Taupin, René, 24, 26n., 34, 36, 47, 48,
    49, 50, 55, 56n., 75, 91, 123, 124n.
Tennyson, Alfred, 29, 151
Time, significance of time in Eliot's
  poetry, 98, 119, 125, 137–40, 146,
    153, 161, 180, 181; in modern art,
    4; in Symbolist poetry, 125;
    time—progression of history, 127
    (*See also* Bergson, 'durée', 'temps
    clos')
Tourneur, Cyril, 6

Unger, Leonard, 93, 94n., 116, 140n.,
    142, 172

Verlaine, Paul, 125
Vermeer, 93
*Vers libre*, 39, 81, 118
Villon, François, 75
Vorticism, 62, 75

Weaver, Harriet Shaw, 27
Webster, John, 119, 126
Whistler, J. M., 52
Whitehead, Alfred North, 4, 50
Williams, William Carlos, 72, 74, 84
Williamson, George, 1, 105
Wilson, Edmund, 41
Wimsatt, William K. & Cleanth
    Brooks, 40n., 41, 42n., 44n., 46n.,
    52n., 166n., 171
Winters, Yvor, 44, 50, 52, 72 (*See also*
    Qualitative Progression)
Worringer, F., 95
Wright, G. T., 103, 116, 131, 156

Yeats, W. B., 3, 47, 82, 173